NEW PERSPECTIVES OF BRAZIL

NEW PERSPECTIVES OF BRAZIL

EDITED BY
ERIC N. BAKLANOFF

VANDERBILT  UNIVERSITY PRESS

F
2510
B23

51411

TO MY FATHER, NICOLAS W. BAKLANOFF

ACKNOWLEDGMENTS

During my fellowship year at the Center for Advanced Study in the Behavioral Sciences I received valuable assistance in the preparation of this volume from several members of the center's staff. I am particularly indebted to Mrs. Betty Callaway, librarian, and to Mrs. Irene Bickenbach of the secretarial staff. Dr. David Maybury-Lewis, a colleague at the center, was kind enough to read the manuscript in its formative stage and to offer comments and suggestions.

Dr. Russel Whitaker of the Department of Geography, Peabody College, and Dr. Donald Huddle, member of the Economics Department of Rice University, also offered critical evaluations of parts of the volume.

The chapters by Professors Baer, Lopes, and Ludwig are based upon lectures delivered by them at Vanderbilt University under the auspices of the Graduate Center for Latin American Studies. To Mrs. Thelma Mills, my former secretary at Vanderbilt, I am grateful for typing the completed manuscript.

CONTENTS

INTRODUCTION

THIS collection of essays is an attempt to illuminate recent and contemporary Brazilian processes and problems from the several perspectives of the behavioral sciences and humanities. To my knowledge, this is the first such enterprise in a decade and a half. *New Perspectives* derives its unity from the examination of salient aspects of Brazilian society undergoing transformation—in its economic, political, social, demographic, psychological and linguistic elements. We do not pretend to provide a comprehensive view of Brazil: for example, there are no chapters on literature, the fine arts, or on such specific topics as transportation and agriculture.

The time-focus of our several approaches to Brazilian reality is the period following World War II—a period marked by an exponential rate of change, not only in this hemisphere, but on a global scale. Each author is familiar with Brazil, has lived there, and brings his special discipline to the analysis and interpretation of an aspect of that nation's development. Wherever relevant, the contributing writers have made interim assessments of the military-civilian *coup* of March 31, 1964, and of the Castelo Branco administration which has followed it.

Brazil is one of the large nations of the world. Given its current population of about 80 million and a rate of demographic growth twice that of the United States, there will be nearly 100 million persons in Brazil by 1970. The country occupies half of the South American continent, or an area roughly equal to the United States without Alaska. A semi-industrialized country, Brazil is vitally linked to the Free World economy by trade, investment and technical assistance arrangements. Indeed, the Free World has a significant stake in the modernization of Brazil within the Western frame of development, characterized ideally by the "open society," broadly shared material benefits and individual freedom.

New Perspectives appropriately begins with Professor John W. F. Dulles's chapter, "Post-dictatorship Brazil, 1945–1965," a chronicle of the interplay between politics and economics, including portraits of Brazil's leading public personalities, such as Vargas, Prestes, Lacerda, Adhemar de Barros, Kubitschek, Goulart, Brizola, and Quadros. The dramatic events of postwar Brazil are sharply illuminated and the country's marvelous capacity for compromise and adaptation confirmed. Dulles writes that the Brazilian electorate "took pride in feeling that the nation adhered to the constitutional way—a way indicating orderliness and maturity." On the other hand, the increasing strains of social dissatisfaction so evident in the early sixties placed a heavy burden on the Brazilian Constitutional system. "It can well be argued," according to Dulles, "that in the early 1960s the Brazilian electorate received packages which rather differed from those ordered and that the crack-up of March 1964 would have been avoided had the voice of the electorate been carefully heeded in the presidential palace." Quadros's wholly irresponsible resignation "opened the door for much that his successful candidacy opposed." And Goulart, who followed him, chose "not to administer but to agitate." At the end of Dulles's chapter the reader will be pleased to discover an exceedingly useful glossary of Brazilian terms.

In his perceptive essay, "Some Basic Developments in Brazilian Politics and Society," Dr. Juarez R. B. Lopes offers a lucid analysis of the profound changes in Brazil's social and political structures in the last half century. In the "Old" or First Republic the "real protagonists of the political system were oligarchical regional (state) groups whose power was based, locally, on the economic, social, and political power of the large landowners (the *coronéis*) " and national politics was a process of adjustment and compromise among oligarchies, the so-called *politica dos governadores*. A new system of urban power resting on the more differentiated oligarchies of São Paulo and Minas Gerais, including the new industrialist group, and on an enlarged and partly new urban middle class and an urban working class has "unleashed new political and economic forces which spread to the local traditional communities and led to the slow and irreversible corrosion of their patrimonial organization." Notwithstanding the widespread political transformation of Brazil, "no associations that mediate between individuals and presidential and gubernatorial candidates have yet appeared." Lopes concludes that the accelerated breakdown of traditional patterns of social organization at regional and local levels has fed back into the national political structure and "solidified the focuses of resistance to change in the national power structure."

Following an historical sketch of Brazil's foreign policy, including the stages of territorial diplomacy and extra-continental initiation, Dr. Reisky de Dubnic centers his analysis on Brazil's experimentation in world politics. The focus is on that nation's recent quest for international nonalignment: "Brazil's search for a different model for her foreign policy, imitating a sort of Nasserism under Quadros and Titoism under Goulart was not merely unproductive in terms of gaining for Brazil distinct economic or prestige advantages, but was also against the cultural and ideological fiber of the largest Catholic country in the world." Reisky demonstrates that the Castelo Branco administration restored Brazil's traditional alliance policy, but Brazil is outgrowing its hemispheric role. He contends that "Brazil is too large a country to be boxed within the Inter-American system. An Atlantic triangle of interests would better suit Brazil's needs and aspirations."

In my own chapter, "Foreign Private Investment and Industrialization in Brazil," I look at the arguments offered for and against the participation of foreign venture capital in Brazil, examine these in the light of theory and data, and define the groups in Brazil which have entered the controversy. I demonstrate that the massive infusion of private capital and "know-how" from abroad was an indispensable factor sustaining Brazil's industrial growth after 1954 when the coffee boom faded. The technically advanced industries (including those producing capital goods), which have formed the growing edge of the Brazilian economy's forward thrust, have been importantly associated with foreign investment. I maintain that "The burden of evidence suggests that the earnings of foreign direct investments in Brazil were a modest price to pay for the powerful, growth-promoting impacts of the foreign-controlled enterprises." In conclusion I outline the measures taken by the Castelo Branco administration to regain the confidence of the international financial community (which was badly shaken during the Goulart regime) to reactivate the inflow of private capital and secure official assistance from abroad —conditions essential for the fulfillment of that government's three economic objectives: growth, stability, and reform.

In "Socio-Economic Imbalances in Brazil," Dr. Werner Baer demonstrates the relationship between official Brazilian policies and the drastic change in the structure of the country's economy between the early postwar years and the early sixties. A concomitant of Brazil's rapid industrialization through the technique of massive import substitution was a concentration of resources in the industrial sector at the expense of other sectors. "By the early sixties the neglect of agriculture, education, regions outside of the dynamic center-south of the country, certain infrastructure investments, and the diversification of exports, were producing economic and social strains which were endangering the further growth of the economy."

Among the more dynamic aspects of the many changes which Brazil has been experiencing recently are those involving her population. In his chapter, "Changes in the Geographic Distribution of Population in Brazil, 1950–1960," Dr. Roland E. Chardon examines the dimensions of Brazil's accelerated rural-urban migration and the factors underlying the population increase in the "pioneer zones" of the country. He analyzes the striking population increases in the ten largest urban agglomerations, the medium-sized cities, including "boom towns," and the significant regional changes in demographic growth. He ties the future progress of Brazil to that nation's capacity to overcome serious structural problems in its traditional agricultural posture and considers the Paraná Basin to be one of the brightest spots in Brazil's social and economic prospect. Chardon concludes that, "recent changes in the geographic distribution of population in Brazil, while reflecting a *Marcha para o Oeste,* seem to indicate an even more dominant *Marcha para o Sudeste.*"

How has the newly created federal capital of Brazil reshaped the regional landscape of that nation? In his chapter on Brasília, Dr. Armin K. Ludwig sets out to answer this question, at least in a preliminary way. The idea of removing the federal district to the interior has behind it a constitutional tradition. The Constitution of 1946, especially, "played upon a growing national state of mind which imagined fulfillment of Brazil's centuries-old *Marcha para o Oeste,* or manifest destiny," through development of the interior. A second rationale offered by its proponents was the need for the creation of an "antiseptic" environment—far removed from the cosmopolitan atmosphere of congested, polyfunctional Rio de Janeiro—to serve as the seat of federal power. Brasília, which became a reality during the administration of President Jucelino Kubitschek, has become a national focus for the construction of roads with strong links to the "economic densities of São Paulo–Belo Horizonte–Rio de Janeiro heartland and to the core of the productive Goiás axis." Ludwig ties the future growth of Brasília to the possibility of extensive, mechanized agriculture integrated with processing plants and associated activities concentrated in the Federal District. In the context of these possibilities, Ludwig foresees few opportunities for the unskilled thousands now flooding into Brasília.

In "Religious Movements and Culture Change in Brazil," Professor Emilio Willems considers the rise of three religious mass movements in Brazil—Pentacostalists, Spiritualists, and Umbandistas—and the attendant changes of the traditional social structure. An important social function of these non-Catholic religious movements is to integrate the raw migrant into the urban social system and lead him to accept more democratic (as opposed to paternalistic) attitudes. "In any of the three movements, particularly in the Pentacostal sects, a person encounters the opportunity to rebuild his personal community." In this way, the migrant who, back in his home town or village, was a member of a highly integrated group of kinsfolk and neighbors, can, when confronting his strange urban environment, resist severe cultural shock leading to anomic behavior.

There is too often a tendency in discussion of Brazil and her problems to overlook a most important factor, namely, the Brazilian himself. Dr. John Santos, in his chapter "A Psychologist Reflects on Brazil and Brazilians," gives us an insight into "The Brazilian Way of Life," and the demands it places upon the individual. Real and permanent solution of Brazil's most complex problems, according to him, can only come from a restructuring of forces and realignment of values. Notwithstanding the recent changes in the Brazilian personality, which was a concomitant of rapid urbanization and industrial development, the Brazilian continues to invest little "energy, emotion, and concern beyond the self, the family, and the close circle of friends." The frequent groping for external solutions to internal difficulties will have to give way to more mature approaches, according to Santos.

In the final chapter, "Emerging Patterns of the Brazilian Language," Professor Earl Thomas shows how the Brazilian language has been enriched by additions from Amerindian and African sources to the word stock imported from Portugal, and borrowing from modern languages. Most recently, American English has become a source of many new words, especially in popular speech in the field of sports and, concomitantly with Brazilian industrial development, in science and technology. "The Brazilian," says Thomas, "loves words, learns new ones easily, uses synonyms in great numbers, and forms new derivatives with astonishing facility." In the emerging patterns of the Brazilian language, Thomas finds evidences of the increasing democratization of Brazilian society.

ERIC N. BAKLANOFF

1/ POST-DICTATORSHIP BRAZIL, 1945–1964
BY JOHN W. F. DULLES

> *Editor's note: Translations or meanings of Portuguese or Brazilian terms used herein are indicated in a glossary following this chapter.*

W HEN the year 1945 opened in Brazil, Getúlio Vargas was at the nation's helm. The short, stocky, sixty-one-year-old dictator from the plains of Rio Grande do Sul had directed that nation's destinies since 1930, and except for three and a half years in the middle of that decade he had done so without a congress.

The genial cigar smoker and attentive listener who appeared to cherish reason and compromise had always made his moves with the calculated care of one who abhors gambling and who will not be rushed. It would have been difficult in 1930 to have found any other man in Brazil so well equipped to master those forces which in the ensuing years, in disappointment, became bent on overturning the regime. Vargas maintained his position by skillfully arranging to preside over contending factions, avoiding becoming the pawn of any one of them; inevitably, he had to alienate some groups in which disenchantment was blended with a liberal measure of ambition. He was careful in his relations with the army, and he was often agreeable to the idea that former foes should make up with him. Pleased with his role as Father of the Brazilians and convinced that Brazil's well-being depended on his continued

3

tenure, Vargas had shown an aversion to popularly elected legislative bodies.

Both the Vargas dictatorship and the nature of the republic that preceded the 1930 revolution meant that Brazil in 1945 had no strong background in the democratic processes. Key political, fiscal, and foreign-policy decisions had been made by a few elite who had usually put other considerations ahead of the immediate reaction by any great body of public opinion.

All this was changed in the period to be reviewed chronologically here. Top decisions came to be influenced profoundly by estimates of what the majority would like to hear.

The demand for manufactured goods was increasing in Brazil. The difficulty of making imports during and immediately following World War II accentuated the country's desire to diminish its reliance on other nations for manufactured products. It was further accentuated when the price tags on these imports were compared with prewar prices and by Brazil's foreign-exchange situation. In any event, the concept of Brazil exporting raw materials and importing manufactured goods was hardly in keeping with the passionate urge to join the envied society of industrially developed nations—a society whose attractions were becoming more and more widely heralded with advances in communications.

The state enacted measures to promote industrialization. The cost was sometimes high, but the progress in certain regions went on at a pace hardly to be appreciated by the outsider reading headlines about various "crises" of the period. The political base of the nation thus continued to move away from the old rural aristocracy. The growing mass of industrial workers became a force of increasing importance and was warmly courted by the proponents of a political *populismo*.

The postwar period was also characterized by currency inflation and growth of nationalist sentiment. Some Brazilian industrialists regarded these phenomena as not incompatible with their own designs. But inflation and nationalism had deeper roots.

Inflation in Brazil during this period of emphasis on the speedy creation of new industry and impressive government construction may be explained technically, if such items as available resources, the agricultural picture, and balance of payments are considered.

But before long the simple fact came to be that the alternative to new currency issuances and decreed wage increases seemed to the average politician in office too unpopular a course to follow. Just as the first taste of inflation may stimulate the economy, the measures required to curb it may be initially painful. While the disease was unpopular, the politicians feared that the remedy might be more so.

When inflation pinched (and it often did so, vigorously), the simplest expedient appeared to be the inflationary one of raising wages. Wage increases were largely brought about by government action; and, with no influential group holding savings which were tied to the purchasing power of national currency, it became more and more difficult to prevent even an increase in the rate of inflation.

The Vargas dictatorship had done much to draw Brazil together into one whole. In the years that followed there developed a healthy nationalism—a justified pride in Brazil and its accomplishments, mingled with a keen desire to enhance the nation's status. But this climate also favored the introduction of an extremist ramification, which, like the extreme inflation, hampered Brazil's economic progress.

The Communist Party of Brazil encouraged a strong anti–United States ultranationalism. Communists also infiltrated strategic spots in the Brazilian society. Among these were organized labor groups and organized student groups.[1]

Despite these accomplishments, Brazil's Communist party had little popular following. A Brazilian far-leftism was stealing its thunder. The far-left movement was sometimes disunited, but it had more appeal than a foreign-directed communism.[2] Brazilian far-leftism, which included a Brazilian national Marxism, noisily insisted that the nation would benefit in adopting more socialist

1. Corruption and Communist infiltration in Petrobrás (the Government-owned monopoly for oil extraction) is discussed in Glycon de Paiva's article, "Petrobrás como banco da subversão nacional e escola prática de corrupção" in *Jornal do Brasil* (Rio de Janeiro, Feb. 16, 1964).

2. See Rollie E. Poppino, "Communism in Postwar Brazil" (Paper presented at American Historical Association session, Chicago, Dec. 29, 1962).

concepts; it also sought to turn nationalism into a crusade against what it called United States "imperialism."

LAST MONTHS OF VARGAS'S DICTATORSHIP, 1945

For Brazil 1945 was a year of unusual political drama in which steps were taken which were highly important to the country's future. What unfolded reflected, not only world events on battle-fields and at international conferences, but also a nervousness which Getúlio Vargas's past behavior justified.

American Secretary of State Edward R. Stettinius, reaching Rio de Janeiro in the heat of mid-February 1945, was driven to the summer colony at Petropolis. There he brought the Brazilian dictator up to date on the changing world picture. Stettinius had come from Yalta, and he spoke of the planned new world organiza-tion in which the Soviet Union, until then never diplomatically recognized by Brazil, would have a strong voting position.

Stettinius and Brazil's foreign minister sped from Rio to the inter-American conference in Mexico City. At this conference, Brazil and other nations of the Americas pushed for arrangements which would provide a regional association for the settlement of hemispheric disputes.

Brazil had sent an expeditionary force of 25,000 to northern Italy. More than 15,000 were now engaged in difficult but success-ful combat at the side of the United States forces.

A democratic world seemed at last to be emerging in all its glory. At home in Brazil there was restlessness springing from a public desire for a return to democratic government—a restlessness shared by important army leaders who for the most part felt they had sustained the dictatorship long enough.

Brazil's first Congress of Writers, held in São Paulo late in January 1945, called for liberty of expression and a government elected by the direct secret vote of the people. The press, long controlled by the censorship and propaganda of the Departmento de Imprensa e Propaganda (DIP), decided soon afterward not to wait for the dictatorship to take the hint. Accordingly, on February 22, the interview which José Américo de Almeida gave to the young newspaperman, Carlos Lacerda, appeared in Rio's *Correio da Manhã*. The liberal politician from the northeast, whose aspirations had been snuffed out when Vargas canceled the 1938 election, cited during this interview principles which had been formulated at the Writers' Congress.

The DIP did not take action against the journal, and from that moment on Brazilian newspapers seethed with articles such as had not been seen since 1937. Men who had broken with Vargas, and some who had been considered still close to him, clamored for democratic freedoms, an election, and a new constitution. Francisco Campos, author of the controversial "constitution" of 1937, stated that Vargas had never properly used the instrument. He declared that it was time for Vargas to think of Brazil and not of himself.

Still in February 1945, many of those who were enjoying this opportunity to lift their voices in discontent followed a suggestion of José Américo and pushed for the election of Brigadeiro Eduardo Gomes to the presidency. The austere Gomes was the only surviving officer of the historic rebellion of the "18 of the Fort" on Copacabana Beach in 1922. He had made a name for himself in the air force after the successful revolution of 1930; and during the war he was Brazil's top man at the important air bases in Brazil's northeast. His candidacy became the rallying point of the now enthusiastic foes of the dictator. It was early supported by Osvaldo Aranha, Vargas's long-time friend and—until he broke with the dictatorship in 1944—invaluable associate.

Whatever Vargas did was held suspect by the press and by politicians who were willingly or unwillingly out of office. They had had their fill of the *gaúcho's* moves which kept him on top and of what they felt was his propensity for procrastinating on matters which might bring democracy nearer. They smiled when Eduardo Gomes turned down suggestions from the government which would have taken him out of the presidential race. They frowned at juridical intricacies which seemed to delay an election decree and at some of the proposed decrees that were rumored to be in the mill. When Vargas stated that he was not interested in running for president in an election they felt he was being evasive.

The old master named the faithful João Alberto Lins de Barros police chief of Rio, a rather important post. To the presidential candidacy of the air force hero, Vargas replied with a sword to fight a sword: he advanced the candidacy of War Minister Eurico Gaspar Dutra, who was quick to show interest. Dutra had once been known for his admiration of the German army and for having made the Brazilian dictatorship possible. He now reflected the general view that the dictatorial *Estado Nôvo* had become outmoded. Although not a brilliant intellectual, he was much more astute than some might have thought. Benedito Valadares, who governed the state of Minas Gerais, sponsored this new, somewhat official candidate just as he had sponsored the somewhat official candidacy of José Américo early in 1937. So did Fernando Costa, Vargas's appointee as federal *interventor* of São Paulo state.

Pressure for amnesty was strong in the press and in legal circles. After a large group of lawyers advanced the cases of outstanding Vargas foes still in exile, the Supreme Court in April granted writs of habeas corpus allowing them to return at last. So the *paulista*, Armando de Sales Oliveira, who had annoyed Vargas by running for the presidency in 1937, came back from abroad to a warm reception. But he was a sick man and died before the year was out.

Of the more than five hundred political prisoners who remained in jail, many had participated in the unsuccessful Communist rebellion of 1935. The sentences of most had not much longer to go; besides, their detention was irritating to Russia and to the new mood.

The most prominent was Luís Carlos Prestes, who from 1925 to 1927 had gained enormous prestige as the "Cavalier of Hope" when he led about twelve hundred men of the *Coluna Prestes* on a tough march of rebellion through Brazil's neglected interior. Instead of backing the 1930 revolution which substituted Vargas for the old political machine which Prestes and *tenentes* had been fighting, Prestes had followed the Communist path; and in the Communist rebellion of 1935 he had tried to unseat Vargas.

Since his capture in 1936 his seventeen-year sentence had been increased by thirty years because, as a prisoner, he had been held partly responsible for the brutal slaying of a girl who had been informing on the Communists.

In April 1945 the jails were emptied of such prisoners. An intermediary had been negotiating between Vargas and Prestes, and now tall Police Chief João Alberto smilingly escorted to freedom the pale little man who had been his revolutionary leader in the mid-1920s.

With politics openly occupying everyone's attention for the first time since 1937, the words of the celebrated ex-prisoner were anxiously awaited. Particular interest was shown by Communist party members, many of whom had been praising the Gomes candidacy because it was anti-Vargas. But when Prestes spoke he assailed both military candidates. At the Vasco da Gama football stadium on May 23 he spoke again, this time after the war in Europe had ended. In all he was now saying, he seemed to be playing a game dear to Vargas: the election should be postponed and a third candidate was needed.

Vargas, however, did on May 28 sign a decree calling for the election of a president and congress on December 2. Under this decree women would vote directly for president for the first time although they had received the right to vote as far back as 1932. Henceforth all political parties would have to be national. (From the turn of the century until the 1930 revolution each state had been pretty well dominated by one local party, and two such parties—those of São Paulo and Minas Gerais—had usually dominated the presidency to the annoyance of the other states.)

Today's leading Brazilian political parties began in this setting during the months before the election decree was signed. At Vargas's instigation, politicians who had been serving with him began organizing the *Partido Social Democrático* (PSD). This party was to carry on the political machinery developed under the dictatorship and was to foster the candidacy of Dutra in 1945. Gomes supporters gathered on April 7 at the Brazilian Press Association auditorium in Rio to launch the *União Democrática Nacional* (UDN) and to bring together all factions unhappy with Vargas and his group.

Besides creating the PSD, Vargas brought about the organization of the *Partido Trabalhista Brasileiro* (PTB), which was founded at his suggestion by officials of his labor ministry, such as Alexandre Marcondes Filho and José Segadas Viana. Vargas

hoped for the incorporation of the great masses of workers, bene-
ficiaries of the social legislation of his "short period of fifteen
years," within the ranks of this labor party. Labor Minister Marcondes Filho's weekly broadcasts during the last years of the dictatorship had been a constant reminder of the existence of this
legislation. The PTB, designed to attract some who might otherwise have followed Prestes, strengthened Vargas's own political
position.

Early in August 1945, while bombs were falling on Japan,
Dutra resigned from the war ministry to run for president as the
PSD's candidate, although Vargas had by this time become cool
toward his candidacy. Brazilian troops were beginning to return
from Europe; and Vargas, as he greeted them, received surpris-
ingly enthusiastic acclaim. As the "Father of the Poor," the dictator
was finding himself the hero of the working classes. *Queremistas,*
those who cried out their support for Vargas, were loud in calling
for a *Constituinte com Getúlio,* that is, the suspension of the presidential election and the election of a constitutional assembly
which would draw up a new constitution and select Vargas to
serve under it as president. Neither the Communist party, which
was reorganized by Prestes, nor the PTB had any announced presidential candidate; and members of both these parties did much
to put on the *queremista* demonstrations in favor of Vargas.

By late September, Vargas was showing definite displeasure
with Dutra, whose presidential campaign was floundering badly;
at the same time he complained that the strong-minded Gomes
backers were planning a military coup. The presidential guard,
headed by younger brother Benjamim Vargas, was preparing
Guanabara Palace against possible attack. Adolf Berle at the American Embassy was worried about trouble at the air bases should the
dictatorship set aside the presidential election. Both Gomes supporters and United States military personnel were at the bases.

Ambassador Berle made a speech expressing hope that the
election would be held as scheduled. Vargas had approved the
speech shortly before it was delivered, but when the dictator later
read excerpts in the press he became indignant at United States
"intervention." He called in War Minister Pedro Aurelio de Góes
Monteiro and expressed his anxiety.

This emphasis by Vargas on agitated conditions and his disparagement of the presidential candidates brought back memories of 1937 and caused many persons to be concerned. There were, however, two outstanding differences: the world of 1945 was not that of 1937; and the military, with two presidential candidates in the field, now had a real interest in the election. With the merging of the military leaders and the democrats, Getúlio, the expert at presiding over conflicting factions, saw his position collapse.

Queremistas, on whose support Getúlio could now count, ignored João Alberto's orders on October 3 when they swarmed around Guanabara Palace. Although Vargas did not agree to cancel the planned presidential election or to be a candidate himself, he made it clear that he sympathized with the views of the demonstrating workers. Events, he said, no longer depended on his will, which was the will of the people; and he offered to resign if this would help prevent disunity.

A week later he did tamper with the election law—an encouraging sign for *queremistas.* Yielding to the pressure of the federally appointed state *interventores,* he signed a decree providing that state elections for governors and assemblies take place on December 2, 1945, instead of May 6, 1946, as originally scheduled. The *interventores* and their political machines might well be out by May, but on the earlier date the machines would still be in power and the Vargas appointees could probably assure themselves of election as governors. The UDN, once hopeful of some governorships, let out a howl.

Juan Perón victoriously entered Buenos Aires on October 17, 1945. Vargas, who had been calling on Brazilian workers to join the PTB, referred to the event with enthusiasm, citing the political power of the working masses. The Brazilian Communist party ruled that there should be no attacks against Perón.

All the anxieties of preparing for what would be Brazil's first popular election for president since 1930 came to a head on October 29. Vargas, without having advised his war minister or the other military leaders, appointed João Alberto mayor of the Federal District. In his place as police chief he put his brother Benjamim Vargas (known derisively as *O Beijo,* meaning "The

Kiss") .[3] Benjamim's appointment, a victory for *queremistas* whom the police had recently prevented from holding meetings to oppose the presidential election, astounded many, particularly in the military. There were rumors that the prison camp at Ilha Grande was being prepared to receive hundreds of new political prisoners.

Góes Monteiro, expressing a lack of confidence in the dictator, resigned as war minister but accepted the suggestion of some army men that he assume the supreme command of all the military and take necessary steps to prevent civil strife. Troop commanders were alerted and key communication points in the capital taken over by the military. While Vargas was insisting that he had the right to name the police chief, the presidential candidates and most of the military leaders went along with Góes's plan to force the dictator's resignation.

On Góes's orders, Osvaldo Cordeiro de Farias took the ultimatum of the military on the evening of October 29 to Guanabara Palace, which had already been surrounded by army tanks. Luís Carlos Prestes had been hovering near the presidential palace in case Vargas, with the help of such Army men as Newton Estilac Leal and Osvino Ferreira Alves, chose to resist.[4] But the dictator, after a short hesitation, agreed to resign. The next day he issued a manifesto stating that history would speak favorably of his record and appealing to the workers and humble people. Bitter at being unceremoniously dumped and promising to return, he was flown on the thirty-first to a ranch of his older brother at São Borja in Rio Grande do Sul.

ELECTION OF DECEMBER 1945

Chief Justice José Linhares, quite surprised, became acting president of Brazil on October 30, 1945, after both presidential candidates quickly agreed on his name. At a meeting of the new cabinet, which included Góes as war minister, it was confirmed that the presidential election should take place on December 2 and that the federal legislature, to be elected at the same time,

3. Hernane Tavares de Sá, *The Brazilians* (New York: The John Day Co., 1947) p. 211.

4. Interview with Luís Carlos Prestes, Rio de Janeiro, Sept. 5, 1963.

should draw up a new constitution. But the elections for state governors and assemblies were postponed. New federal *interventores* were named for the states, most of them judges suggested by Justice Minister Antônio de Sampaio Dória.

Brigadeiro Gomes and the UDN campaigned confidently in November. The removal of the state *interventores* of the old regime hurt the Dutra cause, and there were even rumors that Dutra might withdraw. The Communist party forsook its objection to the election and came forth with a presidential candidate, Iedeo Fiuza, an engineer who was not a Communist but who, as mayor of Petrópolis, had been a personal friend of Vargas. The PTB put up the name of Vargas as candidate for a place in the constitutional assembly from numerous states, and the Communist party did the same with Prestes's name.

Some friends of Dutra and Vargas were alarmed at the prospect of a UDN victory. João Neves da Fontoura, who had done much for the 1930 revolution but had broken with Vargas in 1932, and Hugo Borghi, a *queremista* of the PTB who had acquired considerable wealth in cotton speculation in the last months of the dictatorship, were finally able to persuade Vargas to sign a message supporting Dutra. With the substantial aid of this message of November 28 assuring organized PTB support, Dutra was victor at the polls on December 2.

The popularity of Vargas's name within the laboring class now became evident. The ex-dictator was himself elected senator from Rio Grande do Sul and São Paulo and federal *deputado* from six states and the Federal District. Luís Carlos Prestes had a somewhat similar although less glorious experience. They could accept only one mandate each (Vargas became senator from Rio Grande do Sul), but since the distribution of legislative seats to party members was based on the party vote received for those seats these names helped strengthen their parties in the constitutional assembly. Besides electing Prestes senator from the Federal District, the Communists had the satisfaction of electing 14 *deputados* out of a total of 286. The Communist presidential candidate, even without the hoped-for support from Vargas, received 570,000 of a total of 5,870,000 votes. In the Federal District, where Gomes received 184,000 votes and Dutra 166,000, Fiuza captured 135,000 votes.

THE DUTRA ADMINISTRATION, 1946–1951

Dutra took over on January 31, 1946; and, while the constitutional assembly under the presidency of Senator Fernando Melo Viana wrestled with the job of creating a new constitution, he ruled by decree as had Linhares and Vargas before him. Again the states received new *interventores*. Foreign exchange regulations were liberalized in order not to handicap foreign investors. The National Coffee Department was ended. Gambling was made illegal and thus the fancy casinos were closed.

The relative peace for which the Dutra administration became known was not always apparent in its first months. In March Prestes was reported to have stated that he and his followers would fight for Russia in case of a war between Brazil and Russia. After the police forbade a mass meeting in Rio on May 1, Prestes used inflammatory words in Pernambuco. All known Communists were thrown out of positions in the federal executive branch of the government. The first Russian envoy in twenty-nine years reached Brazil in May 1946 at a time that the Brazilian police were trying to bar all Communist public meetings and were dealing with railroad and port strikes.

The 1946 Constitution, largely the work of the assembly's *Comissão da Constituição,* was pronounced effective on September 18. It provided for five-year terms for presidents, with no immediate re-election. Much of the social legislation of the *Estado Nôvo* was included. The right of property was upheld, but property could be expropriated for public need or social interests "with prior and just indemnification in money." Brazil, under the 1946 Constitution, was assured a plentitude of election years; for presidential and congressional elections were not to be held simultaneously.

Marshal Dutra adhered so carefully to the new constitution that he became known as Brazil's "foremost civilian president." After the document became effective, UDN President Otávio Mangabeira (a consistent enemy of Vargas and one of the prominent exiles to return in 1945) agreed on co-operation between the UDN and the Dutra administration. It was a co-operation useful to the nation, although it was not favored by everyone in the UDN or the PSD. Dutra took two UDN Party members into his cabinet and had a congress with which he could generally work.

The PSD-UDN partnership showed more strength than the PTB in the January 1947 state elections, but the President's PSD Party lost the governorships of São Paulo and Minas Gerais, the two largest states. With Communist support, Ademar de Barros, once an *interventor* named and then fired by Vargas, was elected governor of São Paulo, running as candidate of the *Partido Social Progressista* (PSP), in which his own influence was considerable. The PSD of Minas Gerais had an internal fight, with the result that Milton Campos of the UDN was elected governor.[5] Otávio Mangabeira won in Bahia.

Vargas, taking his seat as a federal senator somewhat belatedly, heard his recent regime attacked. In the face of what he considered a campaign by politicians and the press to "humiliate" him, he returned to São Borja rather than remain in Rio for the signing of the new constitution. But he made an appearance on the political scene late in 1947, campaigning personally on behalf of Cirilo Júnior who was running for the vice-governorship of São Paulo. Cirilo had some PTB and PSD backing and support from Communists, who accused Ademar de Barros of welshing on agreements made; but Ademar's candidate, Novelli Júnior, son-in-law of President Dutra, won the election. After this defeat, Vargas returned to São Borja where he was left alone, ignored except for visits from his young neighbor, João ("Jango") Goulart, and, starting early in 1959, the visits of Samuel Wainer, reporter for the Chateaubriand chain of newspapers.

Inflation was fairly well stalled in 1948 and 1949, since the federal government, in contrast to Ademar de Barros's São Paulo state government, lived close to its income in 1947 and 1948. But as the 1950 presidential election approached congress ignored the pleas of budget balancers, and new money issues again became necessary as they had been in 1946. Credit expansion, which had started toward the end of 1948, continued in 1949 as coffee prices

5. Carolina Nabuco, *A vida de Virgílio de Melo Franco* (Rio de Janeiro: Livraria José Olympio, 1962), pp. 211–215.

rose, and this also contributed to the 6 percent increase in the cost of living in 1950.[6]

Import difficulties during World War II forced Brazil's reserves of gold and foreign exchange to an all-time high soon after the war, with a value equivalent to more than 800 million dollars. Of this amount, about 350 million dollars were in gold reserves, about 260 million dollars in blocked British sterling, and about 50 million dollars in other blocked currencies. The remainder was mostly in United States dollar reserves, and these were used up in large measure for badly needed rehabilitation work on the transport system. There was considerable importation of agricultural machinery, trucks, buses, automobiles, and luxury goods. All of these items had increased in price since the Brazilian balances were created. Construction was begun on the Paulo Afonso hydroelectric plant on the São Francisco River in the northeast. Debts to foreign bondholders were reduced. Of Brazil's gold reserves of about 315 tons, 33 tons were turned over to the International Monetary Fund as Brazil's quota.

On account of exchange difficulties in Europe, Brazil's blocked balances in pounds and francs continued frozen, and the British had to devalue the pound. Brazil's frozen sterling balances were used to purchase and nationalize some port facilities and four railroad companies in Brazil which had formerly been controlled by British owners.

During the first part of Dutra's administration, Brazil went along with the free-trade policies being advocated by the United States; but late in Dutra's term, in view of the foreign exchange situation, Brazil instituted a system of requiring government licenses for imports. This action was taken in accordance with Article XIV of the International Monetary Fund Articles of Agreement and in accordance with the corresponding articles of the General Agreement on Tariffs and Trade, of which Brazil had become one of the original members in 1947.

A favorable trade balance, traditional with Brazil until the 1950s and necessary for the servicing of foreign debts, was realized during the five-year Dutra period, chiefly because many imports

6. Cost of living figures from Oliver Onody, *A inflacão brasileira* (Rio de Janeiro, 1960), p. 25.

were not available in 1946 and because of the considerable improvement which took place in the coffee picture. The government
sold the coffee stockpile which had been in the hands of the National Coffee Department and used the revenue to pay off the
foreign Coffee Realization Loan which back in 1930 had been
made with coffee as security. The world found itself short of coffee
as backlogs became largely exhausted. The price shot up to fifty
cents per pound late in 1949, then went higher. Brazilian coffee
exports set an all-time record of 19.4 million bags in 1949.

Dutra was not noted for being a loquacious president, but
when he did speak he was apt to say something against the Communist movement in the world. At the same time, there were press
attacks in Moscow against Brazil and its president—attacks which
Brazil blamed on the Russian government. Diplomatic relations
with the Soviets, established in 1946, were broken by Brazil in
1947. The incidents which led to this break were not earth-
shattering, but the break itself was welcome to the anti-Communist
military close to Dutra and defined the administration's position
early in the Cold War.

Within Brazil steps were taken to set back the Communist
movement in the fields of politics and organized labor.

In the January 1947 elections for state assemblymen, the
Partido Comunista do Brasil (PCB) obtained more than 9 percent
of the total vote, a slight improvement over its 8.6 percent of
the total vote cast for the federal congress in December 1945.
Its greatest strength continued to be in the cities of Recife and São
Paulo, and in the Federal District (where it seated eighteen of the
district's fifty aldermen). But in May 1947, on the basis of its internal statutes, the PCB was declared illegal by a 3-to-2 vote of the
Tribunal Superior Eleitoral (Supreme Electoral Court). In January 1948 congress ruled to eject Communist Party members from
state or federal positions to which they had been elected, so Prestes
lost his senate seat.

With the paternalistic dictatorship ended and with industry
going ahead, Brazilian labor syndicates were expanding rapidly in
size and number. In order to throw Communists out of their posts
in labor unions, the Dutra administration made use of an article
in the labor law which required that union officials profess to

support no ideology opposing the democratic regime. Communists became rabid opponents of the *impôsto sindical,* the fee collected from workers and employees for supporting the government-sponsored system of *sindicatos, federações,* and *confederações.*

There was no place in this arrangement for a general labor confederation such as the *Confederação dos Trabalhadores do Brasil* (CTB) , and it was suspended in a decision confirmed by the Federal Supreme Court in 1947. In the case of unions which were legal, the Dutra administration had *Juntas Governativas* take control, and no labor union elections were allowed between 1947 and 1950. An effort was made to have workers look to employers for the achievement of social service benefits, this being the idea behind *Servico Social da Indústria* (SESI) , established in 1946 and financed by taxes placed on employers of industrial workers at the rate of 2 percent of their payrolls. Similarly *Serviço Social de Comércio* (SESC) was created for the purpose of providing benefits for commercial workers.

In 1949 Dutra traveled to Washington, reciprocating a visit made to Brazil by President Truman in 1947, in which year the Treaty of Rio was born. Known also as the Inter-American Treaty of Reciprocal Assistance, it was an important step forward in a system of regional organization, and in 1948 it was followed by the creation of the Organization of American States in the Charter of Bogotá.

The year 1949 ended with a harsh attack on the Dutra government issued by Vargas in his message from São Borja to the Brazilian workers, "especially the poor and humble workers." Maneuvering for the October 1950 election was getting under way, and Vargas, "elder statesman" of the Labor Party, was beginning to receive a stream of visiting politicians at São Borja.

ELECTION OF OCTOBER 1950

Two currents were notable during the complex interparty negotiations which occupied much of the first half of 1950. One, in which Dutra showed interest, was an effort to have the PSD and the UDN, which had been collaborating in the administration, agree on supporting a presidential candidate. The focal point of this effort was Minas Gerais, where politicians were insisting on placing a *mineiro* in the presidency and where one wing of the PSD had co-operated with the UDN in the state election three years earlier. Another effort was going forward simultaneously. Vargas had many friends in the PSD, and to them the PTB proposed elaborating a common program to be followed by the selection of a joint PSD-PTB candidate.

Although many a name was mentioned, in Minas the UDN and the two wings of the PSD could not agree on a candidate. On the national scene, there were many in the PSD who preferred to look to Vargas than to the UDN. And so in April UDN leaders gave up negotiating with the PSD and decided once more to back Eduardo Gomes, who had been campaigning since March 1 as candidate of the *Movimento Nacional Popular*. The failure of the PSD and UDN to join forces left the way clear for Vargas to make his bid to return to the presidency "on the arms of the people" and as candidate of the PTB.

Ambitious Governor Ademar de Barros of São Paulo had been on such poor terms with the Dutra administration that it took all the president's reverence for the constitution to hold back those in Rio who favored a federal intervention in São Paulo. Ademar's government, getting what it felt to be insufficient financial assistance from the federal administration, began issuing short-term bonds (*bônus rotativos*), which damaged the state's credit. But the state stepped ahead industrially, and the governor kept busy inaugurating highways, hospitals, and schools.

To become a presidential candidate, Ademar would have had to turn over the state government on April 3 to vice-governor Novelli, who was by then very much his political foe. Instead, Ademar gave the support of the PSP to Getulio Vargas, with the understanding that the PTB would support his PSP candidate for the São Paulo governorship. Ademar also understood that Vargas would give him a taste of the fruits in case of a PTB-PSP victory in 1950 and would support Ademar for president in 1955. Vargas's running mate became João Café Filho, newspaperman and politician who had been exiled late in 1937 for denouncing Vargas's dictatorship and who in 1945 had founded the PSP in Rio Grande do Norte.

Mineiros of the PSD, who had been disagreeing about a candidate but insisting that the PSD put up a *mineiro,* got their wish by turning to Deputado Cristiano Machado, who had worked for the 1930 revolution in Minas but was not particularly well known outside the state. A wing of the UDN, led by Juraci Magalhães, liked Machado and now sought unsuccessfully to have a single Machado-Gomes ticket to oppose Vargas.

That which followed has been described as the "Cristianization" of the PSD: the PTB and Vargas supported a number of PSD gubernatorial candidates, and Vargas in return received some votes which might have been expected to go to Cristiano Machado.[7]

The Communists were told by Luís Carlos Prestes to vote in blank because the principal candidates were "reactionaries," and during the campaign Prestes came out with his party's August 1950 manifesto. This call for an agrarian revolution and the confiscation of key enterprises, especially foreign ones, was even stronger than the party's radical manifesto of January 1948; and when the new manifesto was published in a Brazilian Communist paper the edition was seized by the justice ministry.

Although much of the press supported Brigadeiro Eduardo Gomes, the vote for Vargas came close to equaling the combined vote for his opponents, thus giving the ex-dictator, sensitive to public criticism, the vindication he so much wanted. With Minas Gerais's votes about equally distributed among the three candidates, Machado came out in third place over-all, with Gomes in second place. Vargas rolled up an impressive majority among the working classes in São Paulo, where Lucas Nogueira Garcez, Ademar's PSP candidate, was elected governor. In a close race for the vice presidency, Café Filho was victor despite the opposition of the *Liga Eleitoral Católica* to his candidacy.

THE VARGAS ADMINISTRATION, 1951–1954

With the inauguration of the sixty-seven-year-old Vargas on January 31, 1951, an event at which high expectations and the approach of Carnaval were jointly celebrated, João Neves da Fontoura took over the foreign ministry. This was at the time of

7. Lourival Coutinho, *O General Góes Depõe* (2ª edição; Rio de Janeiro: Livraria Editôra Coelho Branco, 1956), pp. 501–502.

the Korean War; and, although Brazil would not agree to send forces overseas, it did enter into a new United States–Brazil Defense Agreement, which irritated not only Perón but also Communists and some of the PTB members of the Brazilian Congress.

The Brazilian northeast, affected in 1951 by its first severe drought since 1942, was visited by Finance Minister Horácio Lafer, who criticized the traditional emphasis on hydraulic works as a remedy for the various problems of the northeast and persuaded Vargas that the establishment of a regional credit institution would be useful. Lafer also sought to balance the federal budget, but the anti-inflationary effects of this effort were scuttled by the credit policy at the Bank of Brazil, whose president was Ricardo Jafet, another São Paulo industrialist who had aided the Vargas presidential campaign. In 1951 and 1952, while the official budget showed a surplus, there were large new currency issuances and increases in Bank of Brazil loans.

Getúlio, who as a political campaigner had offered to end the inflation, granted wage increases late in 1951 and these helped send living costs up 23 percent in 1952, and Vargas used radio broadcasts and public appearances to place the blame on speculators and "exploiters." Late in 1951 he accused foreign investors of "bleeding Brazil," and early in 1952 he ruled that the 8 percent limit on profit remittances was available only on the capital originally brought in and registered, not on reinvested earnings.

Meanwhile, United States and Brazilian experts were working together in Rio on a joint Brazil–United States Economic Development Commission. The group convened in mid-1951 as had been suggested the previous year by Raul Fernandes, then Dutra's minister of foreign affairs. This commission, which had the advantage of groundwork prepared by the Abbink mission of 1948, was to approve the financing of projects, particularly those in the fields of transportation and electric power. Upon the commission's recommendation, the National Economic Development Bank (BNDE) was established in Brazil to accumulate and provide local currency required for approved projects. This new bank later provided guarantees in the case of some foreign loans. Eventually, the bank itself became a direct borrower for some lines of credit. The fiscal experts saw from the beginning that foreign currency needs of the development program would be financed by the Export-Import Bank and the International Bank for Reconstruction and Development (World Bank). Before Lafer increased taxes to raise local currency requirements, members of the commission were expecting for their projects about 300 million dollars from these Washington lending institutions.

Since the outbreak of the Korean War in 1950 Brazil had been placing orders abroad for items which might have been impossible to obtain had the war spread. This policy was continued on a large scale, and Brazil, whose foreign exchange reserves had become exhausted, found herself at the end of 1952 with foreign exchange arrearages of more than 600 million dollars, of which 370 million dollars were owed to United States exporters.[8] These figures increased during the first months of 1953. Early in the Eisenhower administration, the Export-Import Bank provided 300 million dollars, and Brazil arranged to provide the balance to liquidate the arrearages in the United States. Brazil was also dealing with the governments of the United Kingdom and West Germany for the liquidation of commercial arrearages owed in those countries.[9]

With this decision of the Export-Import Bank and its practical withdrawal from the field of economic development financing, the outlook for receiving foreign loans for all the joint commission's projects became less encouraging. Although in February 1953 the Vargas administration established a "free" cruzeiro market which could be used for the unlimited remission of profits, this did not diminish the World Bank's concern at the deterioration of Brazil's "credit worthiness" nor prevent expressions that Brazil should put its house in order.

The joint commission had been a well planned and well executed exercise in international co-operation; but, contrary to hopes, it did not end its days in 1953 in a blaze of glorious goodwill. Projects approved by the joint commission called for 387 million dollars in foreign currencies and a larger amount of cruzeiros. Foreign currency of 181 million dollars was made available to Brazil during 1952 and 1953 for fifteen of the projects,

8. Banco do Brasil S.A., *Relatório de 1953* (Rio de Janeiro: Jornal do Commercio, Rodrigues & Cia., 1954), p. 62.

9. Hawthorne Arey, memorandum of Dec. 11, 1963, to Samuel C. Waugh.

leaving, at the end of 1953, twenty-six projects, calling for 206 million dollars, awaiting action.[10] Most of the balance was eventually provided, but the slowdown was vexing at the time to Brazil and to members of the commission, particularly in view of earlier understandings.[11]

The conditions under which the joint commission ended its days contributed to a feeling in Brazil that an unsatisfactory change had been taking place in the attitude of the United States toward Brazil. Brazil had for years been the important South American nation, traditionally friend and supporter of the United States, which in turn had accorded Brazil the role of key nation on the South American continent. Brazil had co-operated in the recent war as had no other South American nation, but with the war ended the days of a special role for Brazil in United States policy appeared also to be ended.

The United States was preoccupied with the Marshall Plan, with its focus away from the Americas. That nation was deeply concerned with the struggle against international communism on other continents. Vargas missed Franklin D. Roosevelt and Latin America missed the Good-Neighbor Policy.

While Washington rumbled with McCarthyism and Senator Guy Gillette's resentment toward rising coffee prices, nationalist sentiments were making headway in Latin America. Brazil was no exception. The days were long past in which almost everything foreign had been regarded as good. The United States, which was receiving sincere criticism from some of its friends in Brazil, came also to be a target of some of the less rational aspects of Brazilian nationalism.

The Vargas presidential regime was troubled from the start, not only by inflation, but also by Communist activities and labor unrest.

Luís Carlos Prestes was indicted, but the police chief reported that he could not be found. Communists, crying, "Not one soldier for Korea," worked against the ratification of the United States–

10. See *The Development of Brazil; Report of Joint Brazil–United States Economic Development Commission* (Institute of Inter-American Affairs, Foreign Operations Administration, Washington, D. C., 1954).

11. Merwin L. Bohan letter, Dallas, Texas, Dec. 17, 1963.

Brazil Military Aid Pact. Although the pact had been signed on March 15, 1952, by Ambassador Herschel V. Johnson and Foreign Minister João Neves, it did not get through congress until late in April 1953 after considerable debate. Communist activity was such that both Foreign Minister João Neves and Justice Minister Negrão de Lima expressed serious apprehension. An abortive raid on an army ammunition depot in Natal in March 1952, as the Communist Party of Brazil prepared to mark its thirtieth anniversary, brought an army alert against possible Red outbreaks.

The sternness of the Dutra administration toward communism in organized labor was relaxed. With Danton Coelho heading the labor ministry, a decree of September 1, 1952, struck out the requirement that union officials profess to support no ideology hostile to the democratic regime.[12]

Communist sympathizers in the army found a friend in War Minister Estilac Leal. Euclides Zenóbio da Costa, commander of the troops in the Rio de Janeiro sector (First Military District), resigned in protest. Vargas sought in March 1952 to settle the feud which was notable throughout the army by accepting the resignations of both Zenóbio and Estilac. The head of the presidential *Casa Militar*, Espírito Santo Cardoso, became war minister.

The Brazilian Communist party, always in contact with Russia, came around in 1953 to changing its line drastically from the violent revolutionary one called for in 1948 and 1950. It would limit its attacks on "imperialism" to "attacking American imperialism and not all imperialisms." [13] The Brazilian Communists' new nonviolent tactics reflected the realities of Brazilian politics better than the earlier program which had remained in force until Stalin died. There would be an emphasis on encouraging all anti–United States nationalists.[14]

Vargas assured a disappointed people at the end of 1952 that the economic crisis had been virtually overcome and that better times lay ahead. However discontent with the government and with increased living costs marked the first half of 1953. Rises in

12. Interview with Arnaldo Sussekind, Rio de Janeiro, Sept. 11, 1963.
13. Osvaldo Peralva, *O retrato* (Rio de Janeiro, Pôrto Alegre, and São Paulo: Editôra Globo, 1962), p. 27, footnote 4.
14. R. E. Poppino, "Communism in Postwar Brazil," pp. 4–5.

living costs exceeded those that took place in the closing period of the Dutra regime. By June 1953 Vargas was determined to revamp his cabinet.

The changes began early in June when José Américo, coordinator of the northeast drought control program, disagreed with Transport Minister Souza Lima and was named to replace him. Bank of Brazil President Jafet and his successor had both resigned after squabbles with sound-money-man Lafer, who was, in turn, the target of sniping. Critics accused Lafer of opposing relief in the northeast, where Communists were active and where the United States was trying to assist in the drilling of wells through its Point Four program. Vargas accepted the resignations of Lafer and Labor Minister José Segadas Viana, replacing them with two *gauchos:* Osvaldo Aranha and João Goulart. A few days later resignations were accepted from Justice Minister Negrão de Lima, Foreign Minister João Neves and Agriculture Minister João Cleofas.

Aranha had his work cut out. In addition to living-cost increases, the nation was suffering from transportation tie-ups and balance-of-payments difficulties.

One of his earliest actions, for the conservation of foreign exchange, was well received. This was SUMOC Instruction 70 of October 1953, ending the system of import licenses. (The issuance of these licenses had become corrupt after Luís Simões Lopes had left the Carteira de Exportação e Importação, or CEXIM; the pressure on the control organ had become too great at the time of increasing overvaluation of the official exchange rate.) Now, with SUMOC Instruction 70, the possibility of acquiring foreign exchange for imports was made available to all by means of the government's auctioning of the rights to buy such exchange. Categories of these auctions were established according to the nature of the goods to be imported. Similarly, exporters received bonuses above the official rate of 18.50 cruzeiros per dollar, exports also falling into categories with different bonuses for each. The smallest bonus went to the coffee exporter.

The Aranha policy of "protecting" coffee was less successful. The purchases on the New York Coffee Exchange made by firms of specialists on behalf of Brazil seemed to have a favorable effect for a time; but world production had caught up with consumption, and in spite of a lot of buying done on Aranha's instructions a New York price of about eighty-seven cents per pound could not be maintained. The "defense" was switched from New York to Brazil early in July 1954. The recently created Brazilian Coffee Institute (IBC) would buy in Brazil all coffee that producers and merchants could not sell at the equivalent of an eighty-seven-cent price in New York. The corresponding price in Brazil was paid by the IBC in cruzeiros. Although Brazil started filling warehouses and keeping coffee off of the world market in this manner, the world price continued to fall. Colombians and Africans were among those who increased their exports.

The nationalism of which Vargas had made use while he was out of power became fairly popular. So much was this felt to be the case that UDN legislators were among those responsible for modifying Vargas's projected Petrobrás law in 1953. This action gave Petróleo Brasileiro, S.A., the Brazilian government petroleum company (Petrobrás), a monopoly in exploring for and extracting petroleum in Brazil. Those close to Vargas felt that he had no strong objection to the monopoly.

Twenty army colonels and sixty-two lieutenant-colonels signed a memorandum early in 1954 written by Jurandir Mamede, one of the 1930 *tenentes*. Many of them were associated, as was Mamede, with the Escola Superior de Guerra (National War College), which had been established during Dutra's presidency. Their target was Labor Minister Goulart, who was very close to Vargas but whose behavior in the 1953 maritime strike had, they believed, pleased the Communists. They also resented any tendency they felt would encourage undemocratic or anti-constitutional forces to bring about social-economic changes. And they feared the influence on Goulart of Perón, working to bring Brazil into an anti–United States bloc (ABC) with Argentina and Chile.

Goulart was striving at this time to achieve a 100 percent increase in the minimum wage. Vargas, faced with the warning from the colonels, accepted Goulart's resignation. He called in a new war minister, Zenóbio da Costa, who two years earlier had complained of communism around Estilac Leal. Goulart's influence nevertheless continued; and his wage increase, a May Day 1954 present for labor, brought minimum wages for workers up to the pay for army second lieutenants.

Opponents of the regime intensified their attacks with the approach of a congressional election. So did the press. Among the few daily newspapers which defended Vargas in the capital was *Ultima Hora,* managed by Samuel Wainer and founded earlier at Vargas's suggestion, financed by the Bank of Brazil and certain industrialists. Most violent in attacking Vargas and Goulart was the *Tribuna da Imprensa,* owned and directed by Carlos Lacerda, who was to run for congress against Vargas's son, Lutero.

Vargas and Goulart were charged with receiving assistance from Perón for the election campaign of 1950, with reaching an international understanding with Peron without consulting the senate, and with planning to turn Brazil into a syndicalized state. The administration's opponents later switched their emphasis to charges of mishandling public funds. Vargas himself was reported worried about the talk of improper handling of the Social Security Institutes and the lack of respect for the government. Living costs were about 170 percent of what they had been when Vargas was inaugurated.

Besides running for congress, Lacerda was defending himself against a slander suit brought by Lutero Vargas. The shots which one night early in August 1954 wounded Lacerda and killed an air force major accompanying him were disastrous to the president.

It developed that the shooting had been ordered by Gregório Fortunato, head of the presidential guard and crony of Benjamim Vargas. Gregório's files were seized by investigators with the result that, shortly after Vargas's return on August 13 from a short trip to inaugurate the Mannesmann steel tube plant in Belo Horizonte, there were sensational disclosures of wrongdoings and influence peddling in Catete Palace.

Gregório, the "Black Angel" of Catete, who had recently been decorated by the war minister, was found, not only to have received commissions for arranging import licenses and Bank of Brazil loans, but to have himself borrowed three million cruzeiros from the Bank of Brazil to purchase the São Manoel ranch in São Borja from Vargas's son Manoel. Getúlio was stunned at the disclosures, and political enemies had a heyday.[15]

Thirty air force *brigadeiros* came out with a written resolution calling for the resignation of Vargas. They were backed by admirals. Then a manifesto dated August 22 calling for the resignation of Vargas was signed by twenty-seven of the eighty army generals in the capital. Some of the remaining generals came to regard a presidential "leave of absence" as the best solution. Vargas, however, remarked that he was now too old to end his days amidst "the iniquities and injustices with which they try to hurt me," and he insisted he would shed his blood resisting rather than be forced unconstitutionally out of office.

In the early hours of August 24 Vargas held a dramatic cabinet meeting at Catête Palace. This unusual meeting, which was joined by a number of the president's friends and relatives, ended at 4:00 a.m. when Vargas announced that he would request a leave of absence provided that order be maintained and the constitution respected. Two hours later War Minister Zenóbio da Costa, at a meeting of generals, was trying to dispel some misgivings about the conditional aspects of the leave of absence; and Catête Palace, shortly after 7:00 a.m., received word that Zenóbio had told the generals that Vargas's withdrawal was definite.

An hour later, in his Catête Palace bedroom, Getúlio Vargas killed himself with a bullet. The crowd around the palace had been very hostile to Vargas, but now in a sudden about-face it became full of devotion to the late president.

Vargas left for posterity several copies of his now-famous farewell letter. One he had given to João Goulart. The second copy, signed before the last cabinet meeting, was found at his bedside. This emotional message, which was made public at once, emphasized a strong nationalist sentiment and what Vargas called his continual struggle on behalf of the Brazilian people, for whom he said he was sacrificing his life. "My blood will be the price of your ransom," Vargas's letter declared. Vargas stated that the "underground campaign of the international groups became as-

15. See F. Zenha Machado, *Os últimos dias do govêrno de Vargas* (Rio de Janeiro: Editora Lux Ltda., 1955).

sociated with national groups in a revolt against the regime which was providing guarantees for the worker." [16]

PRESIDENTS CAFÉ FILHO, CARLOS LUZ AND NEREU RAMOS (1954–1956)

Vice President João Café Filho, who earlier in the month had suggested a joint resignation of himself and Vargas as a solution to the situation, was now in the presidency. His socialistic tendencies had given way on a trip to Europe and the Middle East in 1951 to a profound respect for free enterprise.[17] He surrounded himself with a cabinet which represented a considerable break with *getulista* influences. It included War Minister Henrique Lott, who had signed the August 22 manifesto of the generals against Vargas but who had the reputation of having involved himself little in politics.

Professor Eugênio Gudin, who had called the large May 1 wage increases a disaster, became finance minister and presided over difficult times for Brazilian coffee. He initiated discussions which led eventually to agreements between coffee-producing nations. In spite of some popular opposition, Gudin was able to eliminate the large subsidies which made gasoline prices unreasonably low. To impede the expansion of bank credit, he and his advisers issued SUMOC Instruction 108, raising the deposits of private banks with the Bank of Brazil. SUMOC Instruction 113, issued a little later, allowed foreign capital equipment to enter Brazil without the need of first purchasing exchange coverage at unfavorable rates. This instruction became an important stimulant to the flow of foreign investment into Brazil.[18]

Before he turned the finance ministry over to José Maria Whitaker in April 1955, Gudin brought credit expansion to a halt and formulated a budgetary economy plan. Faced with foreign

16. Ch. 13 of Alzira Vargas do Amaral Peixoto, *A vida de Getúlio*, appeared in *Fatos & Fotos* (Rio de Janeiro) of Oct. 15, 1963. In this the author writes of her father and the famous *carta-testamento*: "That he authenticated it with his signature, there is no doubt."

17. João Café Filho, memorandum, Rio de Janeiro, Sept. 6, 1963.

18. Regarding SUMOC Instruction 113, see Lincoln Gordon and Engelbert L. Grommers, *United States Manufacturing Investment in Brazil* (Graduate School of Business Administration, Harvard University, Boston, 1962).

exchange payments of 300 million dollars, he arranged for a five-year loan of 200 million dollars, secured by gold, from New York bankers.

Whitaker terminated SUMOC Instruction 108, and during his administration of the nation's finances credit expansion to the private sector by the commercial banks and the Bank of Brazil got under way again, at equal rates in both cases.[19] He cut out minimum coffee prices and government local coffee purchases which restricted exports.

One of his main concerns was a reform to bring an end to multiple exchange rates. After a meeting of cabinet ministers, who had various opinions about this exchange reform project, Café Filho suggested submitting the proposal to congress, and Whitaker forthwith resigned in October 1955.

Café Filho's labor minister, Napoleão Alencastro Guimarães, had belonged to the PTB, but he had been critical of that party's leader, João Goulart. During Alencastro Guimarães's term as labor minister, illegal unions in which Communists were active, the *União Sindical do Rio* and the *União Sindical de São Paulo*, were finally closed. These unions had been closed by the courts during the Dutra administration but had renewed operations when Goulart was Vargas's labor minister. Alencastro Guimarães's efforts to keep Communists out of high union posts earned him the reputation of being a reactionary. These efforts were handicapped by the law change made during Vargas's recent presidency.

As early as October 1954, Minas Gerais's energetic governor, Juscelino Kubitschek, was hard at work campaigning for the presidential election of October 3, 1955, even though he did not have the support of everyone in the PSD. Juarez Távora (chief of the presidential *Casa Militar*), the military ministers, and the chiefs of staff prepared a memorandum in January 1955 saying that it would be inadvisable to have any military man run for president. Referring to the economic and social crises, they suggested inter-party co-operation as a means of avoiding a violent campaign. This message was read on the radio by Café Filho in one of his frequent undemagogic talks to the nation. Many regarded some of

19. Alexandre Kafka, memorandum, Charlottesville, Va., November 21, 1963.

its passages as the voice of the military against Kubitschek, but it did not slow the Kubitschek bandwagon.

Work within the administration to produce a single candidate of "national union" was unsuccessful, and parties went their own ways. The PSD nominated Kubitschek, the PSP nominated Ademar de Barros, and the UDN nominated Etelvino Lins. A military man became a candidate when the Christian Democratic Party (PDC) and Brazilian Socialist Party (PSB) nominated Juarez Távora. Another candidate was Plínio Salgado who had headed the *integralista* green-shirts in the thirties and had returned from exile in Portugal after the events of 1945, letting it be known that he was a democrat. The *Tribunal Superior Eleitoral*, after studying the statutes of the Party of Popular Representation (PRP) which he founded, let the party exist. In 1955 the party nominated Salgado for the presidency.

Jânio Quadros had been elected governor of São Paulo on October 3, 1954, when he ran as the candidate of some small parties. Early in 1955 he took over this debt-ridden state. There was a moment when Quadros, who had never lost an election, seemed ready to resign the governorship to run for the presidency. Instead, good arrangements were worked out between the administration of São Paulo and the federal government.[20] The state's debts to federal entities were revised in a manner satisfactory to the state, which at this time placed two men, José Maria Whitaker and Otávio Marcondes Ferraz, in the Café Filho cabinet. Quadros campaigned in favor of Juarez Távora, who also became the nominee of the UDN when Etelvino Lins withdrew.

At the suggestion of Aranha, the PTB joined forces with the PSD, bringing the two Vargas-created parties together behind Kubitschek for president and João Goulart for vice president. According to this arrangement, Goulart, if elected, would have a free hand in the labor ministry and the social security institutes.

Távora, like Eduardo Gomes, had been one of those *tenentes* who revolted as far back as 1922 against the old order. As a hand-

20. Castilho Cabral, *Tempos de Jânio e outros tempos* (Rio de Janeiro: Editôra Civilização Brasileira, S.A., 1962), pp. 64–70; Viriato de Castro, *O fenômeno Jânio Quadros* (3ª edição; editor, José Viriato de Castro; distribuidores, Palácio do Livro, São Paulo, 1959), pp. 129–139.

some youth he participated dramatically throughout most of the twenties in jailbreaks, conspiracies, and revolution, becoming in 1930 the "Viceroy of the North." Now, in 1955, he was the *tenente do cabelo branco* (*tenente* with white hair), pushing for a "revolution by means of the vote." He emphasized in his campaign that "I have nothing to offer except sacrifices."

Lacerda's *Tribuna da Imprensa* stormed against Kubitschek and Goulart and headlined Admiral Pena Boto's interview: "It is not possible that there return to authority men who have humiliated this nation; Ademar and Juscelino Kubitschek do not have the moral requirements for the presidency." The *Tribuna* suggested dismissing congress, postponing the elections, and having the cabinet elaborate a new constitution to be voted on by a constitutional assembly.[21] Zenóbio da Costa and other army men who opposed any such *golpe,* organized the *Movimento Militar Constitucionalista* (MMC).

After Juscelino Kubitschek and "Jango" Goulart swung into the lead with the votes reported on October 10, 1955, their opponents voiced a number of objections. "Even with Communist support," wrote Pena Boto on October 14, "the J-J ticket has only about one-third of the vote." There was again discussion of whether the 1946 Constitution required an absolute majority, and some wanted to investigate the large vote reported from Minas Gerais for possible fraud.

The funeral of General Canrobert Pereira da Costa, who had been a leader of the Military Club and Dutra's war minister, occurred at a time when feelings were running high in the army. Colonel Jurandir Mamede's funeral oration, a cry against the "victory of the minority," was such a public political pronouncement that War Minister Lott made up his mind to punish Mamede. In this he was opposed by Carlos Luz, who on November 8 had temporarily taken over the presidency while Café Filho withdrew for medical treatment. Acting President Luz, aware of Lott's expressed wish to resign if nothing were done about

21. Joffre Gomes da Costa, *Marechal Henrique Lott* (Rio de Janeiro, 1960), pp. 233–246.

Mamede, picked out a new war minister, General Fiuza de Castro. Luz and Lott conversed on November 10, after Lott had been kept waiting 40 minutes in the presidential anteroom, and thus Lott learned about his successor. Fiuza accepted Lott's suggested timing for the change: Lott would step down on the afternoon of the eleventh.[22]

Fearing that the Luz administration, together with air force and navy leaders, was preparing to impede the January 31 inauguration of Kubitschek and Goulart, Lott agreed on the night of November 10 to head the MMC's work. This consisted in taking military action. Fiuza was made prisoner. While Catête Palace was being surrounded by troops, Acting President Luz and some of his cabinet got to the navy ministry. There Transport Minister Marcondes Ferraz telephoned Quadros in São Paulo. Then the presidential party, joined by Mamede and Carlos Lacerda, got aboard the Tamandaré. The ship's defective equipment was partially repaired, and it set forth at a slow pace in the fog for Santos after shots from Rio's forts had missed it.[23]

The MMC dominated the military picture, and at Santos the Tamandaré was threatened by coastal artillery and could not dock. By the time the ship got back to Rio on November 13, congress, surrounded by Lott's soldiers, had declared Nereu Ramos, vice president of the senate and the next in line, to be acting president of Brazil.

A new crisis arose on November 21 when Café Filho, back in his modest Copacabana apartment from the clinic, prepared to reassume the presidency. This was perfectly agreeable to Nereu Ramos, but Lott, who had been named war minister by Nereu Ramos, placed army tanks to prevent Café Filho's getting to the presidential palace. Lott was not alone in deploring the insistence shown by anti-Kubitschek people for the return of Café Filho. The PSD-PTB congressional majority voted that Café Filho should not return, and the courts failed to support the excellent legal case he presented.

22. Interview with Henrique Lott, Rio de Janeiro, Aug. 27, 1963.
23. Interview with Otávio Marcondes Ferraz, São Paulo, Aug. 9, 1963.

THE KUBITSCHEK ADMINISTRATION, 1956-1961

Nereu Ramos, on January 31, 1956, turned the presidency over to Juscelino Kubitschek. With Vice President Goulart handling labor matters, *getulista* and Communist labor union leaders looked forward to better days than those of Café Filho's administration.[24]

In the course of his election campaign, Kubitschek emphasized economic development targets for Brazil. Engineers and economists such as Lucas Lopes and Roberto Campos, who had worked on the Joint Brazil–United States Economic Development Commission and with the BNDE, restudied these five-year goals after Kubitschek's election; as members of the National Development Council, they did much to draw them up in final form.

With the inauguration of the Três Marias Dam on the São Francisco River in Minas Gerais in 1960 and with work started in 1958 on the huge Furnas hydroelectric project, also in Minas Gerais, steps were taken to increase significantly Brazil's installed electric energy capacity. Steel production was almost doubled between 1955 and 1960. The automobile industry, which prior to 1957 had been limited to assembling vehicles, came into its own with the production in 1960 of 133,000 vehicles, of which almost 90 percent by weight consisted of parts manufactured domestically.

Food production received less attention than industrial production, and the wheat-production goal remained as unrealistic as statistics on wheat produced. In the face of some difficulties in producing wheat economically, and with the increasing use of wheat bread in the growing cities, wheat imports reached a new high, exceeded in value only by petroleum and petroleum products.

In addition to the development council's thirty economic development targets, another goal, mentioned in the constitutions of 1891, 1934, and 1946, loomed large during the Kubitschek administration: moving the nation's capital from Rio de Janeiro to Brasília in the central plateau. The new site had been de-

24. Robert J. Alexander, *Labor Relations in Argentina, Brazil, and Chile* (New York: McGraw-Hill, 1962), p. 65.

termined in studies made during the Dutra administration and those which followed. In September 1956, congress, at Kubitschek's request, created *Companhia Urbanizadora da Nova Capital,* or Urbanizing Company of the New Capital (NOVACAP), with the hope that it would eventually sell enough lots to finance its tremendous construction program; Israel Pinheiro, *mineiro* politician, became NOVACAP's president. Professor Lúcio Costa's design for the new capital was chosen in March 1957 by a panel of eminent international experts as the best. Oscar Niemeyer was placed in charge of planning government buildings.

Kubitschek always seemed to be in a hurry about the many projects he had for giving Brazil "fifty years of progress in five years." Speed was required above all if he was to finish his term of office at Brasília as he planned. After decades of talk and planning, the physical work now commenced in a sudden burst. Work began in 1957 on a road to the site of the new capital from the nearest rail point, Anápolis, about seventy-five miles away. At the same time, building materials were flown in by plane to start construction of the presidential palace. Something of the rough atmosphere of the old American West was recaptured in Cidade Livre, wooden buildings thrown together hastily for housing about thirty thousand who went to work on a three-shift basis each day of the week at relatively good pay. In addition, twenty thousand found work on the challenging, fourteen hundred-mile Belém-Brasília highway, and fourteen thousand on the 1,060-mile Fortaleza-Brasília highway. The highway between Belo Horizonte and Brasília, more than four hundred miles, was paved in time for Brasília's inauguration on April 21, 1960, and much was done on the highway connection between Santos and Brasília.

Kubitschek and his foreign affairs advisers realized that the demonstrations of hostility toward Vice President Nixon in Lima and Caracas in May 1958 were in part reflections of discontent at economic conditions in Latin America. The Brazilian president lost little time in suggesting to President Eisenhower the urgency of "revising fundamentally the policy of mutual understanding in this hemisphere." [25] When Kubitschek's close friend, Francisco

25. *Operacão Pan-Americana, Documentário* (Rio de Janeiro: Presidência da República, Servico de Documentação, 1958), I, 12.

Negrão de Lima, took over the foreign ministry from aging José Carlos de Macedo Soares in July 1958, he said he was doing so in order to carry out Brazil's foreign policy as enunciated when Kubitschek spoke of Operation Pan-America.

Kubitschek was speaking of the need for attacking underdevelopment jointly "so that, jointly, Pan-Americanism can be saved." That year, Negrão de Lima stressed Operation Pan-America when he spoke at the United Nations and when he attended meetings of foreign ministers of the American Republics held in Washington also in September 1958. These meetings resulted in the birth of the Committee of Twenty-one to study Latin American development programs. This new committee, on which Augusto Frederico Schmidt represented Brazil, deliberated much about ways to improve the Latin American economies, the need for additional loans and capital, and the need to stabilize the prices of basic products. Brazil was well aware that considerable United States aid was flowing to Europe and Asia, some of it to former enemy nations.

The United States, besides putting up 450 million dollars of the original capital of the Inter-American Development Bank, agreed to co-operate with Latin American efforts to fight underdevelopment. The Export-Import Bank's capital was increased. In July 1960 President Eisenhower announced a new program of loans and grants, and in August 1960 the United States Congress authorized his suggested appropriation of half a billion dollars for a special Inter-American Social Development Fund. This was just before the Committee of Twenty-one issued its Act of Bogotá which was "a statement of measures for social improvement and economic development within the framework of Operation Pan-America." [26]

Kubitschek, like many presidents before him, earmarked new expenditures and established new organizations to deal with Brazil's northeast. This was after the drought of 1958 had caused another disaster in this region, which includes roughly 15 percent of Brazil's land area and more than 30 percent of its population.

26. J. Lloyd Mecham, *The United States and Inter-American Security* (Austin: University of Texas Press, 1961), p. 384.

Superintendência do Desenvolvimento do Nordeste (SUDENE) was created late in 1959 to supervise the various federal agencies concerned with bettering the northeast. Under Celso Furtado it built up a staff of technicians and drew up an ambitious program.

The program included large sums for roads and electric power expansion, most of which were expected to be provided. It also gave much attention to "transforming the agricultural structure." Progressive irrigation and partial mechanization were to be advanced in the eastern humid belt, where sugar was being produced at a low yield per acre and per man-hour. Both in this belt and in the semiarid interior, irrigation was to help develop horticultural farming by many families, each of which was to work a relatively small area for the production of foods badly needed in the region. The marketing of such foods was to be improved. Some families had been moving from the northeast's semiarid region to more humid land in the state of Maranhão. Such a movement was to be fostered by SUDENE on a more scientific basis.

The northeast's fishing industry was to be developed; and, particularly in the state capitals of the region, water and drainage systems and popular housing were to be installed. Swampy lands in urban areas were to be reclaimed. Brazilian industry was to be attracted to the northeast by favorable tax and exchange arrangements; and special attention was to be given to reopening plants in the textile industry, the most important industry in the region.[27]

United States officials, irate at Castro and concerned with news of Francisco Julião's Marxist peasant leagues in Brazil's northeast, began to visit the region in increasing numbers.[28] But

27. SUDENE Five-Year Plan transcribed in *O Estado de S. Paulo*, July 23, 1961. The program is discussed in Stefan H. Robock, *Brazil's Developing Northeast* (The Brookings Institution, Washington, D. C., 1963), and Albert O. Hirschman, *Journeys Toward Progress* (New York: The Twentieth Century Fund, 1963), pp. 66–91. William W. Gorton in "The Northeast of Brazil" (December 1959, a report transmitted to the State Department by the American Embassy, Rio on March 11, 1960) states that there has been an overemphasis on irrigation as a cure-all and that more attention should be given to better dryland farming.

28. See comment by Gilberto Freyre on last page of his article "Misconceptions of Brazil" in *Foreign Affairs* (Council on Foreign Relations, Inc., New York), April 1962, pp. 453–462.

Furtado's main problem was getting the necessary Brazilian political support for his program. This he ably did, although congressional approval did not finally come until December 1961, after Kubitschek had left office. While proposing the development of the northeast so that the traditional relief might become less necessary, Furtado argued that this region's economy had been penalized in the past by federal exchange policies which had stimulated industrial development elsewhere.

Much of the money for Kubitschek's "fifty years of progress in five" was obtained by printing currency. Money in circulation increased from 69 billion cruzeiros at the end of 1955 to 202 billion early in 1961. Sight deposits of banks climbed from 112 billion cruzeiros to 507 billion, and the dollar on the free market went from 70 cruzeiros to 210. Living costs in January 1961 had more than tripled since the end of 1955. This was more inflation than Brazil had been experiencing before, and there was some complaint about the speed with which Brasília was constructed. Kubitschek's successor estimated the cost of projects "completed and in execution at Brasília" at 72.6 billion cruzeiros.[29]

The IBC bought and stored a large part of the Brazilian coffee crops, and coffee-producing nations entered into agreements about exports. Yet, coffee prices during the Kubitschek administration were quite unsatisfactory compared with those in the days of Presidents Dutra and Vargas, and they contributed to the balance of payments deficits which occurred after 1956. The balance of payments deficit was particularly large in 1960.

During Kubitschek's administration Brazil obtained some foreign exchange by drawings on the International Monetary Fund. A dispute arose, however, when Brazil sought to increase the drawings and when the IMF expressed grave concern at Brazil's methods of financing its economic development program. Kubitschek at length broke dramatically with the IMF, and among his supporters was Celso Furtado. Nationalists hailed this step, maintaining that economic principles applicable to developed nations are not appropriate for underdeveloped ones. A "reasonable" amount of inflation came to be regarded as good.

29. Jânio Quadros message, Brasília, Jan. 31, 1961, quoted in *O Estado de S. Paulo*, Feb. 1, 1961.

In the first six months of Kubitschek's administration, the Export-Import Bank authorized credits of more than 200 million dollars for Brazil. Of these, the largest item was 100 million dollars for railway rehabilitation equipment, and its announcement in July 1956 was made with Brazil's pledge to adopt means of bringing inflation under control. Again in 1958, after the World Bank had given Brazilian government representatives a cool reception, the Export-Import Bank was approached, this time in connection with arrearages of 158 million dollars on payments due the United States. The Eximbank furnished 100 million dollars and private United States banks 58 million dollars. But the malady persisted, aggravated by the large 1960 balance of payments deficit, and the Kubitschek administration had to leave an imposing number of unpaid short-term foreign currency obligations for its successor to deal with.

ELECTION OF OCTOBER 1960

A rhinoceros won 90,000 votes in the October 1959 São Paulo municipal council election. This incident was recognized as a protest against politicians, high living costs and some shortages of black beans and meat. Even the great projects which were giving Brazil a better place in the sun, even a world's soccer championship and a Wimbledon tennis title could not eradicate a growing discontent. The pains which inflation brought to large sectors and the agricultural community's lack of participation in the progress caused such dissatisfaction that even admirers of the optimistic and high-flying Kubitschek conceded that in the October 1960 presidential election the chances of the PSD were not great. Marshal Henrique Lott, who had served as Kubitschek's war minister, agreed to make the effort; and again the PSD-PTB combination nominated Goulart for Vice President.

Much of the opposition looked to Jânio Quadros. São Paulo had been helped by the Kubitschek administration's industrialization program, and Quadros had concluded a successful, if sometimes turbulent, governorship there and seen his useful finance

30. Export-Import Bank of Washington, press release of July 30, 1956, for morning papers, July 31, 1956.

secretary, Professor Carvalho Pinto, succeed him. Quadros was hardly a party organization man. He had run against the UDN and other large parties to gain the São Paulo governorship in 1954. But he had many qualities which appealed to the UDN. These included a good administrative record and a spirit of opposition akin to that of the UDN. Above all, Quadros had an ability to get through to the poor classes, which was by no means typical of the UDN.

Disheveled, thin, and indignant, Quadros would rant against the "corruption of the politicians" and promise to govern sternly. A good showman who liked to be known as temperamental, he attracted multitudes rather than made friends.[31] Quadros was reserved in office, suspicious of the opinions of others, and sure of his own infallible touch; at times he seemed to regard opposition to his will as something bent on destroying the dignity which he sought to give to the post in which the people had placed him.

At the convention of the UDN, Quadros was opposed by Juraci Magalhães, a 1930 *tenente* who was Bahia's governor. Juraci had long been associated with the opposition party and had recently been its president. But with the support of Carlos Lacerda, Quadros became the UDN's nominee for president. He also became the candidate of some minor parties and of an independent *janista* movement which sought to steer clear of political parties: the *Movimento Popular Jânio Quadros*. Now Quadros's broom, the promise of greater morality in government, became a widely accepted symbol.

Like Távora in 1955, Quadros included, among his offers, the promise that hard work and sacrifices would be required of all. Besides facing Marshal Lott, Quadros faced long-time arch-rival Ademar de Barros, who again ran for the presidency on the ticket of the PSP. Ademar's lawyers had successfully defended him against being jailed for financial irregularities, and he had returned from exile to be elected mayor of São Paulo city in 1957 in the face of Governor Quadros's opposition.[32]

31. Castilho Cabral, *Tempos de Jânio e outros tempos* (Rio de Janeiro: Editôra Civilização Brasileira, S.A., 1962) , pp. 142-145.

32. Viriato de Castro, *O ex-leão de São Manoel: Ademar* (editor, José Viriato de Castro; distribuidores, Palácio do Livro, São Paulo, 1960) , Chaps. III, IV, V.

Early in the 1960 campaign Quadros resigned "irrevocably" as a candidate. To the many who wanted the changes he was promising, it was a relief to learn that the resignation was, after all, not irrevocable but, rather, the political maneuver of one who sought to be independent of political bosses. Soon afterward, Quadros made a short visit to Cuba, which Marshal Lott had refused to do.

Quadros's 5.6 million votes almost equaled the combined totals of Lott and Ademar de Barros. By a narrow margin Goulart was re-elected vice president against two opponents.

THE QUADROS ADMINISTRATION, 1961

A few hours after his inauguration on January 31, 1961, Quadros stressed the financial problems he had inherited, and he named commissions to investigate what he termed previous wrongdoings. Lacerda accused some minor officials of the outgoing administration of having participated in lucrative contraband activities. He had been elected governor of Guanabara, the state which includes the city of Rio and which replaced the former Federal District.

The names of those who were selected by President Quadros to handle financial matters were reassuring to businessmen and international financiers. Also encouraging to some was the new administration's step to eliminate multiple exchange rates. A less popular aspect of this was the ending of subsidized exchange rates for importing wheat, gasoline and paper. Quadros's well-chosen negotiators in the United States and Europe renegotiated large foreign debt payments which were coming due and could not have been met. The general optimism was reflected in the package deal announced in Washington in May 1961, in which the Eximbank rescheduled payments about to fall due and made possible sizable new credits. Other new credits were offered by the Treasury Exchange Stabilization Fund and the new United States foreign assistance program. The IMF also agreed to help.[33]

Quadros left no doubt who was running Brazil. Notes to ad-

33. Gertrude E. Heare, *Brazil, Information for United States Businessmen* (Department of Commerce, Washington, D. C., 1962), pp. 161–162.

ministrators signed by him and bearing instructions on all sorts of matters appeared daily in the press. He banned cockfights, upset the jockey clubs by limiting horse racing to Sundays, and outlawed "bikini" bathing beauty contests. He insisted on a strict adherence to working hours by government employees.

Brazil's new president received a visit in March 1961 from American Ambassador John Moors Cabot and Adolf Berle. Berle, then special representative of President Kennedy, had come from Washington with worries about the Cuban situation and wanted Brazil to join the United States in pressing for inter-American action in the Caribbean.

To this Quadros would not agree. He was just about to unveil a new Brazilian foreign policy which would be profoundly "independent," abandoning "the dependent and ineffectual diplomacy of a nation tied to worthy but alien interests." This new policy, described as a hardheaded drive for power, was pictured by Quadros as being in keeping with, and useful to, a fast-growing Brazil which was making "gigantic strides in breaking the barrier of underdevelopment." Specifically, Brazil rejected "the ideological prejudices of the capitalistic democracies, ever ready to decry the idea of state intervention"; Brazil would renew diplomatic relations with Russia and the Soviet Bloc countries, look for new trade relations anywhere, push for close ties with the emerging nations of Africa, insist on nonintervention in Cuba, and support the proposal that the United Nations General Assembly take up the question of "the representation of China." [34] This new program went forward amid heated discussions by the press and public.

United States Treasury Secretary Douglas Dillon's visit to Quadros, made just before the Punta del Este Conference of August 1961, indicated a vast Alliance for Progress program. The visit was apparently a friendlier one than that of Berle and Cabot. There was no dramatic withdrawal from the Punta del Este Conference. Quadros did, nevertheless, have the opportunity to em-

---

34. See Jânio Quadros, "Brazil's New Foreign Policy" in *Foreign Affairs,* Oct. 1961; also Frank Bonilla, "Operation Neutralism," *American University Field Staff Report,* IX, No. 1 (New York, Feb. 1962); and Maria Y. Leite Linhares, "Brazilian Foreign Policy and Africa" in *The World Today,* XVIII, No. 12 (London: Oxford University Press, December 1962).

phasize his "independent" foreign policy when he decorated Cuba's "Che" Guevara with the highest order of the *Cruzeiro do Sul*. Lacerda, now critical of the president's foreign policy, then presented keys to the city of Rio to Cubans who had defied Castro.

On the night of August 24, Lacerda, reflecting on an unsatisfactory visit he had had in Brasília with a difficult Quadros, made serious accusations on television and radio. He charged that Justice Minister Pedroso D'Horta had spoken to him in the president's name and asked him to seek the support of one of the military ministers for a reform which would increase the presidential authority. Lacerda thus accused Quadros, unhappy with congress (a carry-over from the previous regime), of plotting against the existing form of government. Congress resolved the next morning to investigate and called Pedroso D'Horta to appear. Under these circumstances Quadros resigned, to the surprise of his closest associates. Quadros told one of the generals with whom he was celebrating "The Day of the Soldier" that he could not govern in the face of constant attacks on his honor, his family, his policies and administration.

The dramatic, the unorthodox had been among Quadros's political tools. He saw himself as indispensable to the salvation of Brazil and highly popular with the common people. Much in his resignation letter of August 25 recalled Vargas's farewell words. Quadros's "indefatigable" efforts for everything good and against "appetites and ambitions of individual groups, including foreign ones," were being overwhelmed by "terrible forces." Confronted by these, Quadros advised that he did not lack the "courage" for making the great sacrifice. But, unlike Vargas, Quadros planned to be alive to enjoy the fruits of the popular manifestations aroused by his sacrifice.

Although he spoke of returning to law and teaching, he expected to be lifted back sooner or later as a great political force, stronger than ever. He was not called back quickly, however, as he had been when he resigned as a presidential candidate. True, those who then headed the armed forces had no confidence in Vice President Goulart, but it was up to congress to deal with the situation. Legislators departing for a weekend away from Brasília were called back by their leaders. They expressed no comments when

Auro de Moura Andrade, vice president of the senate, announced the voluntary resignation and prepared to have Ranieri Mazzilli, president of the chamber of deputies, take over provisionally in view of Goulart's absence from the country.

The ex-president was described as tearful when he sailed for Europe, and his tears were attributed to this lack of a great popular wave of support. But as he departed he quoted Vargas in 1945: "Though they send me away, I shall nevertheless return." On his trip to Cuba as a candidate, Quadros had been impressed with the popular support which Castro had derived by an absence from the scene—support which the Cuban prime minister had then used to advantage in his squabble with the Cuban president.

THE GOULART ADMINISTRATION, 1961–1964

People were mostly annoyed and shocked, and they quickly became concerned with the nation's serious political and military crisis. The military ministers "vetoed" turning the presidency in any way over to Goulart, Labor party head, who was on an official visit to Red China at the time. They instituted censorship of the press. Against them were those who felt that Brazil should abide by her constitution. These included Lott, who was made prisoner for expressing his opinion, and came to include enough of the army to make civil war quite possible. There were also Goulart's own noisy supporters. Among these were organized labor and Goulart's brother-in-law, Leonel Brizola. Brizola was governor of Rio Grande do Sul and there the commander of the Third Army prepared "on behalf of the Constitution" to combat the orders of his superiors.

Goulart learned in Montevideo on September 1 about the political situation from his friend, Deputado Tancredo Neves, who had served with him and after him in the last Vargas cabinet. Then he sped to a warm welcome in Rio Grande do Sul. By this time congress was putting the finishing touches on a constitutional amendment which would give the nation a parliamentary form of government. Under it congress was supposed to control the cabinet through the newly created post of prime minister. Labor party members and other Goulart supporters were cool to this change, but when military leaders somewhat reluctantly agreed to accept Goulart under this arrangement, the immediate crisis was over. Brazilians congratulated themselves upon this latest example of the traditional use of compromise to avoid bloodshed. One of the few senators to vote against the new restrictions on the president was Kubitschek, recently elected senator from Goiás. For one thing, he was interested in running for president again in 1965.

Although it turned out that President Goulart still had considerable power, he was, to put it mildly, far from enthusiastic about the new form of government. Political cartoons showed him in the dress of the Queen of England. Tancredo Neves was Goulart's first prime minister for nine months, and during this period it seemed that the system was not conducive to getting much done. The inflation continued with more force than ever.

To succeed Tancredo Neves, late in June 1962 Goulart nominated San Tiago Dantas who, as the parliamentary regime's foreign minister, had been carrying forward vigorously the "independent" foreign policy inaugurated by Quadros. San Tiago Dantas, a clever lawyer and labor party member, did not get the support of the PSD and UDN in congress, and his nomination was rejected.

July 1962 was hectic. Strikes were staged in support of a "popular nationalist government." Unnecessary food shortages in some metropolitan areas touched off riots and looting which caused deaths. Congressmen, anxious to start campaigning for the October 1962 elections, agreed to accept Brochado da Rocha as prime minister, but they would not agree to support him. Brochado da Rocha had been Brizola's justice secretary in Rio Grande do Sul.

Unrest and agitation continued as Brochado da Rocha asked that voting rights be extended to Brazil's illiterates, estimated at 50 percent of the population. He presented to congress a request for extraordinary powers to enact a program hardly agreeable to what he called "an international capitalism linked to reactionary domestic groups." [35] Congress turned down most of the twenty-two-point

35. Brochado da Rocha's address to Congress, July 9, 1962. The full program is given in *Mensagem ao Congresso Nacional*, Brasília, Aug. 10, 1962 (issued by Departamento de Imprensa Nacional).

program. Many regarded the "reforms" which the program was to bring about as interesting to the executive branch for the vast powers provided. But the request for these powers helped pave the way for a compromise which revealed Goulart's political ability and did not disappoint Kubitschek. PSD Leader Ernani do Amaral Peixoto agreed at length with War Minister Nelson de Melo that there ought to be an early plebiscite to determine whether Brazil should return from the discredited "parliamentary" system to a presidential one. This settled, harassed congressmen could resume their campaigning.

Quadros, perhaps reflecting that Vargas had blamed his 1945 downfall on Berle, came back from Europe and explained his resignation in a speech critical of Berle, Cabot, Dillon and the West German ambassador. But it was not a particularly effective performance, and when he campaigned for the São Paulo governorship his opponents declared that whiskey had been among those terrible foreign forces that had overcome him. Ademar de Barros, waving the anti-Communist flag, won the governorship by a close vote in October 1962. At the same time, Brizola, no friend of the American businessman, was voted federal *deputado* from Guanabara by a large margin, although his candidate to succeed him as Rio Grande do Sul's governor was beaten.

In the January 6, 1963, plebiscite, those who went to the polls rejected, by a majority of roughly five to one, the so-called parliamentary regime, blaming it for agitation, inflation and a lack of leadership. Most of the Brazilian people, regardless of where they placed the responsibility for economic and other difficulties, hoped that with the return to presidentialism the administration would turn to that which needed attention.

They wished success to San Tiago Dantas when he went as finance minister to negotiate in Washington in March 1963. There David E. Bell, AID administrator, made 85 million dollars available at once and offered an additional 300 million dollars in steps over the following twelve months, each step depending on financial or economic measures to be taken by Brazil in accordance with the Brazilian government's Three-Year Plan. The Three-Year Plan listed attractive objectives, such as a rate of growth in national income of 7 percent annually (3.9 percent per capita), a progressive and large reduction in the rate of inflation; and a better distribution of the development's benefits among the people. The plan, with its many statistics, was considered helpful in justifying politically difficult measures which the government was to take for reducing the inflation and bettering the nation's financial and credit position.

To the detriment of the execution of such measures political pressures and maneuvers had the upper hand in Brazilian government circles. The entire cabinet was replaced in June 1963. Nor did Carvalho Pinto, then appointed to succeed San Tiago Dantas as finance minister, remain in his post until the year was out.

The sixty-five-year-old Luís Carlos Prestes hailed the defeat of the Three-Year Plan. He was heading that part of Brazil's splintered Communist movement which was Moscow-oriented and which for ten years had been "peacefully" but actively at work in Brazil, attacking United States "imperialism" and espousing the redistribution of large landholdings. Prestes could see the possibility of local forces, with which the Communists co-operated, bringing about what he called a popular-democratic-nationalistic government "without bloodshed, without the need of civil war." These forces had programs similar to those of the Brazilian Communist party, and they had the greater appeal of being more genuinely Brazilian.

The influence of such forces in the land was evident but not such as to control congress. The president, fond of blaming inflation on what he called the country's "obsolete feudal structure," was often critical of congress. Some but not all of the frequent changes he made among administrators were pleasing to far-leftists. Furthermore, in making them, the president seemed to be alert lest any one far-leftist group, such as that headed by Pernambuco's Governor Miguel Arrias, gain a political position too strong in relation to his own.

"Trial balloons" and numerous rumors about changes had an unsettling effect in 1963. The possible meanings of possible changes were everywhere discussed.

A bill to limit the remission of profits abroad, which had been receiving active attention of the lawmakers in 1961 and later, was awaiting a regulating decree from the executive branch. This was in the last half of 1963, by which time both foreign private capital and much Brazilian capital were wary.[36] Arrearages on debts owed abroad were uncomfortably high, and the United States had cut assistance sharply, insisting that development in Brazil required more effort on Brazil's part than that being put forth by the Goulart administration. On the brighter side, the coffee price was beginning to pick up.

In 1963, a poor year economically for Brazil, the gross national product showed a per capita decline for the first time in years. The cost of living in cruzeiros went up at least 80 percent, reaching 340 percent of its 1961 average. Brokers at the end of 1963 were getting 1,200 cruzeiros per dollar, compared with less than 300 when Goulart took over from Quadros. Currency in circulation increased during 1963 from 509 billion cruzeiros to 890 billion. The federal payroll grew fivefold between 1961 and 1963.[37]

The 1965 presidential election was, in the latter part of 1963, a topic of conversation. Prominent candidates included Kubitschek (who spoke of increasing agricultural output) and Lacerda; but many combinations appeared possible, there was a fair amount of uncertainty in the air.

Governors Lacerda and Ademar de Barros were not in the good graces of the chief executive. Some believed that the silencing of these two, particularly the combative Lacerda, was one objective of a "state of siege" which the executive branch asked congress to declare in October 1963. This request followed the curbing of a revolt by army sergeants in Brasília and came at a time of frequent strikes.

The executive branch was warning of possible conspiracies, somewhat as Vargas had warned before he ended democracy in

36. Speaking at the Rotary Club of São Paulo in July 1962, San Tiago Dantas said that the total of Brazilian capital in the United States, Switzerland and other countries was 150 percent of the maximum that the Brazilian Government could hope to obtain from the entire Alliance for Progress program.

Regarding foreign capital, *Análise e Perspectiva Econômica*—APEC (Rio de Janeiro) stated on Sept. 27, 1963, that "the balance of the movement of foreign capital in Brazil was a mere five million dollars for the first half of 1963. For the same period the balance was 154 million dollars in 1961, and 36 million dollars in 1962."

37. Ranieri Mazzilli, address to the nation, April 13, 1964.

1937. But a majority of congressmen, although aware that all was not tranquil, did not favor bestowing on Goulart the temporary special powers which a "state of siege" would provide. The request was withdrawn. Memories remained of those strokes whereby Getúlio Vargas in the thirties set constitutions aside and perpetuated himself in office. With Vargas's ambitious "political heir" in the presidency, these memories were particularly vivid; and Goulart did little to discourage the suspicion that he wished to provoke a coup in order to lead a countercoup.

The polarization of far-left and anti-far-left forces was augmented in 1964. Goulart turned to demonstrators as he had in 1962, to bring influence to bear on congress and his opponents. This turn was also inspired by the president's determination to assume for himself the leadership of far-left groups at a time that San Tiago Dantas's *Frente Unica* was being promoted to attract such groups.[38]

On March 13, 1964, after preparing decrees expropriating private oil refineries and providing for the expropriation of lands near highways and railways, Goulart appeared before a noisy crowd. It had been organized by the illegal General Labor Command (*Comando Geral dos Trabalhadores,* or CGT) in front of Rio's Dom Pedro II Railway Station. Brizola also spoke on this occasion and urged a "populist and nationalist" government and a congress "composed of peasants, workers, sergeants, and nationalist officers." When Goulart spoke, he called the constitution obsolete and attacked business leaders and "reactionaries." Public tranquility and social peace, he declared, depended on the enactment of his favorite reforms.

Some of these reforms were presented to congress when it met a few days later; they included voting rights for illiterates and

38. The San Tiago Dantas *Frente Unica* proposed to improve Brazil by such reforms as enfranchisement of illiterates, legalization of the "Communist party," expropriation of private oil refineries, use of bonds to pay for expropriated lands, amnesty for sergeants who rebelled in 1963, establishment of "a unilateral foreign debt moratorium if a renegotiation were not made available," "abrogation of excessively rigid strike regulations," and cancellation of "mining concessions that might be deemed not in the national interest." Quotes are from p. 175 of the April 1964 issue of Stanford University's *Hispanic American Report* (which covers the matter more fully).

expropriations of property without prompt indemnification in cash. Plebiscites wherein all Brazilians over eighteen could express their opinions on issues were also suggested. A "popular front" cabinet was said to be in the making, and the General Labor Command was reported planning a general strike if congress proved difficult.

Luís Carlos Prestes claimed credit for having suggested the lively March 13 meeting, and there was talk about the possible legalization of the Brazilian Communist Party. In any event, the meeting pleased the president, who announced he would appear at street meetings elsewhere.

This prospect of more unrest further weakened the currency; a dollar would buy 1,500 cruzeiros. Another repercussion was one of Dutra's rare political pronouncements: he urged respect for the constitution and condemned disorder. *Paulistas* were quick to organize a large anti-Communist demonstration at which Senate President Auro de Moura Andrade spoke and where a "manifesto of São Paulo women" on behalf of Christianity and democracy was read. A similar mass meeting was planned for April 2 in Rio.

Goulart had a healthy respect for the military. He believed his attention to promoting officers faithful to himself as a person or as president had considerably improved his position since Quadros's resignation, and he was offering a large increase in military salaries. Before submitting his reform message to congress he cleared it with commanders of military sectors.

Some below the rank of commissioned officers chose, like sergeants of the 1963 revolt, to break discipline as a means of seeking political rights denied them by the constitution. Their ardor whipped up by recent developments, about three thousand sailors in Rio mutinied against their superiors on March 25, 1964.

Goulart had found it tempting all along to back the enlisted men. By now, the only support upon which he could rely lay in the forces he had encouraged at the March 13 rally, and he did not intend to relinquish this support. After the General Labor Command spoke of calling a general strike to back the fourteen hundred sailors who were still striking on March 27, Goulart let it be known that the sailors would not be punished. Many of these sailors then marched victoriously through Rio's streets on Good Friday, carrying on their shoulders the two "leftist" admirals who had refused to punish them.

This "shocking exhibition" was condemned in a memorandum signed by twenty-seven high navy officers. The Military Club also protested, pointing out that the disorderly sailors had been "insidiously indoctrinated by union leaders at the service of Moscow."

ADVENT OF THE CASTELO BRANCO ADMINISTRATION, APRIL 1964

Goulart seemed to be inviting a showdown. Emotionally addressing a group of military police sergeants, he declared himself to be on the side of the sergeants and the people, against foreign trusts and dishonest tradesmen. Referring to the navy crisis, he said that reactionaries were defending discipline by committing breaches of discipline.

Some of his words were too much for commanders of federal forces. Those who had been worrying about Communist infiltration and for this or other reasons had felt it imperative to remove Goulart now finally got the additional support they needed. It came from commanders who had been reluctant to see the armed forces upset a constitutional president. Such a step now seemed preferable to military indiscipline and national chaos.

Having put their reluctance aside and drawn up their plans, the military leaders acted effectively on March 31 in a practically bloodless movement. They had the support of important governors. No sooner had army forces in Minas Gerais gone into action and been backed by Governor Magalhães Pinto, than General Amauri Kruel, head of the Second Army in São Paulo, led a march on Rio. (Kruel, a signer of the 1954 memorandum of the colonels, had in 1962 been Goulart's war minister.) Goulart fled from Rio to Brasília and from there to his home state of Rio Grande do Sul. Activities of the General Labor Command and students sympathetic to it were no match for the military. In the south, too, there was a quick collapse of the pro-Goulart resistance which Brizola tried to organize. Brazilians are not prone to shoot at fellow Brazilians, and some Third Army units under General Cordeiro de Farias were able to occupy Pôrto Alegre on behalf of the movement without firing a shot. Goulart was in exile in Uruguay on April 2, the day which Rio anti-Communists had set aside for a "Family with God for Freedom" procession. The planned protest of these *cariocas* against Goulart became, instead, an impressive victory celebration. There were enthusiastic popular expressions of relief elsewhere.

While the recent military victors and Goulart's strongest political foes were hailed, steps were being taken to eliminate the influence of those believed to have played important roles in making the military action necessary. Some suspects fled the country, and some sought asylum in embassies. Many more were jailed. These included not only Pernambuco's Governor Arrais, but also many who had been involved in the Petrobrás corruption. Subversive material, such as papers which schemers had not had time to burn, were made public to show that infiltrators with ties to foreign communism had been active along with Brazilian Marxists and "Far Leftists."

This time military leaders felt they had more to do than simply step aside quickly in favor of politicians. They hoped to repair some of the damage created by a government which, they said, had "deliberately sought to bolshevize the nation." With the acquiescence of congress, they placed one of their own leaders, General Humberto Castelo Branco, in the presidency to fill out the unfinished term of Quadros and Goulart. The new president surrounded himself with able civilian technicians. Upon assuming office on April 15, he listed his modest material assets, thus implying that there would be a healthy change from practices of the recent past.

The military gave the new president exceptional powers which were to last until January 31, 1966—powers which Quadros and Goulart would have dearly cherished. The "Institutional Act," issued by the "Supreme Command of the Revolution," did not limit itself to enumerating these special presidential powers. It allowed the supreme command, "in the interest of peace and the national honor," to remove congressmen and to suspend for ten years the political rights of individuals. Forty-four federal congressmen were promptly deprived of their mandates, and more than 250 Brazilians lost their political rights for ten years. Among them were João Goulart, Jânio Quadros, Luís Carlos Prestes, Leonel Brizola, Miguel Arrais, Celso Furtado, Francisco Julião, and Samuel Wainer; also Osvino Ferreira Alves, who had become known as "the Marxist Marshal" after the Goulart administration promoted him to the rank of marshal and put him in charge of Petrobrás.

There were weeks of suspense while the fate of ex-President Kubitschek was being decided. This exuberant PSD candidate for the 1965 presidential election declared in May 1964 that the time had come for him to defend himself against attacks—attacks which included some talk about his personal wealth.

On June 8, six days before the end of the period which the new government was allowing itself for the summary cancellation of political rights, Castelo Branco followed the recommendation of the National Security Council. Kubitschek's political rights were canceled for ten years and he was thrown out of his senate seat. Hundreds of thousands of Brazilians had just signed a petition asking the president not to do this.

As in 1955, "J.K." had become the hope of forces which liked *getulismo* and Goulart. But members of the military who were investigating the case felt that the possibility of Kubitschek's returning soon to the presidential palace might be harmful to Brazil. It might, they felt, mean reopening the doors of the palace to concepts which the movement of March 31, 1964 had opposed.

CONCLUDING REMARKS

From September 1946 until late March 1964 Brazil had persevered along the path of democracy established by the 1946 Constitution.

That constitution had no greater devotee than the first president to serve under it, a man steeped in military ways. Asked for his opinion, Dutra's custom had been to turn the pages of the small book which had become his constant companion. "What does the Constitution say?" he would ask.

Most of the electorate took pride in feeling that the nation adhered to the constitutional way—a way indicating orderliness and maturity. This is not to say that the political institutions were immune from scratches. The military, when pretty well united, could act as a sort of extra legal authority whose infrequent but awesome utterances and deeds were defended as necessary for safeguarding democracy itself. Under the pressure of rare circumstances and strong force, Brazil's Magna Carta was adaptable to hasty patchwork, symbolic of a heritage rich in compromise. But until April 1964 this flexibility was not regarded as something for enhancing executive authority at the expense of powers conferred on congress by the 1946 Constitution.

In its seventeen and a half years of life, beginning in September 1946, the system faced the increasing strains of social dissatisfaction. The "population explosion" had been making headway. Advancing communications invited comparisons. Voices, local and foreign, friendly and unfriendly, emphasized the need for some alteration of the status quo. Brazil required a good measure of prosperity and the widespread sharing of its benefits.

The problems were not easy. Steps to distribute better the gains of economic development needed handling in a manner which would not jeopardize that development. But the problems were not so difficult as politics made them. In the latter part of the period reviewed, some were asking whether the system established in Brazil by the 1946 constitution permitted the solution of the economic and social problems.

Numerous political parties operated within the system. Twelve of them were represented in the 1960 federal congress, but of the 326 *deputados,* 251 belonged to either the PSD, UDN or PTB. Runoff elections of top contenders for executive offices were not practiced, so that victory did not necessarily indicate a great popularity. (Goulart, with two opponents for the vice presidency in 1960, received 36 percent of the total vote in spite of the support of two of the large parties, the PSD and PTB.) Split oppositions, interparty deals, and the inability to make such deals considerably affected outcomes. Coalitions worked out in state elections indicated that parties had a greater concern for expediency than for principles.

Quadros suggested a profound difficulty when he remarked that pursuing a program which would benefit Brazil would make him highly unpopular. If Quadros was right, the practice of democracy itself would seem to be a deterrent to necessary measures.

But Quadros may have underestimated a people who had come to find few reasons to rate politicians highly. It is conceivable that serious attention within the law to the problems at hand, rather than a prima donna complex, would have enhanced the popular image of more than one chief executive. Be this true or not, there was an evident need at the top for the kind of courage and patriotism which is not necessarily flamboyant nor swayed by slogans of the moment.

That this need was insufficiently satisfied can of course be blamed on the democratic process as it was carried out under the 1946 Constitution. But to dismiss the matter with this thought would not be fair. One has to recognize the role played by sheer bad luck. It can well be argued that in the early sixties the Brazilian electorate received packages which rather differed from those ordered and that the crack-up of March 1964 would have been avoided had the voice of the electorate been carefully heeded in the presidential palace.

Quadros's wholly irresponsible and reckless act could hardly have been predicted by voters who, favoring his broom, the sacrifices he called for, and the administrative talent his record seemed to imply, elected him by a large vote. His resignation opened the door for much that his successful candidacy had opposed. Men whom electors had rejected in 1960 state elections reappeared in high national posts because they were friends of Goulart and perhaps because there had been no federal congressional election in 1960.

Confronted with the crises of 1961 and 1962, Brazilians continued to favor a fair chance for the constitutional democratic institutions. Goulart was able to achieve the top office in September 1961 because of a widespread desire to see those institutions honored. But once it suited him he shed his respect for this concept. Choosing not to administer but to agitate, Goulart fostered an unfortunate struggle which had some of its roots in October 1945, when noisy *queremistas* clamored for the cancellation of an election decree, wanting the continuation of a government headed by Getúlio Vargas.

GLOSSARY

BNDE. *Banco Nacional do Desenvolvimento Econômico;* National Economic Development Bank.

Brigadeiro. Brigadier. High air force rank.

Carioca. Pertaining to, or native of, the city of Rio de Janeiro.

CEXIM. *Carteira de Exportação e Importação;* Office of Exports and Imports.

Casa Militar. Military household; the military staff of the presidential office.

Cidade Livre. Literally, Free City.

Coluna Prestes. Prestes Column. (Miguel Costa-Prestes Column.)

Comissao de Constituiçao. Constitutional Commission. The Assembly's commission to draft a constitution.

Confederaçao. Confederation. As used here, a national confederation of employee or employer federations in a rather inclusive realm of endeavor (such as commerce, industry, etc.) (Part of an officially sponsored arrangement.)

Confederaçao dos Trabalhadores do Brasil. Confederation of Brazilian Workers. (Not a part of the officially sponsored arrangement.)

Cruzeiro. Brazilian unit of currency.

Cruzeiro do Sul. Southern Cross, Brazilian Government decoration.

Deputado. Congressman.

DIP. *Departamento de Imprensa e Propaganda;* Department of Press and Propaganda. This controlled incoming and outgoing news during the Vargas dictatorship.

Escola Superior de Guerra. National War College.

Estado Nôvo. "New State." Term to denote the dictatorial state ushered in by Vargas in 1937.

Federaçao. Federation. As used here, a federation of *sindicatos* in a particular branch of endeavor in a particular region. (Part of an officially sponsored arrangement.)

Frente Unica. United Front. Used here with reference to a sort of Popular Front, headed by San Tiago Dantas early in 1964 and known more formally as the Front Supporting Basic Reforms (*Frente de Apôio às Reformas de Base*—FARB).

Gaúcho. Pertaining to, or native of, Rio Grande do Sul (southernmost state).

Getulista. Connected with Getúlio Vargas.

IBC. *Instituto Brasileiro do Café;* Brazilian Coffee Institute.

Impôsto Sindical. Tax on all wage- and salary-earners (established by the Estado Nôvo at one day's pay per year) for supporting the set-up of syndicates, federations and confederations.

Integralista. Member of *Ação Integralista Brasileira* (Brazilian Integralist Action), a movement and political party established late in 1932 along lines considered fascist. Dressed in green shirts, the *Integralistas* put on some imposing parades until the party, like others, was outlawed late in 1937.

Interventor. Governor of a state appointed by Brazilian president as his direct agent. During the Vargas dictatorship all states were governed by such appointees, although the appointee in Minas Gerais (an exception) was known as "Governor."

Janista. Connected with Jânio Quadros.

Juntas Governativas. As used here, government bodies used to intervene in, and control, labor unions.

Liga Eleitoral Católica. Catholic Electoral League. This was established late in 1932 by Cardinal Sebastião Leme and others to educate Catholic voters and, at the time, to provide votes for all candidates who would agree to certain Catholic social principles.

Mineiro. Pertaining to, or native of, state of Minas Gerais.

Movimento Militar Constitucionalista. Constitutionalist Military Movement.

Movimento Nacional Popular. National Popular Movement.

Movimento Popular Jânio Quadros. Popular Movement for Jânio Quadros.

NOVACAP. *Companhia Urbanizadora da Nova Capital;* Urbanizing Company of the New Capital.

Partido Comunista do Brasil. Brazilian Communist Party.

Partido Social Democrático. Social Democratic Party.

Partido Social Progressista. Progressive Social Party.

Partido Trabalhista Brasileiro. Brazilian Labor Party.

Paulista. Pertaining to, or native of, state of São Paulo.

Petrobrás. *Petróleo Brasileiro, S.A.* Brazilian government petroleum company, with monopoly on petroleum extraction.

Populismo. This term in Latin America usually refers to the political position which supports popular causes as opposed to minority interests or oligarchies. In literary usage, it connotes an interest in and defense of the common people, their sufferings, tastes, desires, etc.

Queremistas. Term applied to those whose slogan was *"Queremos Getúlio"* ("We want Getúlio").

SESC. *Serviço Social de Comércio;* Social Service of Commerce.

SESI. *Serviço Social do Indústria;* Social Service of Industry.

Sindicato. Syndicate. Labor union or employers' group. To become official, these have to be approved by the Labor Ministry.

SUMOC. *Superintendência da Moeda e do Crédito;* Superintendency of Money and Credit.

SUDENE. *Superintendência do Desenvolvimento do Nordeste;* Superintendency of the Development of the Northeast.

Tenente. Literally a lieutenant. Specifically one of the army officers who participated in the movement which resulted in the revolutions of 1922, 1924 and 1930.

Tribunal Superior Eleitoral. Supreme Electoral Court. Top court in the electoral justice system.

Uniao Democrática Nacional. National Democratic Union.
Uniao Sindical de Sao Paulo. São Paulo (Labor) Union Alliance.
Uniao Sindical do Rio. Rio (Labor) Union Alliance.

EXCHANGE RATES, CRUZEIROS PER U. S. DOLLAR
(selling rate for the dollar)

	Cr.		Cr.
1945[a]	19	ave. Jan. 1957	66
1946	19	ave. July 1957	73
early July 1947[b]	22	ave. Jan. 1958	96
early Jan. 1948	23	ave. July 1958	135
early July 1948	23	ave. Jan. 1959	147
early Jan. 1949	25	ave. July 1959	151
early July 1949	30	ave. Jan. 1960	189
early Jan. 1950	30	ave. July 1960	186
early July 1950	32	ave. Jan. 1961	219
early Jan. 1951	32	ave. July 1961	263
early July 1951	29	ave. Jan. 1962[d]	369
early Jan. 1952	31	ave. July 1962	469
early July 1952	34	early Jan. 1963[e]	805
ave. Feb. 1953[c]	40	early July 1963[f]	802
ave. July 1953	43	early Jan. 1964	1285
ave. Jan. 1954	54	Mar. 29, 1964	1700
ave. July 1954	60	Mar. 30, 1964	1800
ave. Sept. 1954	63	Mar. 31, 1964	1840
ave. Jan. 1955	75	early Apr. 1964	1420
ave. July 1955	76	early July 1964[g]	1300
ave. Jan. 1956	73	early Jan. 1965	1820
ave. July 1956	80	late June 1965	1850

a. 1945–6. "Free rate."

b. Early July 1947 through early July 1952, "unofficial market," based on information provided by Eric F. Lamb of J. Henry Schroder Banking Corporation.

c. Ave. Feb. 1953 through ave. July 1961, "free market" (inaugurated Feb. 1953); data provided by Eric F. Lamb.

d. Ave. Jan. 1962 and ave. July 1962, "parallel market" (which showed little variation from "free market" until Nov. 1961); data provided by Eric F. Lamb.

e. Early Jan. 1963, "Free market"; data from Brazil *Herald*.

f. Early July 1963 through early April 1964, "unofficial market"; data from Brazil *Herald*.

g. Early July 1964 through early June 1965, "parallel market"; data from Brazil *Herald*.

2/ SOME BASIC DEVELOPMENTS IN BRAZILIAN POLITICS AND SOCIETY BY JUAREZ R. B. LOPES

> *Editor's note: This chapter is based upon a lecture delivered November 12, 1964, at Vanderbilt University under the auspices of the Graduate Center for Latin American Studies. The author wishes to express his indebtedness to Dr. Roger Walker, who kindly read the first draft and offered detailed criticism and suggestions.*

CHANGES in the Brazilian political structure have weakened and broken down the traditional patterns of social organization at regional and local levels. The recent acceleration of this process at these "lower" levels has, in turn, solidified the focuses of resistance to change in the national power structure. This chapter will explore in detail this process and its effect.

Discussions of noneconomic development factors usually focus upon the ways in which specific attitudes, values, and behavior patterns facilitate or resist change in the direction of economic and social development. I contend that such socio-cultural phenomena, rather than favoring or opposing economic development in themselves, may be better viewed as attributes of groups and masses within a changing power framework. At given moments in the process of development they impede or facilitate that process by their stand or action. Thus, if we are to understand development we must understand the transformations of political structure.

THE CHANGING BRAZILIAN POWER STRUCTURE

The main contours of political change in Brazil become clear in contrasting the period before 1930, with its clear-cut oligarchical power structure, to the "composite state" and limited democracy which prevailed from 1945 to 1964.[1] The Brazilian political structure from the perspective of the last half century has undergone a profound transformation. Let us contrast the recent political situation to an admittedly simplified picture of political life in the "Old" or First Republic (from the proclamation of the republic in 1889 to the 1930 revolution).

At that time the real protagonists of the political system were oligarchical regional (state) groups,[2] whose power was based, locally, on the economic, social and political power of the large landowners (the *coronéis*). The power of the *coronéis*, in a predominantly agricultural economy, derived from a highly concentrated agrarian structure. This political system has been called *coronelismo*. In this system the large landowners dominated locally, and the majority of the population, the common people, had no real political participation. The functioning of elections and representative institutions in general—the *votos de cabresto* (voting by agricultural workers, because of the traditional loyalty,

1. I shall leave out for the sake of simplifying the main line of the argument the Vargas period from 1930 to 1945. In important ways, paradoxical as it may seem, it was the gestation phase (with the emergence of the urban masses in Brazilian political scene) for the limited democracy Brazil experienced from 1945 to 1964. It is also clear that whatever else one may think of the recent coup, March 1964 ended that period.

2. The power of an oligarchy rested to a great degree on the control of a state's governmental apparatus. There were local opposition groups, but as they could very seldom control the local government they had eventually won without the support from the state's oligarchy, such groups were invariably completely outside the local power structure. Because it made little or no difference to the oligarchy which local group it supported, the winning local oppositions ended by being co-opted by the oligarchical structure, which was to the advantage of both parties.

for the landowner's candidate), the open ballot, the falsification of election results, the need for "recognition" by congress of those who had been elected, the co-optation by the oligarchy of opposition deputies eventually elected—was such that their consequences were the same *as if* the decision-process had been totally within the state oligarchy with its local ramifications. But it must not be forgotten that in this situation the local political chiefs (the *coronéis* immediate leaders) were part of a regional framework, and the balance of power was not on the side of the local political chiefs but on the side of the state—the seat of the oligarchy. Thus the real protagonists of political life were state oligarchical groups, based locally on the power of the large landowners.

National politics was a process of adjustment and compromise among oligarchies, as indicated by the *política dos governadores* [3], a political device for nominating the official presidential candidate, who invariably won. The oligarchies from economically stronger states [4] had the major voice in this process.

During this period, writes Vieira da Cunha,

. . . the nation is understood as an equilibrium or armistice among local groups of power. The power of these groups, recognized by the monarchy, is extended during the republic to the point where states freely contract foreign loans, collect export taxes, create interstate customs and maintain their own armed forces. National politico-governmental institutions are, not rarely,

3. The classic exposition of the *política dos governadores* is found in the book *Da propaganda à presidência* by the Brazilian president Campos Sales (1898–1902), one of the main architects of this political device. It is well epitomized by his phrase, "What the states think, thus thinks the Union." *Da propaganda à presidência*, p. 252, *apud* João Camillo de Oliveira Torres, *O presidencialismo no Brasil* (Rio de Janeiro: Edições O Cruzeiro, 1962), p. 231.

4. States whose economy was based on the main agricultural export crop: coffee. Afonso Arinos writes about the matter: "During the First Republic the [*política dos governadores*] was, at the last instance, as it could not avoid being, the politics of the great states." He adds: "Furthermore, agricultural production, or better, coffee production, which held unchallenged domination over Brazilian policy of those times, was predominantly concentrated in [São Paulo and Minas Gerais] and demanded a corresponding unification in the political machinery," a unification which expressed itself precisely in the rotation in government of presidents coming from those two oligarchies. Afonso Arinos de Melo Franco, *Um estadista da república* (Rio, 1955), *apud* João Camillo de Oliveira Torres, *A formacão de federalismo no Brasil* (São Paulo: Cia Editora Nacional, 1961), p. 218.

simple emanations of the state powers. The states [governors] are strengthened; and, for the necessary understanding among them, there evolves the *politica dos governadores,* through which they speak for the nation, an abstract entity, with no claims of its own, apart from those of the states.[5]

But new economic and social forces were developing within this political structure, making themselves felt especially during the last decade of the *República Velha.* The main factors and directions of change since the First World War were the processes of urbanization and industrialization which resulted in the slow emergence of new social classes; an industrialist group, an enlarged and partly new urban middle class and an urban working class; and a strengthening of the federal government, mainly through the increasing dominance of the oligarchies of São Paulo and Minas Gerais, and their extension to the national level of the political structure. Control of the federal economic policies had become increasingly crucial to the interests of the great coffee states.[6]

The political system which emerged after what could be referred to loosely as the Vargas period (from 1930 to 1945), was drastically different from that of the Old Republic. The focus of power is no longer the states' governments. Instead, now the focus of power is definitely in the national political structure; the urban masses have an increasingly crucial role in the political process; and with exceptions only in a few areas, the old *coronelismo* system has survived under new guises, and in a *weakened* form.[7]

Let me treat as a unit the period from 1945, the redemocratization of the country, to 1964, when the coup of the First of April ended it, and examine how the Brazilian political system functioned. I shall deal separately with the formation of executives

5. Mário Wagner Vieira da Cunha, *O sistema administrativo brasileiro, 1930–1950* (Rio de Janeiro: Centro Brasileiro de Pesquisas Educacionais, 1963), pp. 16–17.

6. See on this point Furtado's analysis of the mechanism of "socialization of losses," with respect to the coffee economy. Celso Furtado, *The Economic Growth of Brazil* (Berkeley: University of California Press, 1963), Part V.

7. The persistence of the *coronelismo* system and its present form in one of the northeastern states is carefully described in Jean Blondel, *As condições da vida política no Estado da Paraíba,* translated from the French (Rio de Janeiro: Fundacão Getúlio Vargas, 1957), especially Chaps. 3 and 4.

(election of the president of Brazil and of the states' governors), and the formation of the legislatures.

To understand the election of a president, or of a governor of one of the more urbanized states,[8] it is essential that we understand the phenomenon designated by the term *populismo* (populism). In it lies the real basis of the limited democracy that Brazil experienced during the entire period. The political hegemony of the coffee interests (or more precisely, of all agrarian sectors devoted to export crops) had definitely ended. With the greatly increased economic and social differentiation, no other single group in society took their place. There now appears in the political process a constant appeal to the *povo*, the implicit reference of this term being the urban population, or more precisely the urban lower and middle classes; but, as Weffort rightly asserts,[9] this urban population acted not as classes, but as a mass. Most of these people, both middle and lower classes, are of very recent rural origin. The impossibility of acting in the urban milieu, on the basis of traditional ties and patterns of their world of origin has resulted in a thorough process of social pulverization, in terms of political behavior. No associations that mediate between individuals and presidential and gubernatorial candidates have yet appeared. Political parties may be almost disregarded. A direct, charismatic relationship between the populist leader and the urban masses is established. It is important to note, however, that the people are a mass to be manipulated by leaders emerging from the dominant groups as a tool for the acquisition and preservation of power.

O povo participated hardly more than in the Old Republic,

8. As a rough indicator, for the purpose at hand, one may take the states whose capitals (always the largest city) have populations over the half million mark. The capitals of the seven following states were in this category in 1960: São Paulo, 3,776,581; Guanabara, 3,228,296; Pernambuco, 788,580; Minas Gerais, 680,025; Bahia, 655,739; Rio Grande do Sul, 640,173; and Ceará, 514,828. In 1950, only the first three could be included.

9. I am at this point following Francisco C. Weffort's penetrating analysis of the 1962 election in the city of São Paulo, "Política de massas," in Octávio Ianni *et al*, *Política e revolução social no Brasil* (Rio de Janeiro: Editora Civilização Brasileira, 1965), pp. 159–198. See also the article by the same author, "Raízes sociais do populismo em São Paulo," *Revista civilização brasileira*, Ano I, No. 2, maio de 1965, pp. 39–60.

but once the executive was elected he had to take it into account. Every president and governor, whatever his initial identification and backing, tended after his election to move toward popular positions—even to get some leftist coloring.

In congress, especially the Chamber of Deputies, and the state legislatures, the urbanization and industrialization, and the correspondingly greater differentiation of Brazilian social organization, brought about the representation of a greater heterogeneity of interests and groups.[10] The influence of economic interests in the legislatures also increased gradually.

On the one side, the continuing presence of *coronelismo* in many of the rural areas, although less strong than before 1930, produced a substantial number of *coronéis* men, even in the national legislature: deputies whose electoral basis was still the *votos de cabresto* (bridle votes) derived from the traditional social, political, and economic power of the large landholders. One could still say that everything worked as if those landholders had plural votes. These were the deputies who were much the same as those in the Old Republic. Not only were their numbers probably declining, however, but their behavior was being transformed.

Now, side by side with them, were two new kinds of deputies: the economic group representative and the clientele politician, both elected mainly by the growing urban population. To understand both types, as well as the change in the older representative of the *coronelismo* type, we must examine the role of urban *cabos eleitorais*. They acted as intermediaries between the large impersonal institutional framework of the city and the people of a neighborhood, a *favela*, or a recreational club. Most of the lower and middle classes are of recent rural origin and are without the knowledge, the skills, and the relatives and friends to satisfy their needs in the large cities. The *cabos eleitorais* are middle

10. I shall base the discussion at this point, with some modifications, on Singer's typology of politicians of parties of the dominant classes in Brazil. Paul I. Singer, "A política das classes dominantes," in Octávio Ianni *et al, op. cit.*, pp. 63–125. The section on politics in a recent study of Rio de Janeira's *favelas* was also very useful. See "Os processos da demagogia no favela," in "Aspectos Humanos da Favela Carioca," *O Estado de São Paulo* (April 13 and 15), special supplement.

men. From the administration they obtain services for their clients, such as obtaining a job, a place in a school or hospital, bringing water or electricity to a street, getting a public telephone installed, or having a bus route changed. In return the *cabos eleitorais* deliver the votes of their group. They are the foundation on which the "demagogic" urban politics rest. The politicians make the concrete "promises" to "the masses" and to specific individuals and groups. The *cabos eleitorais* deliver the votes and ensure at least a partial fulfillment of the promises. Given the narrow and concrete nature of the interest involved (and consequently the almost complete lack of larger issues, not to mention ideological principles, in the politics for the legislature),[11] one understands the need for the *cabo eleitoral,* someone from the group concerned, capable of transmitting the candidates' promises through a personal network of contacts and relationships and of making sure that the voters made good their part of the bargain.

In this situation, the representatives of economic interest groups easily buy off, directly or indirectly, the *cabos eleitorais* and get themselves elected. The increasing dominance of money in elections and politics is intimately linked to the growth of the urban vote and to the nature of the urban population during the initial phase of a very rapid urbanization process.[12]

The economic interests that achieve representation in this way are usually narrow. The candidate elected to a state legislature or to the Federal Chamber of Deputies in such a manner usually "represents" only a single enterprise, an industrial concern, or a small number of firms controlled by an economic group, often be-

11. One conclusion to be drawn from this analysis is that one can almost entirely ignore parties in trying to account for elections of members of legislatures. Existing correlations of socio-economic status with voting for given parties. Gláucio Ary Dillon Soares, "The Political Sociology of Uneven Development in Brazil," in Irving L. Horowitz, ed., *Revolution in Brazil* (New York: E. P. Dutton & Co., Inc., 1964), p. 188, to my mind, raises the question not of *party preference,* but of why a greater proportion of candidates from given parties (such as the Brazilian Labor Party) make the type of appeal and have the kind of behavior in office that attract voters from these strata.

12. There is a corresponding growth of importance of money in the rural areas. Such a development was linked to the weakening of patrimonialism in those areas, directly or indirectly due to urban politics.

longing to people with kinship ties. They do not usually represent an industry or a sector of industrial or mining interests. Less still are they mouthpieces of industry as a whole. The Brazilian capitalists are not yet organized as a class. The broadening of interests represented in the political system should be studied as part of the process through which a class is organized, with the concomitant formation of pressure groups and such means of making its influence felt as mass media or lobbying.

Another type of deputy is the clientele politician, with a similar mediating role between the newer primary groups arising in urban environment and the insufficient urban facilities. He is really a bigger *cabo eleitoral*—one whose primary community (an ethnic group, the inmates of leprosy hospitals) is large enough to get him elected. In the legislature, his is the narrowest outlook of all. He is there to represent a group of people with a narrow range of interests. This does not necessarily imply any definite position on any other issues, hence his erratic voting behavior on the broader problems. He tends to bend with the prevailing mood.

Singer [13] makes the important point that the nature of economic development in Brazil (growth of capitalistic enterprise and increasing role of the state in the economic system) is increasing the dominance of the economic group representative over the other types of elected legislators. This happens during elections, when economic groups come to finance *coronéis* and clientele representatives; through the exchange-of-votes behavior in legislatures that naturally results from the narrow economic or group interest which most deputies defend; and from the fact that, in an economic situation in which so many opportunities for windfall profits depend upon a timely knowledge of what will be the probable governmental measures and directives, many representatives of *coronéis* and clientele representatives come to invest in capitalistic enterprises and so become somewhat "mixed" types.[14]

13. Paul Singer, *op. cit.*

14. Again, just pointing, to this tendency, important as it certainly is, in a sense begs the real question of the social process through which "interests" represented are broadened. This is connected with the problem of the extent to which the industrialists are already a class in themselves and will be touched upon again later on.

We see therefore that the vote of the urban masses was the really new factor in the changing political situation. Their voting behavior for representatives in the legislature (at the municipal, state, and national levels) is a consequence of their adjusting to a hostile and strange urban world. But their vote for the executive usually goes to a charismatic, populist leader.

The workings of the political system, in a situation of almost no commitment by politicians to general principles and clearly delineated ideologies (derived in the last analysis from the voters' political attitudes and behavior), lead naturally to the formation of amorphous "political groupings" cutting across party lines. The main outline of the process is clear. First, the recurrent *ad hoc* exchange-of-votes behavior in the legislatures gives rise to more stable compromises and alliances. Second, the distribution by the president and governors of the positions in the executive branch of government, in order to form their legislative support, links broader groupings of legislators to the top of the bureaucratic apparatus. Third, people in the several levels of government (municipal, state and federal) become similarly interlocked. From the day-to-day functioning of the political system, therefore, there arise many networks of aldermen, federal and state deputies, ministers, secretaries at the state level, and heads of governmental agencies all based in the last instance on the exchange of political favors among politicians with common or at least nonconflicting interests.

The essential point is that, in this period from 1945 to 1964, Brazil came to have a "composite state," in which many interests (in place of the almost single dominant agrarian interest of the past) developed agreements and compromises and in which the "people," in the sense of the urban lower and middle sectors of the population (with no clear-cut class or ideological orientation), had to be taken into account, although they in no sense directly participated in the power structure. As a consequence of both conditions, the president, some governors and deputies, increasingly began to answer to "popular" interests.[15] To my mind, this

15. Such interests should not be thought of as given or as in any way deriving automatically from the objective conditions of the people. They were being defined as part of an evolving process of public opinion, taking place in the cities and

background is necessary to understand the enacting of laws and the making of governmental decrees and directives with a popular content in a social and political situation in which working-class consciousness and organization was generally low, and left or "popular" political groupings had little social basis.[16]

PROGRESSIVE DISSOLUTION OF THE PATRIMONIAL ORDER

Life in the Empire and the Old Republic has been depicted as part of a patrimonial order. The *coronelismo* system I have already mentioned should be seen as the political aspect of such an order during the Republic. The weakening of this political system is linked intimately to the dissolution of the patrimonial labor relations which prevail in much of the rural areas of the country and which are by no means absent from small industrial towns.

The changing power structure unleased new political and economic forces which spread to the local traditional communities and led to the slow and irreversible corrosion of their patrimonial organization. To the extent that *coronelismo*, as part and parcel of this organization, was also weakened, these changes fed back to the national political system (through the diminishing number of pure *coronéis'* representatives in state legislatures and in congress) and extended the possibilities for new political action based on the growing urban capital and responsive to the growing urban electorate. To illustrate, I shall examine two cases.

First, let us consider the case of small towns where antiquated factories managed to survive through a certain guaranteed regional market for low-priced cotton textiles (resulting mainly from high transportation costs) and low costs of labor. Labor relations

---

having as focuses the campaigns for the executive offices. In this process, which was gaining a rhetoric of "nationalism," not only politicians, but also intellectuals, students, labor leaders and members of the industrial bourgeoisie were getting an increasing role. For a partial account of the political controversy during the last decade in Brazil see Frank Bonilla, "A National Ideology for Development: Brazil," in K. H. Silvert, ed., *Expectant Peoples* (1963).

16. The low level of solidarity of industrial workers in São Paulo and their relative incapacity for collective action, such as strikes, is analyzed in the author's research, "O ajustamento do trabalhador à indústria," in *Sociedade industrial no Brasil* (São Paulo: Difusão Européia do Livro, 1964), pp. 22–95.

had been adjusted to the prevailing patrimonial pattern of the surrounding rural area, from which most workers were recruited; and the administrative staff of foremen and sub-foremen which had been formed was largely a patrimonial, rather than a bureaucratic one.[17]

If one looks for the conditions under which labor relations began to change in these communities, leading to the initial breaking of their patrimonialist character and to the organization of independent unions, one is led at every point to developments and forces originating outside the local communities, which must be interpreted in the context of the changing national power structure. One is bound to look at the impact upon the local level of federal laws and directives, especially in the electoral and labor areas. But one notices that some of these laws, such as that permitting and regulating the organization of unions, were in existence for a long time before they achieved social reality and began to affect the minds and actions of men in these parts of Brazil. The alteration in the local political setting, derived, once more, from the same changing power structure at the national level, made the difference.

During the First Republic, the state oligarchy manifested itself as a power monopoly in the local community by a single political faction. Not that one did not have a continuous political struggle; on the contrary, that was exactly the traditional situation all over Brazil: two political "clans" (extended families) as they came to be called, engaged in a fierce struggle and, with their respective followings, divided society vertically. But at any given moment all power positions of the community were controlled entirely by one of the political factions. The ascent to political dominance of the other faction, when it occurred, meant in a short time a complete change and the occupation of all focal power-statuses by the new group. The dominant group of a given

17. This characterization and the following analysis of the mechanism of its transformation are derived from a research reported in the author's article, "Relations Industrielles dans deux communautés brésiliennes," *Sociologie du Travail* No. 4 (1961), 330–344. The complete analysis is to be published as a book by Difusão Eruopéia do Livro, under the title *Desintegração da sociedade tradicional brasileira: Um Estudo de Caso.*

time had, locally, a virtual power monopoly and was backed by the state oligarchy.[18]

The major result of the political transformation of Brazil for the local *municípios* is that their political structures are no longer monolithic. Now it is very rare that some power positions are not filled by incumbents independent of, or even opposed to the dominant group, although in general terms a single "clan" still dominates the community politically. In other words, as a consequence of the changing national power structure, the patrimonial structure of power of rural and small urban communities was somewhat weakened. The groups politically represented at the state and national levels have become too differentiated for a monolithic local power structure to maintain itself.

Important positions in local offices of social security and welfare agencies are, for instance, often filled by indication of the local opposition chief; and most state judges and public attorneys in the community are no longer so dependent upon the local dominant group. Such a weakening of local patrimonialism is a precondition of the effectiveness at the community level of the electoral and the labor law. The existence of persons at the local level who are "outside" the patrimonial structure and to whom lower-class people can go to for help and advice is essential to the process by which these people come to conceive of themselves as having "rights" derived from the federal laws and to understand why and how they can begin to put forward claims in order that such rights become effective. One can understand how, for instance, change in the electoral law—the introduction in the 1946 Constitution of the secret ballot and the several successive attempts through law to ameliorate the electoral system—have led to a series of adaptations of *coronelismo*. Each one, however,

18. The real meaning of the electoral struggle at the community level was then clearly, as Nunes Leal points out, a contest for gaining the privilege of backing the state government and, as a result, receiving its all-important support. As far as the state oligarchy was concerned, the main interest was getting to its side and to support the majority faction of the *município*. Cf. Victor Nunes Leal, *Coronelismo, enxada e voto. O município e o regime representativo no Brasil* (Rio de Janeiro, 1948) , pp. 25–30.

reveals increasing strains and results in the persistence of the system in modified and weakened form.[19]

The labor law has made itself felt in two interrelated ways: by making possible the establishment by federal decrees of minimum-wage levels, that during the last two decades have meant decreasing wage differentials between the technically antiquated, and paternalistic small industrial towns and the more modern and rationalized industries of the great metropolises of São Paulo and Rio de Janeiro,[20] and by facilitating the organization of independent labor unions.

Industrialists in these traditional areas find themselves facing a rapidly changing economic situation. Having factories less modern than those of their counterparts in the large cities, both in the technological and in the organization sense, they see their major advantage—their low labor costs—substantially taken away from them. (Transportation was improving throughout this period, widening competition.) They react by unsystematic and frequently nonrational means of trying to raise their labor productivity and to reduce general labor costs. They continue

19. At the same time that the traditional methods of manipulating the rural vote (the juxtaposition of an appeal to loyalty and gratitude to the use of sanctions) continues to be used, there is now a more direct use of money and a greater emphasis on ways and means of electoral manipulation and control. Before, the economic element would be disguised as ways of making it possible for rural people to vote (providing transportation to and from the small urban center, for registration and on election day, registering them, giving them shoes and clothes, food and lodging for their stay in town, or giving them money so that they themselves could pay for their needs). Now, not only the rural people, but also industrial workers and other townsfolk, are paid a given amount to vote for the political chief's candidates. Previously, the mixture of appeal to loyalty together with the vague possibility of sanctions were enough to guarantee the proper vote; today the use of the threat of loss of job and other economic sanctions is much more direct and a greater emphasis is put in ways of finding out how people voted and so controlling them.

20. In Brazil, by federal decree, minimum wages are established at different levels (according to costs of living) for the different regions and subregions of the country. The urban unions have persistently pressed for the use of a smaller number of different wage levels. In fact, the several succeeding decrees regulating minimum wages have exhibited a trend toward diminishing wage differences in various parts of the country. Here, therefore, one finds evidence of how the new system of power in the urban areas came to effect the transformation of the more traditional parts of the country.

patrimonialistic practices to a large degree (the "caring for" their workers, the particularistic administrative practices), but they increasingly attempt to speed the work pace, and are sporadically preoccupied with substituting lower-wage (minors and women) for higher-wage workers, and increasing housing rents.[21] Such reactions on the part of the industrialist represent, however, a break with the traditional labor relations and lead to greater tensions in worker-foreman relationships. Such is the background for the organization of the union and the motives for joining it, rather than going to the industrialist or to one of his trusted foremen when the worker has problems or is dissatisfied. Even using the union's president for voicing one's grievances is a disloyal and rebellious act in the eyes of the traditional employer. The ties of obligation and loyalty have been broken. A cumulative circular process of change is established, and behavior and relationships get farther and farther away from the patrimonial patterns. The process is irreversible; the slow dissolution of patrimonial ties results.

A similar process is going on in the rural areas, most clearly in the northeast. The presence of the changing national power structure is also making itself felt in this region, and the tempo of transformation of a still predominantly patrimonial society was and is being accelerated. In a recent analysis of the northeast, Furtado delineates the main outline of the process.[22] He shows the effects of rising prices of sugar during the last decade in the

21. Less often, factories react to the new economic situation in the direction of a much clearer modernization, both technologically (better machines) and in the sense of greater bureaucratization of its administrative structure (e.g. a substitution of all the patrimonial foremen by efficiency-minded supervisors). Two points should be made: first, even in such cases, a great deal of compromise remains for a considerable time between patrimonial practices and the newer technology and organization; second, the amount and kind of modernization measures that then occurs produces similar social tensions as in the other cases. They also represent an initial break in the patrimonial patterns and create dissatisfaction that gives impetus to unionization.

22. Cf. Celso Furtado, "O processo revolucionário no Nordeste" in *Dialética do Desenvolvimento* (Rio de Janeiro: Editôra Fundo de Cultura, 1964), 137–173. Furtado deals separately with conditions and developments in each of the three zones into which the Northeast is divided: the sugar-cane coastal region, the transitional *Agreste,* and the semiarid *Sertão* (the hinterland). I shall take the first of these zones, for very succinct exemplification.

sugar-cane coastal strip in the northeast. Before, rural workers in the area were given small plots of land to plant subsistence crops for themselves, a traditional arrangement tied to the condition that they work several days a week for the landowner in the sugar-cane agriculture. Because of this, they are called *condiceiros*. Later they were increasingly put on a straight-wage basis, in order that all land might be utilized for sugar-cane cultivation. The pressure for higher wage levels became great: they now had to pay inflated prices at the local fairs for the subsistence crops that they had previously produced for themselves. But resistance on the part of the landowners to such an increase was greater: costs of production, due to use of poorer lands, were rising. As a result, the already low standard of living of the rural workers was forced even lower, and this occurred while the sugar industry was having a period of prosperity.

Putting the workers on a straight-wage basis also meant a change in their spatial distribution; from being spread over the plantation, near their small plots, they were agglomerated in hamlet-like settlements alongside the roads. This, as Furtado remarks, made for easier communication among them, for the rapid spread of ideas, and for the emergence of leadership among the peasants themselves. Such were the conditions for the rapid growth of the peasant movements during the last decade, especially during the last couple of years.

For a fuller understanding one should examine the vital role played in the process by politicians, university students, and Roman Catholic priests.[23] Their very presence in the political scene

23. For an intelligent and impressionistic account of the happenings in the rural areas of the northeast and their tempo during 1963, including the role in them of Catholic priests, Communists, and other groups, see the recent book by the journalist Antônio Callado, *Tempo de arraes: Padres e comunistas na revolução sem violência* (Rio de Janeiro: José Alvaro, 1964). An earlier book by the same author is a good source for some of the social and political conditions under which the peasant movement emerged during the middle fifties: *Os industriais da sêca e os "Galileus" de Pernambuco: Aspectos da luta pela reforma agrária no Brasil* (Rio de Janeiro: Editôra Civilização Brasileira, 1960).

An important document contains the grievances presented to the president, by the class association of the sugar growers of the State of Pernambuco in October 1963. It clearly shows that for the landowners the fact of labor organization was by itself proof of "subversive activities" and it indicates the amount of violence

of rural northeastern Brazil, as well as the possibilities of action by them, backed as they were by urban-based organizations and by large segments of the urban electorate, clearly illustrates the changed power structure in Brazil.

The subject deserves a fuller investigation and analysis than it has heretofore received. But it is clear that one must study the present, more "divided" power system, and the resulting possibility of manipulation of diverse groups against one another, to understand the role played by the new political protagonists in the kindling of the agrarian movement and in the gradual formation of peasant leaders.

One must examine, together with social and economic conditions conducive to the emergence of the movement and the role played in it by "outside" political activists, the effect of federal acts, such as the passage by congress in early 1963 of a rural workers' statute, which clarified the rights already valid for rural workers and extended to them rights so far reserved for urban workers. The approval of this legislation by congress indicates in itself the changed national political structure. The effectiveness of the statute, moreover, presupposed both a weakened local patrimonial power structure and the partly related phenomenon of a vigorous social movement to generate pressures for its enforcement.[24] This peasant movement, however, should be studied as an ongoing process; and the hypothesis might reasonably be put forward that as such it would essentially reveal itself to be part of a process of dissolution of patrimonial patterns of labor relations (and their substitution in the long run by a less personal and diffuse kind of employer-employee relationship),

---

which was coming to the fore as part of the process of rapid transformation of labor relations. See "Produtores acusam Arraes de proteger os agitadores" and "Denúncia de agitação em Pernambuco," *O Estado de São Paulo* (October 23 and 24, 1963).

24. This role is all the more surprising when one understands the very great fear that members of the dominant groups have for any independent organization of the masses. Weffort very perceptively remarks in his paper that in all recent political crises, the intervention of the *povo* appeared as an imminent possibility and he points to the almost frantic attempts of the elites (even the most radical among them) to contrive "formulas" in order to forego the participation of the masses in the political process and their eventual radicalization. This, he observes, betokens "the mark of the oligarchic spirit in the new elite." *Op. cit.*, p. 162.

having the same irreversible, cumulative circular-causation character as was identified in the small industrial towns analyzed above.[25]

REPERCUSSIONS OF THE CHANGES

I think that the cases we have examined illustrate a very wide-spread process of change which has been going on in Brazil, during the last decades. These changes were largely a result of a political transformation at the national level, ultimately connected, as was seen, to the urbanization and industrialization of society. This has been the focus of this chapter. I would like, however, to conclude with the suggestion that the recent acceleration of the processes of change at the lower levels of society fed back into the national political structure, causing a reaction. The increasing tempo of change of rural labor relations, with the accompanying unrest, tensions, and conflicts, is clearly connected, especially since 1961, with the growing alarm of the dominant classes. Under this threat they seem to have forgotten some of the conflicts among their interests.

CONCLUSION

Fifteen months after the April 1964 coup there was still considerable uncertainty about the social and political outcome. Here I shall limit myself to brief comment on what is pertinent to the main theme of this chapter: the role of *populismo* in the slow corrosion of Brazilian traditional society. It has been shown that elections in urban areas have been basic to this process during the last decades. Street manifestations and protests could admittedly come to have the same consequences as populism in the trans-

25. Furtado writes about this crucial point: "When this law was passed, and perhaps this was the reason for its approval, it was the general opinion that its effective application would take many years." He goes on to point out that the minimum wage law is not a reality in many instances, even today, for urban workers, especially in the case of those from small industrial towns, where there is an excess of labor. He adds that the existing peasant movement, however, made a great difference: ". . . during the course of a year, agricultural workers in the sugar-cane plantations were able to transform into a reality, objectives that, for several decades, are still dead letters in the law books for an important fraction of the urban working class that got such rights as a paternalistic gift." *Op. cit.,* p. 149.

formation process that was analyzed. Such occurrences, however, presuppose a consciousness and an organization of the masses and/or an extensive disruption of society unlikely in the immediate future. The questions that now present themselves are, what are the short-run prospects of elections, and, more important, what kind of elections?

Castelo Branco's government, reflecting the balance of opinion of the leaders of the insurrectionary movement, has leaned toward the maintenance of the electoral contest—provided that candidates be "acceptable" and populist techniques be ruled out—rather than toward a clear-cut and outright dictatorial regime. Elections, if held, shall be narrowly circumscribed indeed. Populist leaders with few exceptions have lost their political rights; constitutional amendments and laws "redefining" the electoral process have been obtained from Congress through more or less open, mostly military, pressures; with similar processes, the limits within which opposition by the still formally free press is tolerated have narrowed considerably. Two constitutional changes were of crucial importance: first, the requisite of an absolute majority for the election of the president, in the absence of which the choice is to be made by congress, and, second, the specification that conditions of eligibility be established by ordinary law. In the latter case, the law subsequently passed was quite openly designed to make ineligible Hélio de Almeida, at the time the nominated opposition candidate for the governorship of Guanabara state. The precedent may quite possibly be used again.

All such changes therefore will from now on grossly restrict the influence that popular interests had before on the power structure. The government has apparently chosen to maintain the semblances of democracy, attempting to control the political process through not very veiled military pressures on congress, the judiciary, and the parties. The difficulties in so doing are becoming increasingly evident. Clearly the opposition is not to persons but to a renewal of the politics of manipulation of the urban masses. Keeping up elections without mass agitation and populism is no easy matter.

But why this need of the new powerholders for preserving at least the trappings of democracy? Among several possibilities, the fact looms as most important that there is complete lack of unity among the civilian and military participants in the coup, except in opposition to the "return of the subversives and the corrupt." During the last year the government has come under violent criticism from almost every side. The divergences among the leaders, on the other hand, reflect the conflicting interests among the dominant economic groups in the society—a conflict made more severe by the anti-inflationary policy of the government and the threatening prolonged economic stagnation. These conflicts are the greatest and most enduring obstacles to agreement and compromise. Personal antagonisms arising from previous political crises (such as the preventive coup of 1955 and that attending the resignation of Quadros) only complicate the picture further. The point, however, is that as far as no group or alliances of groups is hegemonic, elections would have the important function of arbitrating among their interests—elections, it must be added, which would not unduly reflect interests from below.

The alternatives, therefore, seem to be elections without populism or a power struggle through which a faction among the leaders of the April movement gets enough power, not exclusively, but mainly military, to constitute a stable authoritarian regime. That to me is the principal reason for the almost hopeless quest for an electoral system, a "selective democracy," as it has been called, which would hold no dangers of slipping back to mass agitation and mass politics.

Whatever happens, the short-run prospects seem to be for an eclipse of the politics of populism and a resulting slowing down of the disintegration process of the patrimonial organization in Brazil.

3/ TRENDS IN BRAZIL'S FOREIGN POLICY
BY VLADIMIR REISKY DE DUBNIC

T HE government installed in Brazil by the 1964 revolution brought about marked changes in Brazil's foreign policy. Trends departed from the earlier ones of nonalignment, and those trends bent, not merely toward Brazil's traditional policy of hemispheric alliance, but also toward closer ties with Western Europe.

Historically, Brazil's foreign policy has passed through three stages: territorial diplomacy, extra-continental initiation,[1] and experimentation in world politics.[2] One stage inevitably overlaps another. The era of territorial diplomacy ended during the first decade of this century. The subsequent territorial adjustments were minor ones. Extra-continental initiation began with Brazil's entry into World War I. President Janio Quadros's trial of a nonalignment policy marks the beginning of experimentation in world politics.[3]

The territorial diplomacy stage began with Brazil's declaration of independence from Portugal in 1822. The newly independent nation was preoccupied during this period with preserving and

1. The author gratefully acknowledges permission to use in this chapter some material from his article "Brasilien: Von der Blockfreiheit zur Solidarität mit dem Westen" which appeared in *Europa Archiv*, XX, No. 3 (February 1965).

2. For a concise description of the three stages, see Nelson Sampaio de Sousa's Chapter, "The Foreign Policy of Brazil," in Black and Thompson's *Foreign Policies in a World of Change* (New York: Harper and Row, 1963). Sampaio has described the third stage as "Brazil's apprenticeship to become a World Power" and sets its beginning after 1945.

3. During the Goulart administration, Gilberto Freyre wrote that Brazil's new foreign policy "will necessarily be experimental and extremely difficult." Gilberto Freyre, "Misconceptions of Brazil," *Foreign Affairs*, XL, No. 3 (April 1962), 460.

expanding the vast territory inherited from the Portuguese colonial era.

The four wars in which Brazil engaged during this period were attempts to expand its domain southward and to establish a balance of power with Argentina. Brazil attempted to annex Uruguay and subsequently to prevent Uruguay's being annexed by Argentina.

The fourth war, the Paraguayan War, was a result of Brazil's expansion ambitions. Paraguay, to the south, felt menaced after its offer to mediate between Uruguay and Brazil was rejected. Paraguay declared war on Brazil. In trying to attack Rio Grande do Sul in Brazil, Paraguay invaded Argentinian territory. Argentina thus found itself fighting on the side of Brazil. The war grew into the biggest in South American history, lasting from 1864 to 1870. It ended with the defeat of Paraguay.

This war also ended Brazil's period of conquest by arms. The able foreign minister, the Baron of Rio Branco, settled further boundary questions peacefully and in Brazil's favor. Rio Branco served under four presidents from 1902 to 1912 and gave stability and continuity to Brazil's foreign policy. He was the architect of Brazil's peaceful foreign policy tradition and is still an inspiration to Brazilian foreign policy makers. Rio Branco's diplomatic and legal skill enriched Brazil with territories acquired from Argentina, through the arbitration of President Grover Cleveland, and from French Guiana[4] (the Amapa territory). The Acre territory was acquired from Bolivia by the Treaty of Petropolis in 1903. Rio Branco's acquisition of more than 200,000 square kilometers by peaceful means[5] marked the end of Brazil's territorial quests, and the nation then concentrated on preservation of the status quo.

The role played at The Hague conference in 1907 was Brazil's debut in extracontinental multilateral diplomacy. German submarines sank Brazilian ships and brought Brazil into World War

4. The border with French Guiana was defined with precision only in 1960 on the basis of the work of the mixed Brasil French Demarcation Commission which started its work in 1955. "Frontiera do Brasil com a Guiana Francesa," *Revista Brasileira de Politica Internacional*, III, No. 10 (June 1960), 137.

5. Joseph E. Black and Kenneth W. Thompson, ed., *Foreign Policies in a World of Change* (New York: Harper and Row, 1963), p. 628.

I. This began Brazil's extracontinental initiation. Membership in the League of Nations soon followed, signifying a more sustained effort in Brazil's world diplomacy. Brazil was elected and re-elected a member of the council.

Brazil, however, felt that it was not accorded a voice commensurate with its diplomatic skill and importance as the largest South American country. It lost interest in the League and withdrew in 1926.

Brazil pursued a policy of isolation during the subsequent period, but Communist and Fascist influences made themselves felt. President Getúlio Vargas put down the Communist uprising of 1935 and the Fascist coup of 1938. Pointing to both threats, Vargas found an excuse to establish his own dictatorship.

The attempts by Communists and Fascists during the thirties to take over Brazil were clear demonstrations that Brazil could no longer afford a policy of international isolation, even though isolation seemed desirable during the early years of the Second World War. Brazil's granting of permission to the United States to build air-naval bases in Belem, Recife, and Natal in March 1941, before the United States had entered the war, the breaking of relations with the Axis powers after Pearl Harbor, and the subsequent entry of Brazil into the war on the side of the Allies were fine examples of Brazil's hemispheric solidarity. Vargas hesitated in declaring war for eight months after Brazil's breaking of relations with the Axis. But Brazil was not equipped to enter the war effectively. This time, Brazil's entry into the war would not be just a symbolic gesture as in 1917; it would call for real sacrifices, for which the country had to be psychologically and materially prepared.

A cooling-off period in the Good Neighbor relations with the United States followed the war. Brazil perceived that the United States was concentrating on the European recovery program and neglecting Latin America. Many Brazilians felt that their participation in World War II had not been sufficiently appreciated by the United States. President Juscelino Kubitschek's proposal in 1958 to establish a multilateral program for Latin American social and economic development, the Operation Pan-

America (OPA), was not seized upon in time. The Alliance for Progress, initiated in 1961, was slow in its start. It was built on the assumption that the spirit of the Good Neighbor Policy, dating back to the Hoover and Roosevelt period and by this time almost faded away, still existed.

~ The establishment of the Alliance for Progress fell into the third stage of Brazilian foreign policy: the era of experimentation in world politics. The Brazilian participation in the two World Wars had been more an expression of hemispheric solidarity than one of a particular Brazilian world policy. The psychological foundations for a more dynamic foreign policy were laid during Kubitschek's presidency. His policy of *desenvolvimentismo* (rapid economic development) mobilized the national consciousness and contributed to a wave of optimism and a desire for a greater world-affairs role for Brazil. The mood of the public caught up with the spirit of the Brazilian Foreign Office, whose high esprit de corps was partially the result of the professional foreign office members' long-standing confidence in the future global role of Brazil. While rapid economic development contributed to a spirit of optimism in the great future of Brazil, it also brought about grave economic stresses that increased the need to modify Brazil's foreign policy and to diversify its international economic ties.

During the Kubitschek presidency the Brazilians were interested in a Marshall Plan–type of agreement, although they were not disposed to accept the supervision and guidance clauses of such an arrangement as had Western Europe in 1949. Even had Brazil been more flexible on this point, however, the Republican administration was not willing to inaugurate a program with the scope of the Marshall Plan. The direction any Brazilian government's foreign policy would take was conditioned by the nature of the new national consciousness, by past and present United States policies, and by the Brazilian President's assessment of what policy best served the country's national interest. In many cases, as during Goulart's presidency, it was also conditioned by the president's own subjectively evaluated domestic power interests.

PRINCIPLES AND OBJECTIVES
OF BRAZILIAN FOREIGN POLICY

There are certain principles to which governments profess to adhere in their international relations. What could be considered the principles fundamental to the post–1964 Brazilian foreign policy? The first republican Brazilian constitution of 1891 declares, "The United States of Brazil will in no event commit itself to a war of conquest, directly or indirectly, for itself or in alliance with another nation." [6]

Since then, all Brazilian governments have adhered to this principle. Another tradition of Brazilian foreign policy is nonintervention and adherence to the principle of self-determination.[7] These two principles were the justification of the governments of Jânio Quadros and João Goulart for not participating in any sanctions against Castro's regime and for maintaining good diplomatic relations with Cuba. The government of President Humberto Castelo Branco installed by the revolution of 1964 defined the principle of self-determination in a democratic way: "All those peoples that would wish to be free through representative democracy will have the support of Brazil in their self-determination." [8]

Thus, while the Quadros and Goulart governments defended the rights to self-determination of Castro's regime, the revolutionary government of 1964 defended the right of self-determination of the Cuban people and broke relations with Castro because Castro's government had violated the principle of noninterference by engaging in subversive activities in Brazil. The Revolutionary Government of Brazil, to justify breaking relations with Cuba, thus invoked the same principles upon which the previous government based its pro-Cuba policy. The Goulart government, besides adhering to the principle of self-determination (of governments) enunciated a threefold objective of Brazilian foreign policy: *desenvolvimento, desarmamento, decolonizacão* (develop-

6. *Ibid.,* p. 628, quoting the first republican constitution.
7. João Goulart, *Mensagem ao congresso nacional 1962* (Rio de Janeiro: I.B.G.E. 1962) , p. 45.
8. *President Humberto Castelo Branco's Inaugural Speech* (Press Release of the Brazilian Embassy, Washington, D.C., undated) .

ment, disarmament, decolonialization). Development had already been the key objective of Kubitschek's administration.

The second objective, world disarmament, was emphasized by the Quadros, Goulart, and Castelo Branco governments. (Regionally, Brazil was formerly engaged with Argentina in a naval armaments race, but this was an expression of a policy of prestige rather than a part of any warlike design.)

Brazil's ambassador in Washington, Juracy Magalhães, stated:

> Brazil's attention is also sharply focused on the objective of world disarmament, both because it is of fundamental interest to the preservation and strengthening of world peace and because it will also constitute an efficient means towards the liberation of economic resources so vitally necessary to the development of vast areas throughout the world. Conscious of its assigned role, Brazil has rendered full co-operation, both in the United Nations General Assembly and to the Disarmament Conference itself, in Geneva, and will continue to do so in the hope that in due course the sum total of the partial agreements reached will enable the world—on the basis of a foolproof system of international control and inspection—to banish its weapons of destruction and to devote itself entirely to the fight against poverty, against diseases and against illiteracy.[9]

Brazil engaged very actively in diplomacy on behalf of the effort to make Latin America a denuclearized zone. Brazil presented to the Seventeenth General Assembly of the United Nations a proposal for the denuclearization of Latin America. In April 1963 the governments of Brazil, Bolivia, Chile, Ecuador, and Mexico in a joint declaration stated their readiness to "sign a multilateral Latin American agreement not to manufacture, receive, stock or test nuclear weapons or instruments for the launching of nuclear weapons."[10]

Former Foreign Minister Afonso Arinos told this author that when he was head of the Brazilian delegation to the United Nations in 1962 he attempted, in his conversations with the Cuban

9. Remarks on Brazilian foreign policy by Ambassador Juracy Magalhães, School of International Studies, the American University, Washington, D.C., February 10, 1965. (Mimeographed.)

10. "Declaracão Conjunta de 30 de Abril de 1963, dos Presidentes do Brasil, Bolívia, Chile, Equador e México." *Revista Brasileira de Política Internacional* (Vol. VI, No. 22. June 1963; Rio de Janeiro: Instituto Brasileiro de Relações Internacionais), p. 310.

ambassador to the United Nations, to persuade the government of Cuba to support the projected Latin American agreement to establish Latin America as a denuclearized zone, but the Cuban ambassador to the United Nations, upon direct instruction from Fidel Castro, declined to support such an agreement.

The third objective, decolonialization, loomed significantly in Quadros's foreign policy. While Brazil was always anti-colonial, militancy on this issue was mitigated by strong cultural ties to Portugal. The Kubitschek government, whenever it came to the question of Portuguese colonies, had no desire to antagonize Portugal. The Quadros and Goulart regimes' declarations in favor of freedom for the Portuguese colonies were a departure from the past policies of Brazil. While this position was not inconsistent with the philosophy of Brazil, it was nevertheless a departure from the traditional friendly policies to Portugal. It was hoped that by a dynamic African policy Brazil might assume a significant role in the Portuguese colonies after they gained independence.

If one were to single out the overriding national interest of Brazil, it would be that of accelerated development. Other objectives are conditioned by this interest. The experimentation in world politics had its origin in the design to use foreign policy as a tool for economic development.

THE TREND TOWARD NEUTRALISM

Toward the end of Kubitschek's administration Brazilian leaders came to believe that more detached relations with the United States might be in the national interest. This belief was based on the theory that some allies are "more equal than others" and that the faithful ally is often the neglected one. They also felt that detachment might alert the United States to Brazilian objectives. The 1960 Brazilian presidential election campaign indicated that Brazil was preparing to assume a third-force position. Quadros's foreign-policy platform was a mixture of neutralism and of pro-Cuba and anti-colonial sentiments, with an open-door policy for foreign investors and a profession of friendship for the United States.

During the years from 1961 to 1964, while still formally

anchored to its hemispheric commitments by its membership in the Organization of American States and by the Rio Treaty of Inter-American Defense of 1947, Brazil tended to experiment with a nonalignment policy. Brazilian officials generally felt that the foreign policy was due for a revision, with the aim of solving Brazil's economic problems.

President Quadros's foreign policy may have been a puzzle to many, but it had a certain logic in following this aim. He had assumed the leadership of a Brazil already awakened from the complacency of underdevelopment and acquiring a new national consciousness but facing the gravest social and economic problems of its history.

Quadros came out in support of Kubitschek's OPA policy, but it became clear that he would not steer Brazil in the same direction. His repeated declarations about engaging in more trade with the Soviet Union and establishing relations with Communist China were not made merely to gain a certain electoral following. It was apparent that in Brazil's quest for new foreign trade opportunities Quadros and his successors would leave no stone unturned.

Brazil's foreign policy concept during the Quadros period could be defined as a policy of bargaining with East and West; Brazil was no longer United States, or Pan-American, but globally oriented. It would establish ties independently of the ideological and power-political watershed line. Quadros was on record as having said that Brazil must assume a position apart from the existing world power struggle and must not remain linked to any great power.[11] This profession of neutralism was, however, somewhat counterbalanced by another Quadros declaration—that his government would remain within the Inter-American alliance system.

Quadros found it necessary to come out with new Brazilian foreign-policy concepts, not merely because of his conviction that Brazil had outgrown the marginal role it played in world politics,

11. In his article for *Foreign Affairs*, Jânio Quadros wrote: "We had been relegated unjustifiably to an obscure position. . . . We gave up the subsidiary and innocous diplomacy of a nation aligned with worthy though alien interests and to protect our rights, placed ourselves in the forefront." Jânio Quadros, "Brazil's New Foreign Policy," *Foreign Affairs*, XL, No. 1 (October 1962) , 19.

but also because of his own assessment of public opinion. The development of Brazil into a representative democracy and the rising national consciousness of the social classes awakened from ignorance by the industrialization process brought about a situation wherein the military hierarchy and the professionals in the Brazilian foreign office were no longer the only influences on the president in foreign-policy decisions. While the Brazilian military, dependent on United States supplies, was interested in preserving strong ties with the United States, there were forces, primarily those of the political left, which counter-balanced this interest.

Quadros's new foreign policy, while it alienated many military leaders, was supposed to contribute to a certain minimum of national concensus among the diverse political and social groups. The left, frustrated by Quadros's internal economic policies, found consolation in Brazil's turn in foreign policy which induced it to assume a more co-operative stand toward the government. The center forces tended to go along with any policy which appeared to increase Brazil's prestige in the world. Thus the Communists, the nationalists, and the moderates, all for different reasons, believed that Brazil's future lay in diversifying its relations.

In an atmosphere of great national expectations and confronted with economic desperation, a bold new foreign policy served as an escape from grim domestic realities. Rarely in history has a country continued to pursue a traditional foreign policy when faced with seemingly insoluble domestic problems. It was a phenomenon of contemporary international relations, at least until China's aggression against India, that countries adopting a neutralist position generally enjoyed greater international prestige than did countries in a similar stage of development committed closely to one or the other super-power. Brazilian policy-makers from Quadros to his successor, Goulart, believed that a globally oriented Brazil, disengaged from the Cold War as far as practically possible, would give Brazil additional prestige, which in the atmosphere of great national aspirations might make the domestic sacrifices and prolonged austerity more bearable.

A common desire to remain outside of any great power's sphere of influence and the many similar socio-economic problems which accompany rapid industrialization created some affinity between Brazil and the underdeveloped areas of the world.[12] This mutual interest led Quadros to undertake, half a year before his election, a fact-finding tour which included India, Egypt, Yugoslavia, and Cuba, countries which a few years before would have been of only marginal importance to Brazil. Only two industrial countries were included in his itinerary: Japan and the Soviet Union.

Evidently swayed by his trip, Quadros declared that Latin America needed another Nasser. The neutralist countries were eager to bring Brazil into their midst; they could point out that far from being isolated they drew assistance from two sources, East and West.

Neutralism had, however, no precedent in Latin America. Until 1962, many Brazilians had hopes that Castro's Cuba would be able to stabilize its revolution by assuming a neutralist position. Jânio Quadros was interested in the Cuban revolution primarily because Castro seemed to him a symbol of independence from foreign control. Once the total political, economic, and military dependence of Cuba on the Soviet Union became evident, and humiliating for Cuba, after the Soviets withdrew their rockets without consulting Castro's regime, the Brazilian government's hopes for building neutralism in Latin America dimmed. The illusion that Cuba would be able to use the competition between East and West to benefit its development without actually becoming a victim of the Cold War had been artificially perpetuated. The fact that Cuba had moved into the Soviet orbit and become a base for further communization of Latin America was an unpleasant awakening for those neutralists who wished Latin America to assume a unified collective bargaining position toward the United States.

The bargaining position of Latin American countries increased in the early stages of the communization process in Cuba, but the death of the Monroe Doctrine announced by Khrushchev and seemingly accepted by the United States gave many Latin

12. ". . . the economic and technical underdevelopment (of Brazil) leads us to undeniable approximation of interests with the Afro-Asian world." Foreign Minister Afonso Arinos as quoted by José Honório Rodrigues, *Brasil e Africa: Outro Horizonte,* (Rio de Janeiro: Civilizacao Brasileira, 1961), p. 344.

Americans cause for concern. The Monroe Doctrine had never been very popular with the Latin Americans,[13] mainly because it was a unilateral declaration by the United States;[14] but the manner in which it was violated was not one in which they could find cause for satisfaction, for it was not the Latin Americans who terminated it.

When, for the first time, Latin America became exposed directly to the struggle between the United States and the Soviet Union, some Brazilians, paradoxically, based their neutralist stand on the assumption that international communism did not present a real danger to Latin America. This position could not be convincingly maintained for long. It was felt by some, however, that under a good leader, a power such as Brazil could develop a position of approximation to the Soviet Bloc for the sake of faster industrialization of the country without running the risk of winding up in the Communist camp. Some Brazilians considered their ties to the United States, industrially the most advanced country in the world, inadequate for an accelerated development of Brazil. They thus looked for extra-hemispheric links.

Quadros's desire to change Brazil's foreign policy could also be traced to the influence of the general international situation. The possibility of a nuclear war between the super-powers, limited or unlimited, made the peripheral nations feel that a

13. In an article attributed to Foreign Minister Rio Branco, the writer has taken issue with sectors of Brazilian opinion hostile to the Monroe Doctrine: "On several occasions they [some Brazilian writers] showed an ungrateful contempt for the Monroe Doctrine." José Maria da Silva Paranhos, barão do Rio Branco, "Brazil, the United States and the Monroe Doctrine," *Jornal do Comercio*, Rio de Janeiro, January 20, 1908.

14. Brazil's foreign policy showed signs of a great power outlook long before it entered the arena of world politics. It had its own concept of inter-American security in the early years of the country's independence. The government of Brazil would have preferred to complement the Monroe Doctrine with a bilateral alliance with the United States or a multilateral treaty. A note presented to the United States Government in the year 1825 stated that it was not ". . . in accordance with reason, justice and right that the Government of Brazil should accept such sacrifices gratuitously . . ." The note further expressed the Brazilian Government's hope that, ". . . the Government of the United States will also offer conditions for entering into an offensive and defensive alliance with the Government of Brazil . . ." Cited by José Maria da Silva Paranhos, Barão do Rio Branco, "Brazil, the United States and the Monroe Doctrine," *Ibid*.

neutralist position was the more sensible one. Quadros, aware of Brazil's strategically vital position for the continent of Latin America and for Africa, would not have liked to see this position used to the advantage of any power in the Cold (or perhaps hot) War.

While Quadros's period of "innocent" neutralism did not alarm the Brazilian public, the Communist infiltration in the administration of his successor, Goulart, and the design of the extreme left to stage a revolution from above, gave second thoughts to many advocates of nonalignment; for neutralism began to be used by the left as a point of departure for a pro-Soviet and pro-Cuba policy.

The extreme left tried to convince the Brazilian public that Latin America had no true cultural identity with the West. They held that Brazilians did not owe any allegiance to the Western social systems, ethical values, or international security arrangements. They expressed affinity with countries in a similar stage of development, facing similar economic problems, even though these "peripheral" countries were otherwise very different from Brazil. The extremists of the left assumed an ideological position hostile to the West, distinguished from the short-lived government of Jânio Quadros, whose neutralist tendencies were rather a manifestation of domestic frustrations and of a need to demonstrate the independence of Brazilian foreign policy. Brazil had no interest in trading its old peripheral position within the Western community of nations for another peripheral one in the Soviet orbit. This, however, did not mean that it could not have drifted into such a position; for the extreme left under Goulart was gradually capturing the policy-making apparatus.[15]

It was one thing for Jânio Quadros, with the unprecedented national and international prestige he enjoyed while president, to pursue a policy which led toward neutralism; but it was an-

15. U. S. Congress, House of Representatives. *Castro-Communist Subversion in the Western Hemisphere*, Hearings before the Subcommittee on Inter-American Affairs of the Committee on Foreign Affairs. Committee Print No. 95314, 88th Congress, 2nd Session. March 1963, p. 247. At that time, Ambassador Lincoln Gordon stated the Communist influence ". . . is much, much larger than those small numbers suggest. . . . In the Government itself there has been infiltration."

other matter when subsequently Goulart, with a weak parliamentary system and a divided country behind him, tried to solidify this trend. A neutralist policy for a Brazil which faced great political, social, and economic convulsions was not practicable; for neutralism in such a context had not the distinction of a patriotic policy.

The policy initiated by Quadros in 1961 of an open door to all nations to bring more capital into Brazil and foster trade with any nation did not bring the desired results. It failed, not merely because of Brazil's unfavorable economic conditions and political instability, but also because the Brazilian international policy of ambiguity brought misgivings from the United States and gained nothing from the Soviet Union.[16]

The Soviet Bloc did not make full use of Brazil's four years of aloofness toward the United States to establish close economic relations. It was difficult for the Soviets to sound convincing when, in 1963, they offered to sell wheat to Brazil and a few weeks later knocked on the United States' door wanting to buy wheat to alleviate their own shortages.

It was unrealistic for Brazil to assume a policy of disengagement from the United States without first striving to establish strong economic ties with such industrial countries as Britain, Germany, France, and Japan, whose support Brazil needed for further development; but Goulart's government did not try to establish such ties. The parallel Brazilian effort to build up a Latin American Free Trade Area (LAFTA) did not and could not bring results to compensate even partially for the indifference of the European Common Market and United States private capital toward a Brazil alienated from the West. The Latin American economies were neither diversified enough nor strong enough to rely on their own common-market area.

The United States device for development, the Alliance for

16. Octavio Dias Carneiro, Assistant Secretary General for Economic Affairs of the Brazilian Ministry of Foreign Affairs, wrote in an article, "O comércio entre o Brasil e a Europa Oriental": "With the Soviet Union the situation is peculiar, for there are not yet any long-term contracts and Brazil is a short-term creditor of U.S. $4 million to the USSR." *Revista Brasileira de Política Internacional*, V, No. 18 (June 1962), 230.

Progress, had no place in Goulart's strategy. For one thing, his government was not in a condition to comply with its basic fiscal rules. United States assistance under the Alliance was based on a certain economic performance, including an anti-inflationary policy and a more efficient taxation system. The Alliance required a team spirit with the United States in the joint work for economic improvement, and it depended on Brazil's policy of indemnification for nationalized assets of United States companies in Brazil. The United States legislation was clear: there would be no aid to countries which did not offer just indemnification for taking over assets of American firms. Goulart's government showed no will to tackle these technical questions. Political resentment against the Alliance was perhaps even more crucial, for it was this which made it impossible to tackle the technical issues.

A Brazilian Alliance for Progress policy would have meant introducing measures which would tend to lessen the power of the political professional in favor of economic planners and experts; and the latter would, at least for a time, become the economic czars of the country. Goulart's scrapping of the Three-Year Plan and the dismissing of its architects and executors, Celso Furtado and San Tiago Dantas, was a characteristic move of a political leader who would not tolerate sharing effective power with the economic policy-makers. The creation of an Alliance for Progress bureaucracy would have necessitated a government by technical experts with broad powers, rather than by political satellites of the president. The Communists and the communonationalists supported Goulart's aloofness to the Alliance for Progress, since they saw in the Alliance, not merely a means for the United States to preserve its interests in Latin America, but also a recovery and development program not under their auspices, which would not foster an atmosphere for revolution.

Goulart's presidency signified a rapid deterioration of United States–Brazil relations because of Goulart's negative attitude to the Alliance for Progress and his government's lack of co-operation in the Inter-American Security System. Brazil's position at the second Punta del Este Inter-American Conference of 1962 and its negative attitude toward Venezuela's charges made in 1963 before the Organization of American States against Cuba's arms shipments to Venezuela's rebels were two outstanding manifestations of a policy of pseudoneutralism which favored Soviet and Cuban interests.

Brazil's stand at the Foreign Minister's Meeting of January 1962 at Punta del Este could hardly be justified in terms of the Brazilian national interest. The Goulart government's objectives were to preserve Castro's Cuba within the OAS and to oppose economic sanctions against Cuba. The latter aim was unrelated to the internal or external interests of Brazil, since there was virtually no trade between Cuba and Brazil. Goulart's opposition to isolating Cuba clashed head-on with United States objectives. It also angered many Brazilians. Democratic groups protested their country's position at Punta del Este, and the Brazilian Congress submitted Foreign Minister Dantas to sharp questioning and criticism after his return from the conference.[17] Washington chose not to point to the Brazilian government's position as being contrary to the spirit and letter of the Rio Treaty; the United States did not wish to draw even more attention to the then prevailing hemispheric disunity on the Cuban question. When the Brazilian delegation made light of Castro's involvement with the Soviet Union by its vote of abstention on suspending Cuba's membership in the OAS, this attitude was motivated by its government's policy of nonalignment.

Considering Cuba's degree of involvement with the Soviet Bloc, it was unlikely that the Brazilian Government based its policy, as San Tiago Dantas asserted, on the remote hypothesis that Cuba would return to the hemispheric fold if only the OAS would not try to isolate the island.[18] Soviet military advisers were already

17. For an account of Deputy Levy's attack against Brazil's policy at Punta del Este, see San Tiago Dantas, *Política externa independente* (Rio de Janeiro: Civilizacão Brasileira, 1962), pp. 157–163. The criticism of Deputy Herbert Levy (of the União Democratica Nacional Party) made in the Federal Chamber of Deputies on February 7, 1962, that Brazil's position at Punta del Este weakened the system of collective security and was against the interest of Brazil, was heavily applauded from the floor.

18. "It is not true that Cuba (the regime) is lost to the democratic way of life . . . Cuba will complete its revolutionary process, and this process will bring it back to the community of the democratic states of this hemisphere." *Ibid.*, p. 154. This statement was made nine months after Fidel Castro had said that Cuba was definitely a Socialist Republic, and also after Castro's public proclamation of faith,

present in Cuba before the suspension of Cuba's OAS membership.

The strong protest in Brazil of Foreign Minister Dantas's position at Punta del Este and Brazil's continuing formal adherence to the Inter-American Defense Treaty (Rio Treaty) prevented Dantas's explaining Brazil's position in terms of nonalignment; he preferred to explain his stand as the only one which could ease international tension and promote coexistence. Dantas proudly reported to his nation that his action prevented voting of military, economic, or diplomatic sanctions against Cuba, and he considered this a victory for the forces of peace.

The decision of the Soviet Union to install nuclear devices in the form of intermediate ballistic missiles in Cuba was partly influenced, however, by the irresolute stand on the Cuban question of the major Western Hemispheric nations at Punta del Este. San Tiago Dantas's defense of a firm OAS nonintervention position at Punta del Este was made at the expense of United States and hemispheric security. The position of Goulart's government against the expulsion of Castro's Cuba from the OAS strengthened the prestige of the extreme left, which claimed that Brazil's policy was the result of the growing national "anti-imperialistic" conscience. Dantas, instead of rectifying this impression, was contributing to this claim of the extreme left by stating that Brazil's stand at Punta del Este represented a victory for the Brazilian people who were "showing their will." [19]

Goulart and Foreign Minister Dantas underestimated the anti-Communist mood of important components of the Brazilian nation. After the Punta del Este Conference, both were unable to regain their prestige with the center forces. Had Goulart's foreign policy produced positive results for Brazil, he could have strengthened his position at home. His policy of nonalignment, or alignment with all nations which amounted to the same thing under existing world conditions, did not, however, gain any advantages for Brazil. If the Brazilian neutralist tendency was in essence a policy of bargaining, as some Brazilian observers maintained, the question was, where were the practical results? The essence of

---

"I am a Marxist-Leninist and will be one until the day I die." The *New York Times*, December 3, 1961.

19. San Tiago Dantas, *op. cit.*, p. 146.

bargaining is in presenting Partner A with facts of available favorable alternatives with Partner B, in case Partner A's policies do not appear satisfactory. International conditions did not, however, present opportunities for such a policy.

The policy of the Quadros government and the Goulart government had been contradictory. On one hand, it was declared that Brazil pursued an impartial "open-door policy" to all nations; on the other hand, the Brazilian Government showed a distinct affinity for countries of the Soviet Bloc[20] who could not possibly assist Brazil in its struggle for rapid economic development.

This policy was independent in the sense that it was not the result of pressures from abroad; in reality, however, it was influenced at times by persons dependent on non-Brazilian ideologies. It is well to remember that Goulart's prime minister, Hermes Lima, stated, possibly under the pressure of the extreme left, that the Cuban experiment in socialism could not be allowed to die.

The nonalignment policy of Brazil from 1961 to 1964 brought no advantages to the country, and the friendly approach to Castro's Cuba only benefited Soviet and Cuban interests. While this was not the intent of Quadros, who was the initiator of the nonalignment course, it was certainly the result. The essence of the Quadros policies was stressed time and again: an independent foreign policy, and the gaining for Brazil of a global role in world affairs.[21] While San Tiago Dantas tried to preserve these over-all objectives under the Goulart government, the internal weakness of that government and its worsening economic situation made any leadership role for Brazil impossible, and the independent policy became more and more compromised by the interests of the extreme left.

20. In his message to congress, President Quadros stated: "Brazil cannot ignore without injustice to reality the vitality of the dynamism of the Socialist States." To refer to "dynamism and vitality," in the context of the Hungarian regime, only five years after the quelling of the Hungarian uprising, was water on the propaganda mill of the extreme left. See Jânio Quadros, *Mensagem ao Congresso Nacional* (Rio de Janeiro: Departamento de Imprensa Nacional, 1961), p. 94.

21. For the positive results of Quadros' foreign policy see Vladimir Reisky de Dubnic, "A política externa do Brasil no governo Jânio Quadros." *Síntese Política Econômica Social*, Janeiro-Março, III, No. 9 (1961), 67–87.

THE FOREIGN POLICY OF THE
REVOLUTIONARY GOVERNMENT OF 1964

The April 1964 Revolution against the economic and political anarchy of Goulart's administration brought in a government which ended abruptly the unproductive neutralist foreign policy of the Quadros-Goulart era. The new government under the presidency of Castelo Branco abandoned the following aspects and preferences of Goulart's foreign policy: the pro-Castro bias, the objective of organizing the underdeveloped countries against the developed ones for the purpose of creating a world-wide third force, and the effort to strengthen ties with Communist China and the Soviet Bloc.

The discarding of these policies in itself constituted a favorable climate for good United States–Brazil relations. At the Ninth Inter-American Meeting of Foreign Ministers of the OAS which took place in Washington in July 1964, Brazil submitted a draft declaration to the Cuban people which expressed the hope that Cuba would

within the near future free itself from the tyranny of the Communist regime that oppresses it and install in the country a government freely elected by the will of the people and that would assure the respect of basic human rights.[22]

Brazil's foreign policy thus came about full circle from opposition to any sanction against Castro's Cuba to a vanguard position in the move for voting an inter-American diplomatic and economic quarantine against the Cuban regime.

Many observers believed that without the initiative of the Brazilian foreign minister no energetic sanctions against Cuba would have been approved. Brazil's foreign minister stressed that the sanctions voted by the OAS against Castro's Cuba made the decision obligatory for all member states. Brazil's interest in strengthening the prestige of the Organization of American States made her again the champion of inter-American solidarity.

The evolution of Brazil's foreign policy during the four years

22. *Boletim Informativo*, Embaixada do Brasil, Washington, D.C., No. 29 (July 22, 1964).

from the Quadros presidency to the presidency of Castelo Branco might serve as an example that nonalignment and neutralism, in vogue a few years ago, ceased to represent a rational alternative among the developing Latin American countries. Their economic needs and considerations of national security were not served by such a policy.

The first concrete and immediate measures taken by the revolutionary government were these: co-operation in the re-scheduling of external debts, the normalization of relations with France, the renewal of the Great Dialogue with the United States, the review of diplomatic relations with Portugal, and the start of commercial negotiations with the Federal Republic of Germany and with Sweden.[23]

The deterioration of relations with France was not of Goulart's making. The "Lobster War" between Brazilian and French fishing vessels off the northeast coast of Brazil was the main cause of the strained French-Brazilian relations, especially after France dispatched a warship to the area. The dialogue with the United States was sabotaged by Goulart's government in order to oblige the extreme left. The traditional friendly relations with Portugal were also strained. The colonial policies of Portugal in Africa affected Quadros's and Goulart's attitudes, since they gave distinct preference to the friendship of African nationalists. The commercial negotiation by Goulart's government with Western European countries could not have been successful, since Goulart's socializing and supernationalistic tendencies did not provide the climate for foreign investments. The efforts of Quadros and Goulart to develop economic ties with East Germany had an adverse effect on the possibility of expanding economic relations with the German Federal Republic.

Thus the main foreign policy objective of President Castelo Branco's regime was to terminate the isolation of Brazil from the Western powers. The Castelo Branco government put Brazil squarely back into the camp of the Inter-American defense system. Even on issues beyond the Western Hemisphere, Brazil's position

23. According to Foreign Minister Leitão da Cunha's television interview as reported by news from Brazil, No. 28 (July 15, 1964).

became strongly pro-Western, as represented in the pronouncement of the Foreign Minister Vasco Leitão da Cunha, who declared that Brazil's preoccupation in the United Nations with
the conflict in Southeast Asia was the same as that of the United
States and stressed that Brazil would enter the war in Southeast
Asia, should that war be transformed into a world conflict.[24]

While Brazil wants friendly relations with all nations, it has
no political, military, or economic attractions for developing close
relations with the Soviet Bloc, Yugoslavia, and the neutralist countries. The revolutionary government entertained no illusions so
far as their relations with the Soviet Bloc were concerned. The
Brazilian Revolutionary Government's Foreign Minister Vasco
Leitão da Cunha ironically took a position on international communism more resolute than some of the pronouncements of United
States foreign policy representatives who advance the theory of
"good" and "bad" Communist countries. Perhaps in the long run
this discrepancy is all to the good, for one cannot expect a Latin
American nationalist to be enthusiastic about fighting Communist
expansion should the fight be foreign-inspired, that is, United
States–led. Should the defense against communism and a positive
desire for reforms spring from native revolutionary effort, as in
Brazil, it would be of more lasting value. Brazil feels the need for
self-fulfillment in international affairs; that is, to steer a course in
foreign policy independent of United States tactical moves of
the moment and rather to be guided by its own ideological con-
victions, which are founded on native unwavering resentment
against international communism in any form. The aloofness
and hostility to which Marshall Tito was subjected during his
state visit to Brazil in 1963 served as an indication of the mood
of the country. Brazil's search for a different model for her foreign
policy, imitating a sort of Nasserism under Quadros and Titoism
under Goulart, was not merely unproductive in terms of gaining
for Brazil distinct economic or prestige advantages but was also
against the cultural and ideological fiber of the largest Catholic
country in the world. The foreign policy of the revolutionary

24. *Boletim Informativo*, No. 152, 7 August, 1964, quoting from *Diário de
noticias*.

government of Brazil may thus be a durable one. The government has a stake in building a firm ideological base for Brazil's foreign policy because it was formed by a revolution which had as one of its objectives the elimination of Communist and extreme leftist influences from the Brazilian government. While the objectives of Brazilian foreign policy were founded on the principle that foreign policy is to be used as a tool of Brazilian development, the new ideological orientation is a codetermining factor in the foreign policy decision-making process. Any foreign policy which would please the extreme left would strengthen the revolution's internal enemies. The new Government thus adopted a built-in anti-Communist foreign policy with the aim of creating a foundation for a long-range global Brazilian foreign policy not conditioned by the subsiding or intensification of the Cold War according to the East-West coexistence ups and downs as the world may experience them at a given moment, but rather on Brazil's own over-all evaluation of its opportunities and domestic necessities. Brazil found De Gaulle's increasing interest in Latin America, or that of any other Western European country, welcome, because this might lead to assistance and comprehension from sources other than the United States. Brazil's foreign policy is, primarily, a tool of Brazil's aspiration for rapid economic development.

Goulart's nonalignment policy did not lead to the developing of realistic alternatives. While the Soviet Bloc was not in a position to help Brazil economically, the socializing tendencies of Goulart's government and its effort toward closer economic relations with East Germany and Communist China alienated Western Europe and the United States respectively.

The Brazilian revolution of 1964 has scrapped these policies for both economic and political reasons. The new policies, according to the pronouncements of President Castelo Branco, and of his foreign minister, are policies which honor Brazil's commitments to the free world and which will support the hemispheric partnership.

Brazil's breaking of diplomatic relations with Castro's Cuba in May 1964 was the logical result of the country's new international orientation. Brazil's new policy might signify the turning of the tide in Latin America in favor of democratically inspired revolutions instead of Cuban-type revolutions. The leading role of Brazil in the Latin American effort for dynamic economic development was interrupted by the Goulart era, as was the foreign policy of loyalty to the inter-American alliance system. The new regime restored Brazil's traditional alliance policy, but Brazil is outgrowing its hemispheric role and strives also for a true partnership with all the Atlantic nations. It has an opportunity to develop a policy of world significance beyond a Latin American policy of leadership, after putting its economy in order.

The new foreign policy course of Brazil since the April 1964 revolution should mark the beginning of a more productive relationship between Brazil, the United States, Western Europe and the rest of the free world; for Brazil is too large a country to be boxed within the inter-American system. An Atlantic triangle of interests would better suit Brazil's needs and aspirations. While the current revolutionary government has an ideological stake in this policy, thus making the policy more firm, the future Brazilian governments shall judge the new policy of Brazil also on the pragmatic grounds of what advantages they may bring to Brazil; thus Brazil's long-range foreign policy orientation depends very much upon the response it receives from the West.

BIBLIOGRAPHY

BOOKS:

Dantas, San Tiago. *Política externa independente*. Rio de Janeiro: Editôra Civilizacão Brasileira, 1962.

Delgado de Carvalho. *História diplomática do Brasil*. São Paulo: Comp. Editôra Nacional, 1959.

Freyre, Gilberto. *Sugestões em torno de uma nova orientacão para as relacões intranacionais no Brasil*. São Paulo: Servico de Publicacões do Centro e Federacao das Indústrias do Estado de São Paulo, 1958.

Jaguaribe, Hélio. *O nacionalismo na atualidade brasileira*. Rio de Janeiro: ISEB, 1958.

Macedo Soares, José Carlos de. *Brazil and the League of Nations*. Paris: A. Pedone, Editeur, 1928.

Pinto, Bilac. *Guerra revolucionária*. Rio de Janeiro: Companhia Forense de Artes Gráficas, 1964.

Rodrigues, José Honório. *Brazil e Africa: Outro horizonte.* Rio de Janeiro: Editôra Civilizacão Brasileira, 1961.

Sampaio de Sousa, Nelson. "The Foreign Policy of Brazil," Chapter in Joseph E. Black, and Kenneth W. Thompson (eds.). *Foreign Policies in a World of Change.* New York: Harper and Row, 1963.

ARTICLES:

Carneiro, Otavio Dias. "O comércio entre o Brasil e a Europa oriental," *Revista Brasileira de Política Internacional,* Junho 1962, V, No. 19, 227–243.

Freyre, Gilberto. "Misconceptions of Brazil," *Foreign Affairs,* XL, No. 3 (April 1962), 451–462.

Johnson, John J. "The New Latin American Nationalism," *The Yale Review,* LIV, No. 2 (Winter, 1965), 187–204.

Quadros, Jânio. "Brazil's New Foreign Policy," *Foreign Affairs,* XL, No. 1 (October 1961), 19–28.

Reisky de Dubnic, Vladimir. "A política externa do Brazil no govêrno Jânio Quadros." *Síntese Politica Ecônomica Social,* III, No. 9 (Janeiro-Marco 1961), 67–87.

Torres, Garrido. "Operacão pan-americana: Uma política a formular," *Revista Brasileira de Política Internacional,* III, No. 10 (Junho 1960), 33–50.

Valle, Henrique. "Alguns aspectos das relacôes Brasil–Estados Unidos," *Revista Brasileira de Política Internacional,* IV, No. 16 (Dezembro 1961), 5–22.

DOCUMENTS:

"A posicão do Brasil nas questões do desarmamento, desenvolvimento e decolonizacão," *Revista Brasileira de Política Internacional,* VI, No. 23 (Setembro 1963), 518–536.

Goulart, João. *Mensagem ao congresso nacional,* Rio de Janeiro: Servico Grafico do I.B.G.E., 1962.

Kubitschek de Oliveira, Juscelino. *Mensagem ao congresso nacional.* Rio de Janeiro: Departamento de Imprensa Nacional, 1959.
Operacão Pan-Americana, Documentario VII, Rio de Janeiro: Departamento de Imprensa Nacional, 1960.
"Projecto de resolucão sôbre desnuclearizacão da América Latina," *Revista Brasileira de Política Internacional,* VI, No. 22 (Junho 1963), 308–9.
"Declaracão Conjunta de 30 Abril de 1963, Dos presidentes do Brazil, Bolívia, Chile, Equador e México," *Ibid.,* p. 310.

Quadros, Jânio. *Mensagem ao Congresso Nacional,* Rio de Janeiro: Departamento de Imprensa Nacional, 1961.

U. S. Congress, House of Representatives. *Castro-Communist Subversion in the Western Hemisphere,* Hearings before the Subcommittee on Inter-American Affairs of the Committee on Foreign Affairs. Committee Print No. 95314, 88th Congress, 2nd Session. (March 1963).

4/ FOREIGN PRIVATE INVESTMENT AND INDUSTRIALIZATION IN BRAZIL
BY ERIC N. BAKLANOFF

O NE of the major decisions involving the strategy of industrializing a less developed nation centers on the role of foreign capital, private and official, in the economic process of growth. What is the desirable division of domestic and foreign savings and, equally important, the desirable participation (or exclusion) of foreign private investment in the various sectors of the economy—manufacturing, utilities, agriculture, commerce and trade, finance, and minerals? Another important question concerns the particular form of investment desired from abroad and the ability of the country to attract scarce capital resources in competition with other borrowing nations.

The constructive nationalists who helped shape Brazilian economic policy in the period between the framing of the Constitution of 1946 and the termination of President Kubitschek's regime in 1961 generally encouraged venture capital, private credits, and public assistance from abroad. This favorable attitude, manifested mainly in the 1954–1961 period, helps to explain the large flow to Brazil of new loans and venture capital—nearly seven billion dollars—in the decade and one-half between 1947 and 1961.

Notwithstanding the important role of private foreign capital in the postwar economic development of Brazil, especially in expanding and broadening the industrial sector, there emerged in the late fifties an anti-foreign investment coalition which developed sufficient momentum during the Goulart administration to pinch off the flow of venture capital, private credits, and, ultimately, external official assistance to Brazil.

The purpose in this chapter is threefold: we will demonstrate the magnitude and pattern of foreign capital in Brazil, distinguishing the forms of investment entering from abroad; we will attempt to measure the postwar impact of foreign investment on the Brazilian economy, concentrating our analysis on foreign venture capital, quantifying whenever possible; we will look at the various arguments presented for and against the participation of foreign venture capital in Brazil, examine these in the light of theory and available data, and try to define the various groups in Brazil which have entered the controversy. In the final section we hope to draw some relevant conclusions with particular reference to economic decisions taken in Brazil following the military-civilian coup of March 31, 1964.

Much of the empirical support for this chapter comes from the Brazilian Superintendency of Money and Credit (SUMOC); the Getúlio Vargas Foundation, the most important economic research organization in Brazil; the official National Economy Council; and the United States Department of Commerce.

TOTAL FOREIGN CAPITAL IN THE
BRAZILIAN ECONOMY: STOCKS AND FLOWS

The phenomenal postwar economic expansion of Brazil was substantially assisted by foreign capital participation, particularly in the industrial sector which formed the growing edge of the economy and in the financing of the nation's economic infrastructure. Foreign capital flows were especially decisive for Brazil after 1954 when the coffee boom faded and the terms of trade affected the economy adversely. In the period from 1947 to 1961 Brazil received more than 6.7 billion dollars in new capital from foreign investment, comprising 1,438 million dollars in new venture capital (including an estimated 607 million dollars in profits reinvested in the country) and 5,262 million dollars in new loan capital. A little more than half of the loans represented the financing of specific projects, mostly to cover imports of equipment essential to economic development. Official institutions, principally the United States Export-Import Bank and the World Bank, accounted for about a third of these loans; the remaining medium and long-term funds were supplied by private creditors from countries in the following order of their importance: the United States, France, West Germany, Italy, Japan, and others.[1] In the years of accelerated investment inflow, 1954 to 1961, foreign capital accounted for about a quarter of the total amount of Brazil's investment.[2]

An economy grows as the productive capacities of its citizens increase and as the stock of capital available to each worker expands. In turn, the increase of a nation's capital stock—machinery and equipment, plant, inventories—requires that income be withheld from current consumption and that these savings (together with foreign capital) be invested in their most productive uses. Hence, one of the important explanations for the low per capita productivity and income in Brazil compared with that of the United States is the small quantity of capital stock available per worker. It has been estimated that from 1945 to 1952, on the average, an employee in the United States was supported by twenty times more capital stock than his Brazilian counterpart.[3] Foreign capital, whatever its form, represents an addition to the resources of the capital importing country. These external financial savings are transferred to a country fundamentally in the form of imports of goods (or services) and represent therefore an addition to the real resources available to the country. Foreign capital not only increases the margin of savings for investment in income creating activities, but it may also, depending on its form, become a channel for the diffusion of technology and advanced business practices to the host country. One consequence of this diffusion of skills is that the capital-absorptive capacity of the borrowing nation is augmented.

Another way of looking at foreign capital in Brazil is to select a moment in time and estimate the accumulated foreign claims against the country and compare this magnitude with the country's accumulated capital stock. My estimate for total outstanding

1. The writer is grateful to Mr. Fabio Antonio da Silva Reis, economist, Division of International Affairs, Superintendency of Money and Credit, for providing him with these and other SUMOC data.

2. Ministry of Planning, *The 1964–1966 Action Program of the Brazilian Government.* (Analytical summary prepared by Benjamin Higgins, mimeographed) p. v–3.

3. Brazilian Embassy, *Survey of the Brazilian Economy*, 1958. Washington, D.C., p. 81.

foreign capital in Brazil as of June 30, 1963, is given below:[4]

Private Direct Investment ....2,752 million dollars
External Debt ....3,887 million dollars
_____

Total ....6,639 million dollars

A very rough calculation of Brazil's fixed stock of tangible repro-ducible assets can be made on the basis of the country's gross na-tional product in 1962 of about 24 billion dollars and the esti-mated average capital/output ratio of 2:1.[5] A comparison of Brazil's estimated capital stock of 48 billion dollars (the capital/output ratio times the gross national product) with the ac-cumulated foreign capital of 6.6 billion dollars is indicative of the important role of foreign savings in expanding the productive capacity of the country.

The forms of capital investment which have entered Brazil from abroad may be divided into two major categories: venture capital and loan capital. We give the term "venture capital" to any form of investment which provides variable returns, includ-ing the possibility of loss. "Loan capital" refers to an investment which provides a contractual schedule for amortization and a fixed-interest return. Venture capital may take a number of forms, including wholly owned subsidiaries of foreign parent com-panies; joint ventures with Brazilians; equity participation in return for patents, managerial services, or special industrial know-how; and venture capital investment in Brazilian-controlled com-panies. At the present time there are no studies which segregate foreign direct investments (in which the foreign group holds the controlling share) from other forms of venture capital. If we as-sume, with the United States Department of Commerce, that 25 percent of the equity in the possession of a single group or parent company is sufficient to establish de facto control then it would

4. For my estimate of private direct investment please see Table 2. The magni-tude of Brazil's total external debt, including interest, is derived from the Economist Intelligence Unit, Ltd., *Quarterly Economic Review: Brazil*, No. 49 (February, 1964), p. 4.

5. U. N. Department of Social and Economic Affairs, *Analysis y Proyecciones del Desarrollo Economico. El Desarrollo Economico del Brasil*, 1956 (E/CN 12/364/Rev.), p. 24.

appear that the value of foreign venture capital in Brazil, other than direct investment, is still very small.

FOREIGN CAPITAL AND THE CAPACITY TO IMPORT

In postwar Brazil the pace of economic development continues, although in a diminishing degree, to be significantly tied to the balance of international payments—to the country's ability to expand the value of exports and to draw on foreign investments to provide Brazil with the means of payment to import essential commodities and to pay for a variety of services, including interest and dividend obligations abroad. When focusing on the merchandise account only, the capacity of a country to purchase imports is determined by the quantum of exports and the terms of trade (the relationship of export prices to import prices converted to an index). In the immediate postwar period, say between 1948 and 1954, the capacity to import increased 77

TABLE I/ BRAZIL'S CAPACITY TO IMPORT 1948–1961 *1948=100*

Years	Quantum of Exports	Export Prices	Coffee Prices	Import Prices	Terms of Trade	Capacity to Import
1948	100	100	100	100	100	100
1949	90	106	116	86	119	107
1950	78	152	208	78	195	152
1951	82	186	231	96	194	159
1952	64	178	236	106	168	108
1953	75	169	250	98	172	130
1954	75	197	310	84	235	177
1955	82	155	220	85	182	149
1956	83	150	218	88	171	141
1957	77	147	211	89	166	127
1958	74	134	190	83	161	119
1959	86	109	150	79	138	119
1960	90	107	151	73	146	131
1961	102	108	149	74	145	148

Source: SUMOC, *Relatório do Exercício de 1961*, p. 56.

percent. As Table 1 indicates, despite a 25 percent reduction in the quantum of exports in this period, Brazil's capacity to import rose by 77 percent, reflecting a more than doubling of the terms of trade, from 100 in 1948 to 235 in 1954. Brazil's good fortune in this short span of years was, of course, a result of the coffee boom (the price of Brazilian coffee tripled) and of the sharp increase in the unit value of the country's secondary exports. Between 1954 and 1961, despite an increase in the quantum of exports, Brazil's capacity to import declined from 177 to 148, reflecting the weakness of coffee, cacao, cotton and other traditional crops in world markets. Parenthetically, when the entire postwar period is considered, the quantum of exports remained quite stable, and the terms of trade moved in Brazil's favor by 45 percent. The improvement in Brazil's terms of trade meant that with roughly the same quantity of exports the country received in exchange 45 percent more imports in 1961 than in 1948. Objectively, the Brazilians cannot validly argue that their country has suffered in its trade relationships with the industrialized countries on account of a deterioration in its commodity terms of trade. After 1954, because of increased supplies of coffee in Brazil, in the rest of Latin America, and in Africa, coffee prices fell rapidly.

A key to Brazil's continued economic growth after 1954, despite the sharp reversal in the nation's terms of trade with the rest of the world and the accelerating rate of inflation, is to be found in the massive inflow of foreign capital, especially private investment, which helped to sustain Brazil's "total capacity to import." [6] For example, in the five-year period ending in 1961, new foreign long-term capital inflows to Brazil averaged half a billion dollars, and these financed 42 percent (private loan capital contributed 19.3 percent; foreign direct investments, 9.3 percent; and official capital, 13 percent) of the country's average annual commodity imports of 1,252 million dollars.[7]

Taking the years 1960 to 1961 as rather typical, it is useful to break down Brazil's import structure[8] into the following significant components (in millions of U. S. dollars) :

6. Total capacity to import is equal to the value of foreign exchange received from exports plus the algebraic sum of the net balance of service account and net capital inflow.

7. Based on balance-of-payments statistics contained in the SUMOC bulletins. Imports are valued F.O.B.

8. *Revista do Conselho Nacional de Economia*, XI, No. 6 (November-December 1962), p. 658, Table II. Import values are expressed as C.I.F. rather than F.O.B.

Equipment and machinery 520
Raw materials and semi-manufactured
    producer's goods 450
Fuels 280
Food products 200
Consumer goods 25

The country's margin for safety in compressing consumer goods imports had practically disappeared, leaving Brazil's foreign exchange position exceedingly vulnerable to the slightest adverse shift in the terms of trade and to the volume of international capital movements. Thus, if imports of raw materials are cut back the economy will be forced to operate well below capacity; if capital equipment imports are cut back investment will suffer. Notwithstanding the vigorous program of import substitution which has characterized the country's postwar industrializing strategy, the absolute import requirements have remained high: "capital goods to equip the new industries and public works, coal and petroleum to provide energy for industry and transportation, food to supply the deficiencies of Brazilian agriculture, and consumer goods, especially luxuries, to satisfy inflation-born domestic demand." [9] By the early sixties, as already indicated, the volume of luxury imports had been reduced to negligible quantities. The Getúlio Vargas Foundation in an article entitled "Foreign Capital—Elements of a Rational Policy" cited the dependency of Brazilian imports upon the continued entry of foreign capital, no matter what form, on a high level. The author recommended "stimulating as much as possible that which remains in the country (not requiring fixed amortization payments), such as direct investments or official donations." [10]

As Celso Furtado has suggested, the principal factor limiting national investment in Brazil has probably not been the ability to save; rather it has been the difficulty of converting savings into real investment through the import of machinery and equipment. This is another way of saying that the prime factor limiting investment has been the "total capacity to import."

9. Theodore Geiger, *The General Electric Company in Brazil,* National Planning Association, 1961, p. 9.
10. *Conjunctura Economica,* VIII, No. 1 (January, 1961), 35.

Brazil, more than any other nation in Latin America, has been inordinately successful in creating a capital goods industry. This is reflected in Brazil's postwar drive toward the development of heavy industry. Although the country increased the quantum of equipment imports by a third between 1952 and 1961,[11] the nation's relative dependence on equipment imports in overall domestic requirements declined from 53 percent in 1949 to 33 percent in 1958.[12] In 1958, Brazil supplied out of domestic production 49 percent of its requirements for agricultural equipment, 48 percent of its manufacturing equipment, 72 percent of its transport equipment, and 87 percent of its power equipment. It would thus appear that Brazil is achieving greater investment autonomy and "economic independence." The process of import substitution to which foreign capital has made such a notable contribution is progressively putting into Brazilian hands control over "decision centers." Significantly, three-fourths of the foreign direct investments which entered under provisions of SUMOC Instruction 113 and subsequent legislation were concentrated in the heavy-industries sectors. The heavy industries most favored included those producing vehicles and parts, heavy chemicals and petrochemicals, electrical and mechanical equipment, naval construction, and steel. Within the light-industry category the foreign direct investments emphasized small mechanical and electrical appliances, pharmaceuticals, textiles, and food products. The evidence notwithstanding, the Marxist-oriented Brazilian economist, Caio Prado, Jr., contends that his country cannot count on "imperialistic" enterprises to achieve a real development.[13]

THE PATTERN OF FOREIGN DIRECT INVESTMENTS

According to Editôra Banas, a private economic research group in Brazil, foreign direct investments in that country reached a value of nearly three and a half billion dollars at the end of 1959 (see Table II). The Banas estimate covered some two thousand companies that contain varying degrees of foreign capital par-

11. *Brazilian Bulletin,* XIX, No. 442 (Nov., 1963), 7.

12. Presidency of the Republic, *Three-Year Plan for Economic and Social Development, 1963/1965.* (Summary, mimeographed), Dec., 1962, p. 33, table XII.

13. See his *Historia economico do Brasil* (Editôra Brasiliense, 1963), p. 323.

ticipation. By using the arbitrary exchange rate of 100 cruzeiros per dollar,[14] Banas probably overstated the actual dollar equivalent of foreign direct investments in Brazil; on the other hand, as they point out, the cruzeiro balance sheets published by the companies themselves probably undervalued their real capital in a period of rapid inflation. Another approach to calculating the outstanding value of foreign holdings is to take an initial estimate (such as the Banco do Brasil figure for 1951) and add to it the new direct investments from abroad and the earnings reinvested [15]

TABLE II/ FOREIGN DIRECT INVESTMENTS IN BRAZIL,
BY COUNTRIES, 1950, 1959 and 1961
(*Millions of U. S. Dollars*)

Country		1950[a]	1959[c]	1961[f]
Dollar Investments		950.4[b]		
United States	644.0		1,307.4	
Canada	306.4		618.3	
West Germany		—	323.2	
United Kingdom		233.3	257.1	
France		43.5	191.1	
Italy		—	157.5	
Belgium-Luxembourg		43.3	139.9	
Switzerland		13.4	121.9	
Sweden		3.4	64.3[d]	
Argentina and Uruguay		42.0	155.6[e]	
Japan		—	64.3	
Others		12.9	17.9	
Total		1,342.7	3,491.5	2,665

Sources:
a. Banco do Brasil, *relatório de 1950*, p. 162. Conversion rate: 18.72 cruzeiros per dollar.
b. The figure registered for dollar investments failed to distinguish between U.S. and Canadian capital. The amount registered for the United States is the U.S. Department of Commerce estimate. (See *Survey of Current Business*, August 1959, p. 30.)
c. Editôra Banas, *O Capital Estrangeiro no Brasil*, 1961, p. 8. Conversion rate: 100 cruzeiros per dollar. Based on figures published in the "diarios oficiais" of approximately 2,000 foreign companies that hold varying proportions of foreign capital.
d. Nordic countries, including Sweden.
e. Argentina only.
f. My own estimate calculated by adding to the 1950 estimate of the Banco do Brasil the new direct investments from abroad ($751 million) and the estimate of earnings reinvested in Brazil (571 million) during 1951–1961.

14. The theoretical equilibrium rate of exchange for 1959 was 165 cruzeiros per dollar, based on U.S. and Brazilian wholesale price indexes with 1939 as the base year.
15. It should be emphasized, however, that the estimates for reinvested earnings include only the profits of the United States subsidiaries. For 1959–1961 there was

by the foreign subsidiaries in Brazil. By following this method, my estimate for 1961 is only 2,665 million dollars (see Table II). Although the bulk of the capital which is directly invested in Brazil has been channeled into wholly owned foreign subsidiaries, it is significant to emphasize that according to one study published in 1958 there were 1,496 joint-ventures in Brazil, representing somewhat more than one-fifth of total foreign direct investments in the nation.[16] Willys Overland do Brasil, the most celebrated joint-venture enterprise, has about 40,000 stockholders in Brazil, representing more than 50 percent of the voting shares.

Taking the Banas study as the best available indicator of the country-origin of foreign direct investments, we conclude that United States participation leads with 38 percent, followed closely by Western Europe with 35 percent, and Canada with 19 percent of total investment. Of considerable interest is the very substantial postwar growth in the holdings of West Germany, Italy, France, Switzerland, Japan, Belgium-Luxembourg, and of Argentina-Uruguay. The assets of the former Axis powers, Germany and Japan, were confiscated by the Brazilian authorities during the Second World War. The investors of both countries have, since the conclusion of the Marshall Plan, plunged into the economic development of Brazil. Since World War II Brazil has received more West German direct investments than any other country in the world.[17] Of the 791 United States affiliates covered in the Banas study, the 24 largest represent 46 percent of all United States direct investments in Brazil. Among the well-known United States enterprises in Brazil are Willys Overland in autos; General Motors, Ford, and International Harvester in trucks; Du Pont in chemicals; Le Tourneau, Westinghouse, and Caterpillar in construction machinery. The estimate for outstanding United States

---

no data on reinvested profits, and I have therefore calculated these at 32 million dollars annually, the average of the three-year period 1956–1958. To the extent that profits reinvested by European and other foreign companies are not included, the above magnitude of 2.7 billion dollars undervalues the total stake of foreign direct investment in Brazil.

16. See Jose Garrido Torres and Denio Nogueira, *Joint International Business Ventures in Brazil* (New York: Columbia University, 1959).

17. Gertrude Heare, *Brazil: Information for United States Businessmen*, U. S. Department of Commerce, 1961, p. 13.

direct investments in Brazil at the end of 1959, given in Table II, corresponds reasonably well to the independent figure of the United States Department of Commerce for 1958 of 1,345 million dollars.[18] The latter figure includes the following most important activities of United States subsidiaries in Brazil: manufacturing (701 million dollars), petroleum distribution (215 million dollars), public utilities (181 million dollars), and trade (171 million dollars).

The representation of foreign firms in the various sectors of Brazilian business reflects to an important degree the special economic structure of each of the countries from which the investment originated. The affiliates of the United States and the United Kingdom are thus important in petroleum distribution; France, Germany, and the United States in chemicals; Germany and the United States in machines and domestic appliances; Japan, Belgium-Luxembourg, and Germany in steel; Canada and the United States in light and power; Holland and the United States in pharmaceuticals; the United States and Germany in the automobile industry; the United States, Argentina, and the United Kingdom in foodstuffs; Belgium-Luxembourg and the United States in plastics manufacture; and Japan in heavy shipbuilding.[19] Three-fourths of United States investments, for example, are diversified among nine principal branches of the Brazilian economy.

FOREIGN DIRECT INVESTMENTS IN BRAZILIAN INDUSTRY

The rapid industrialization of Brazil has been marked by significant transformations in the structure of its economy, including a rise in the relative importance of manufacturing industry in the share of the gross output; a change in the composition of industrial output in favor of heavy industry; and a decline in the percentage of the active labor force in agriculture. With respect to the second point, 70 percent of the value of manufacturing output in 1939 was concentrated in nondurable consumer goods; in 1961 more

18. *Survey of Current Business*, August, 1959, p. 30. However, net working assets of the American subsidiaries were subsequently written down in order to take account of the depreciation of the cruzeiro, and in 1959 U. S. direct investments were reported to total only 839 million dollars (see Gertrude Heare, *op. cit.*, p. 13).

19. Editôra Banas, *O Capital Estrangeiro no Basil*, 1961, pp. 13–26.

than half of the country's manufactures comprised final and intermediate capital goods and consumer durables.

The government's policy of favoring industry has typically followed a sequence, beginning with the "finishing touches" of product assembly and gradually working backward to include replacement of imports for the product components. Whenever imports of some commodity reached the "threshold" of minimum economic size, additional capital formation (often including a participation of foreign capital) was triggered in that activity. Foreign direct participation in Brazilian industry has been very important; its share increased from one-fourth in 1957 to one-third in 1960.[20] Parenthetically, it is instructive to recall that external participation in Brazilian industrial activities had reached 40 percent two decades earlier, in 1940.[21] As a consequence of the substantial investments entering Brazil from abroad in the postwar period, foreign enterprises at the beginning of 1960 controlled 69 percent of the automobile industry, 62 percent of the pharmaceutical industry, 57 percent of the manufacture of auto parts, 38 percent of machinery manufacture, 37 percent of the chemical industry, 28 percent of plastics production, 22 percent of the cellulose industry, 17 percent of steel manufacture, and 15 percent of the paper industry.[22] And foreign subsidiaries in 1961 controlled 52 percent of Brazil's electric power capacity.[23] A striking indication of the contribution which United States manufacturing enterprises have made to Brazil's industrial growth is given by the rates at which production of United States–owned firms rose, compared with the manufacturing sector as a whole in the period from 1955 to 1960. The average annual advance in Brazilian manufacturing production of 14 percent was paced by the U. S. affiliates which expanded their dollar sales by 19 percent per year during the five-year period.[24]

20. *Ibid.*, p. 8.

21. The 1940 census showed that of total industrial capital of 7,273 million cruzeiros, 2,985 million was foreign-controlled. Cited in J. A. Camacho, *Brazil, An Interim Assessment* (London: Royal Institute of International Affairs, 1954), p. 55.

22. Editôra Banas, *op. cit.*, p. 7.

23. *Conjunctura Economica,* February 1964, p. 137.

24. U. S. Congress, Hearings before the Subcommittee on Inter-American Economic Relationships. *Private Investment in Latin America,* 1964, p. 60.

Although the Brazilian market has provided an expanding effective demand for the creation of new industries, including those turning out consumer durables and capital goods, official protection has been a necessary factor in their realization. Unit costs for most of these consumer durables and capital goods continue to be higher than in the industrially more advanced nations of the North Atlantic. The country has recently become self-sufficient in home appliances, including such familiar products as electric ranges, television sets, radios, refrigerators and sewing machines.[25] The more traditional "vegetative" consumer goods industries, such as textiles and food processing, have exhausted the possibilities of replacing imports; their development is largely limited to the rate of growth in population and per capita income. The greatly expanded automotive industry is "compelling" investment in new industries producing component parts and related services. The Brazilians are learning their skills as a by-product of development and a portion of the extra cost may be considered an investment in human capital. In Hirschman's words, "The economy secretes abilities, skills, and attitudes needed for further development roughly in proportion to the size of the sector where these attitudes are being inculcated." [26]

One of the interesting postwar trends is the shifting balance of economic power between the "Big Two" in Latin America—Argentina and Brazil. In the period from 1948 to 1958, Argentina lost her preeminent position in the area contest for industrial leadership and was successfully challenged by her neighbor, Brazil. On the basis of value added in manufacturing industry in the ten-year span, Argentina's share of Latin American production fell sharply from 30 percent in 1948 to 21 percent in 1958, while Brazil moved up from 19 percent to 23 percent, thus occupying first place in 1958.[27] The realignment in the area's economic balance during the decade was even more pronounced where heavy industry is concerned. Brazil came up from behind

25. Brazilian Embassy, *Press Release*, March 12, 1962.

26. Albert O. Hirschman, *The Strategy of Economic Development* (New Haven: Yale University Press, 1958) , p. 36.

27. United Nations, Dept. of Economic and Social Affairs, *Patterns of Industrial Growth, 1938–1958*, New York, 1960, p. 124.

with 18 percent in 1948 to 25 percent in 1958 to tie Mexico for first place in the output of heavy manufactures in Latin America. Meanwhile, Argentina's commanding lead in heavy manufacturing industry with 34 percent of total Latin American production in 1948 was subsequently lost as that country's share fell to 23 percent in 1958. Between 1958 and 1961 Brazil pushed ahead in manufacturing production at a rate of growth exceeding that of both Mexico and Argentina. One of the critical factors in Argentina's failure to sustain a rapid increase in industrial growth during the Perón era was that country's negative approach to all forms of foreign capital, private and official.

LICENSING AND THE INVESTMENT OF KNOW-HOW

Some foreign companies choose to invest only their intangible assets—their patents, research and development efforts, or management skills. The different kinds of licensing include patent license contracts, know-how contracts, technical assistance contracts (e.g., engineering, management), franchise (distribution) contracts, and a combination of these.[28] Payment for these intangible services may take the form of fees, royalties, or profits from a minority share in the licensee's (the Brazilian company's) stock held by the licensor (the foreign company). In addition to securing a share in the equity of the licensee firm, the investor may succeed in getting a seat on the board of directors in order to have a spokesman inside the company. The licensing agreement usually provides arrangements for controlling quality and for auditing the licensee's accounts.

An appreciation of the importance of the diffusion of foreign technical knowledge and managerial experience to Brazil in the period from 1952 to 1961 can be inferred from the data on remittances in payment for "administration and technical assistance" which averaged nearly 18 million dollars per year and for "patents, royalties, and leasing" which averaged about 15 million dollars. These SUMOC statistics include payments effected by both Brazilian companies and foreign subsidiaries. Together

28. For a detailed analysis of licensing see Lawrence J. Eckstrom, "Licensing in Foreign Operations," *Case Studies in Foreign Operations*, International Management Association, Special Report, No. 1, 1958.

they add up to 33 million dollars per year, a sum equal to average profit remittances of the foreign-owned companies from 1954 to 1961, and are indicative of the considerable dependence of Brazil on the technology and business methods generated in the industrially advanced countries. "In certain cases," writes Senator Mem de Sá, "the technical secret, the chemical formula, is the decisive factor of production." [29]

A number of United States firms have established licensing arrangements in Brazil. For the Westinghouse Company, the decision in favor of licensing was made, not merely to save manpower, but also because the method offers a favorable return with a minimum of investment and a minimum of risk in the face of economic and political uncertainties. In addition to providing the Brazilian firms with its valuable trademark, available only by special arrangement, Westinghouse offers a continuous stream of new processes and products to its licensee partners. Philco International Corporation, which has built up a vast network of licensees, including one in Brazil, usually acquires a stake in both ownership and management. The company's service package includes personnel and sales training, technical assistance, and help with laying out plants.[30] Similarly, Eletromar, a Brazilian-owned enterprise, has been operating since 1949 under a licensing agreement with Western Electric International Company. The latter has provided Eletromar with patents and technical assistance in the construction and operation of its plants and has trained Brazilian personnel in the United States.

IMPACTS OF FOREIGN DIRECT INVESTMENTS: BENEFITS AND COSTS

The section will deal exclusively with foreign direct investments and their impacts on the host economy. It will be recalled that the difference between loan capital and direct investment hinges on management control—the latter involving the combination of capital, technical know-how and management under one unit of control. Foreign direct investment as a form of capital

29. *O Problema da Remessa de Lucros,* Associacão Comercial de Guanabara, Rio de Janeiro, 1962, p. 24.

30. "Middle Way to Profits Abroad," *Business Week* (March 22, 1958), pp. 109–114.

transfer possesses a high degree of adaptability: both the management and ownership functions can be substantially integrated with the host country—the first by promoting qualified nationals to high-level positions in the firm; the second, through the instrumentality of joint-venture, maintaining in the hands of the parent company only enough shares to hold minimum control over basic decisions. Once established, the firm can expand through reinvestment of profits.

Specifically, what are the impacts and relationships that foreign direct investments generate in a developing country? Three broad effects may be distinguished: income effect, foreign exchange effect, and intangible effect. Cash turnover of the foreign-owned companies for local wages and salaries, taxes, interest and dividends paid to local claimants, and raw materials and supplies purchased within the country represent the cost of doing business. From the perspective of the developing country, however, they constitute factor payments and enter the domestic income stream. For example, in 1960 the manufacturing sales of United States firms operating in Brazil were nearly 900 million dollars.[31] The total factor cost involved in the production of these commodities represented incomes to Brazilians. Payments made for imported materials embodied in these commodities did not, of course, become part of Brazil's national income. The more than 2,000 foreign subsidiaries operating in Brazil must have a very significant income effect, particularly in their area of geographic concentration—the south-central states of Brazil. They pay the best wages, provide extensive fringe benefits for their employees, scrupulously pay their taxes, and purchase vast quantities of materials, supplies and services from domestic firms. The nonwage outlays of these foreign companies generally equal 20 to 40 percent of the basic wage costs, and many manufacturing concerns over and above their participation in the National Apprentice System (SENAI) have instituted their own training programs. In contrast to government pension systems, which have proved completely inadequate in the course of growing inflation, many foreign companies have instituted sound pension plans for their employees.

31. Gertrude Heare, *op. cit.,* p. 8.

Some Brazilian writers in their attacks on foreign direct investment, including some economists, direct attention to balance-of-payments transactions by comparing only profit remittances with new capital inflows. Whenever profit remittances exceed the net inflow of private direct investment, as in the early postwar period, it is held that the foreign companies are "decapitalizing" Brazil. This kind of argument, which has much currency throughout Latin America, fails to distinguish between the current account (income flow) and the capital account (net additions to capital stock). Moreover, it fails to take into account the full impact of foreign direct investment on the host country's balance of payments—on capital account, on merchandise account, and on services account. Profit remittances in a dynamic economy tend to constitute only a small proportion of the additional foreign exchange proceeds (or exchange savings) generated by the investment.[32] The balance-of-payments effects of foreign direct investment are analyzed below:

Positive

Inflow of capital plus exports receipts attributable to the foreign companies.

Foreign exchange savings through substitution of imports attributable to the foreign companies.

Negative

Profits and interest remitted abroad.

Value of imports necessary for operation of the foreign companies.

Salary payments transferred abroad.

Profit remittances are properly related to the total sum of existing investments, old and new alike; they represent a factor payment on a stock which has accumulated over many years of investment. Even when profit remittances abroad in a given period exceed the net inflow of capital, the foreign companies are nevertheless adding to rather than decapitalizing the host country's

32. United Nations, *Foreign Private Investments in the Latin American Free-Trade Area*, New York, 1961. (See especially pp. 13–14.)

tangible wealth. And this is even possible when the net inflow of capital registers zero on the balance of payments, so long as part of the profits earned in the course of the year's operation in the country are reinvested rather than paid out in dividends. Profits are not paid out of capital; they represent a variable return (it may even be negative) after costs of production are met, and their origin is production and sale of desired goods and services.

In Brazil, the foreign exchange saved by foreign-controlled companies through the process of import substitution has been much more important than foreign exchange earned from exports. Foreign concerns are involved in the extraction and export of iron ore and manganese, and with their assistance the output of the two mineral products in recent years has expanded. However, it has been the prodigious foreign outlay in the Brazilian manufacturing sector, particularly in the period from 1956 to 1961, associated with President Kubitschek's Program of Goals, that has contributed so importantly to the balance of payments. Had these investments not occurred, either Brazilian incomes would have been insufficient to buy these goods at all or the goods would have been largely imported with a consequent drain on foreign exchange. The outstanding case illustrating this principle is the automotive industry, dominated by European and United States firms, which was firmly established in Brazil under the Program of Goals. Significantly, the motorcar producers have saved Brazil 273 million dollars [33] in foreign exchange since 1957— an impressive positive support for the country's international payments position.

We have shown that about one-third of Brazilian industry is represented by foreign direct investment. Moreover, foreign capital has favored the newer, technically advanced industries which form the growing edge of the Brazilian economy's forward thrust. The foreign companies have implanted an organizational technique that, together with progressive indigenous enterprise, has decisively altered the economic structure of south-central Brazil. In the apt words of Peter Drucker, the modern enterprise is a "new principle of social organization" which acts as "solvent of the traditional social order of pre-industrial society." In Brazil,

33. *Christian Science Monitor*, September 16, 1964, p. 12.

the foreign-owned enterprise, whether German, American, Japanese, or Italian, presents a visible paradigm of a progressive, nonfamily-oriented enterprise directed by professional management. "Under favorable circumstances," writes Henry William Spiegel, "the foreign establishment will have a profoundly disturbing influence on traditional methods of production, with a healthy spirit of emulation taking the place of the sleepy routine of the past." [34] The United States enterprises in 1957, for example, employed 140,000 persons in Brazil and, out of five thousand classified as supervisory, professional and technical, only one thousand were from the United States.[35] In the majority of American subsidiaries operating in Brazil, United States personnel probably continue to dominate the key executive posts.[36] Naturalized Brazilians of European origin are making important contributions in both foreign-controlled and national enterprises, particularly in production management and in engineering. According to the Gordon-Grommers study, all the participating companies are either employing Brazilians in high-level technical and managerial positions or are preparing them to take over such responsibilities in the future, and roughly 60 percent of them state as their policy the future transfer of all managerial responsibilities to Brazilians.[37] The same policies with regard to "Brazilianizing" high-level positions are likely to be followed by other foreign subsidiaries. The Volkswagen Company, for example, has steadily withdrawn its German staff, so that by the end of 1964 the factory was 96 percent Brazilian-operated.[38]

34. "Brazil: The State and Economic Growth" in *Economic Growth: Brazil, India, Japan,* edited by Simon Kuznets, Wilbert Moore, and Joseph Spengler (Durham: Duke University Press, 1954), p. 425.

35. U. S. Department of Commerce, *U. S. Business Investments in Foreign Countries,* 1960, p. 122, Table 34.

36. John C. Shearer, *High-Level Manpower in Overseas Subsidiaries, Experience in Brazil and Mexico,* Industrial Relations Section, Princeton University, 1960. Shearer studied 21 U. S. subsidiaries in Brazil employing 43,300 persons. The citizenship composition of key executives of the companies surveyed indicated a dominant position of U. S. personnel (63 percent), followed by Brazilians (25 percent), and others (12 percent).

37. Lincoln Gordon and E. L. Grommers, *United States Manufacturing Investment in Brazil,* Division of Research, Graduate School of Business Administration, Harvard University, Boston, 1962, p. 110.

38. *Christian Science Monitor,* September 16, 1964, p. 12.

The foregoing comments suggest that "organizing capacity" or entrepreneurship may well be the more strategic factor of production in a country such as Brazil which is moving increasingly toward more capital-intensive and complex kinds of manufacturing. It is precisely at this stage of industrial development that the foreigner can apply the craft of managing large undertakings.[39] As one writer put it:

The most essential human skill in modern economic activity is that of building, maintaining, and energizing the human organization, which can best apply accumulated knowledge to the efficient use of the passive resources that cannot combine themselves.[40]

Private direct investment, in sharp contrast to foreign loans made to government agencies,

. . . carries with it conscientious and industrious follow-through in the management function. This situation emerges from (1) the fact that performance on a private basis is measured by results over the life of the investment rather than in the completion of structural targets as such (determined by Government officials), and (2) devoted attention to detail in production and marketing on the part of men who have the best incentives because they stand to gain a substantial share of the results of high efficiency.[41]

The introduction of a new product or service or the expansion of sales of existing products by foreign investors usually induces local capital to embark on or expand upon all manner of small and medium-sized complementary investments. A celebrated example of this kind of backward linkage is that of Sears, Roebuck and Co., in Brazil. In 1949 the company inaugurated its first two stores in Rio and in São Paulo; today, Sears has nine stores and two huge warehouses. In the first year of operation the company sold mainly imported items, while today 98 percent of its products are made in Brazil by nearly two thousand supplier

39. W. Arthur Lewis suggests (see *The Theory of Economic Growth*, Homewood, Ill.: Richard D. Irwin, Inc., 1955, p. 258) that this "craft" is the foreigner's most important contribution to the less-developed countries.

40. John C. Shearer, *op. cit.*, p. 8.

41. American Enterprise Association, *American Private Enterprise, Foreign Economic Development, and the Aid Programs.* (Washington: U. S. Govt. Printing Office, 1957), p. 27.

firms, many of whom have received technical assistance and financial accommodation from Sears.[42] Without a doubt, Sears has had a profound effect on retail merchandising in the two major cities of Brazil. The United States–controlled firm, in building up local sources of supply, has had a profound effect on the standardization, quality, and cost of domestic manufactures, particularly in the durable and nondurable consumer goods industries. Clearly, the diffusion of production techniques and management methods to a supplier (as in the Sears case) or to a customer of a foreign affiliate are important intangible effects which must ultimately be reflected in the host country's national product. The foreign-owned meat-packing establishments have had similar effects on the cattle-raising industry through the requirement of standardization and quality control. Recent foreign investments in citrus processing in Brazil are having much the same impact on the growers of oranges and grapefruit.

The foreign affiliates over the years have created a reservoir of trained people, the benefit of which has accrued to the Brazilian economy. Theodore Geiger, chief of international studies of the National Planning Association, drew on the experience of the several NPA case studies of United States business performance abroad when he testified, as follows:

Even in a comparatively advanced country like Brazil, many of the top officials of locally owned banks and business firms acquired their early training at the First National City Bank of New York. The American companies studied have in effect continuously replenished reservoirs of semi-skilled and skilled workers, technicians, and potential managers, upon which locally owned enterprises and government agencies could draw as required. Without the training and experience provided by such American companies, the shortages of technical and managerial skills in many underdeveloped countries would be much more critical than they are now.[43]

The burden of evidence suggests that the earnings of foreign direct investments in Brazil were a modest price to pay for the powerful growth-promoting impacts of the foreign-owned enterprises. In the long period of 1947 to 1961 their profits averaged

42. Brazilian Embassy, *Boletim Informativo*, No. 161 (August 20, 1963).
43. U. S. Congress, House Committee on Ways and Means, *Private Foreign Investment*, 1958, p. 465.

80 million dollars a year, and half of this sum was reinvested in Brazil. Profits remitted abroad from 1954 to 1961, the period of accelerated capital inflow, constituted about 2 percent of Brazil's export proceeds and roughly one-fifth of one percent of the country's gross national product. My estimates of the rate of profits on the book value of total foreign direct investments are given in Table III. The rate of profit ranged between 7 percent in the 1947–1953 period and just over 3 percent in the 1954–1961 period; the rate of profit remittances fell from 3.5 percent of investment in the first period to 1.5 percent in the second. It should be noted that I have calculated these rates on the most conservative base, my own estimate for direct investments, rather than the larger Editôra Banas figure.

TABLE III/ BRAZIL: ESTIMATED RATE OF PROFITS AND PROFIT REMITTANCES ON FOREIGN DIRECT INVESTMENTS
(*Millions of U. S. Dollars*)

	1950	1947–1953 Average Annual	1958	1954–1961 Average Annual
Book value of investment	1,343		2,143	
Total profits		93		68
Profits remitted		47		33
Total profits/investment		7%		3.2%
Profit remittances/investment		3.5%		1.5%

Sources: For 1950 the book value of investment is the estimate of Banco do Brasil (see Table II); the 1958 investment was calculated by adding to the Banco do Brasil estimate the new direct investments (including reinvested profits) made in the 1951–1958 period. Data on profits and profit remittances are derived from SUMOC bulletins.

The United States companies in Brazil from 1957 to 1959 earned an average of 7.3 percent on the book value of total investments and 9.5 percent on their investments in the manufacturing sector.[44] During the early phase of the Korean War, in 1950 and 1951, the earnings on all United States direct investments in Brazil averaged 12.7 percent, compared with 14.9 percent for Latin America as a whole.[45] The Gordon-Grommers study which

44. U. S. Department of Commerce, *U. S. Direct Investments in Foreign Countries,* 1960 (derived from Tables 3–4, 42–43, and 45–66).
45. U. S. Department of Commerce. Cited in Banco Central de Chile, *Inversiones Extranjeras en Chile* (Santiago, 1955), p. 77.

covered thirty-six large United States manufacturing subsidiaries in Brazil, including most types of products and fields of activity, indicated that in the 1946–1960 period earnings amounted to 15.9 percent of book value; but of this total two-thirds was reinvested in Brazil while only one-third, or 5.4 percent, was remitted home.

Given the foregoing figures, based on official United States[46] and Brazilian statistics, it is difficult to comprehend how the claims that foreign private direct investments extract an exorbitant cost from Brazil can be justified.

THE ANTI–FOREIGN INVESTMENT COALITION VS. THE CONSTRUCTIVE NATIONALISTS

We now turn to a discussion of the principal adversaries in the debate concerning the role of foreign direct investments in Brazil's economic development. To the forces opposed to the participation of foreign subsidiaries I will apply the term "anti-foreign investment coalition"; for it is essentially a marriage of convenience among three groups: those ideologically opposed, business interests who are against the entry of foreign affiliates for reasons of competition, and those who are simply misinformed. Within the first group are a number of prominent Brazilian writers and academicians occupying positions rather far left of center, including some Communists. Some of them are outright statists; others, probably the majority, would tolerate the participation of local capitalists in the economy within a framework of tutelary guidance by the state. Their ideas have found expression in the weekly journal *O Semenario* and in the *Revista Brasilense*. Many of the

46. These earnings ratios should be compared with earnings of leading U. S. corporations within the United States for the years 1961 and 1962 which averaged 8.9 percent of book value for all economic activities and 10.4 percent on manufacturing investments. (See First National City Bank, *Monthly Economic Letter*, April, 1963, p. 40.) Book values are based upon the excess of total balance sheet assets over liabilities and the amounts at which assets are carried on the books are far below present-day values. According to the U. S. Department of Commerce, when comparing book and market values of U. S. direct investments in Latin America, "the market value of direct investments could be more than double their book value." (See *Survey of Current Business*, August, 1956, p. 15.) Therefore, since profits are stated in current dollars, the percentage relating earnings to equity or book value will tend to be exaggerated.

younger members of this group received their intellectual training from the Instituto Superior de Estudos Brasileiros (ISEB),
which formally came into being in the middle of 1955 as an
autonomous institution within the ministry of education for
study and research at the graduate level. According to Frank
Bonilla, ISEB "shaped the thinking of a substantial number of
importantly placed Brazilians through its extensive publications,
courses, and public lectures." [47] Among political personalities,
the most vociferous opponent of foreign private investment is
Leonel Brizola, brother-in-law of deposed President Goulart and
formerly governor of the State of Rio Grande do Sul.

The leftist ideological position vis-à-vis foreign direct investment in Brazil has found expression in a recent United States
publication by Professor Irving Louis Horowitz.[48] He writes
that the foundation of the balance-of-payments crisis is the con-
duct of foreign corporations (page 213), that United States manufacturers "sap Brazilian wealth" (page 399), and that United
States investors are not "unique in this maintenance of Brazil in
a less-than developed competitive condition" (page 212, footnote). Yet on page 220 he undermines his argument by admitting
that private investors from the United States could considerably
assist the Brazilian economy by fresh investments. And Professor
Horowitz is obviously displeased because these investors "insist
on guarantees that no further expropriation or nationalization be
attempted."

The second group in this unstable coalition is made up of
an undetermined number of local businessmen, among them
some extraordinarily wealthy ones, who supported restrictive
legislation designed to keep out foreign capital whenever it was
believed to threaten a comfortable market position. They wish
to be protected, not only against foreign goods, but also against
the competition of foreign-controlled factories sharing their
markets. According to one economist familiar with Brazil,

47. See his chapter "A National Ideology for Development: Brazil," in K. H.
Silvert (ed.), *Expectant Peoples: Nationalism and Development* (New York: Random
House, 1963.)

48. Irwing Louis Horowitz, *Revolution in Brazil: Politics and Society in a
Developing Nation* (New York: Dutton, 1964).

. . . the rate of industrial expansion is inhibited by the defensive tactics of existing producers who hope to reserve the expanding market for themselves without being under pressure to rationalize their techniques of production or to meet price competition.[49]

Co-operation between these rather short-sighted men of business with extreme leftist politicians worked effectively to exclude the participation of new foreign ventures in the aluminum, tin-can, textile, metallurgy, and iron-ore industries. A leading national industrialist, for example, subsidized a Communist campaign—including student demonstrations—against American Can Company when it proposed establishing a new plant in Brazil. The favorable exchange treatment given to foreign investors with the introduction in 1955 of Instruction 113 and subsequent rulings was not available for substantial numbers of Brazilian firms who were in competition with foreign concerns.[50] It is evident that this differential treatment exacerbated feelings against foreign capital participation and ran counter to the spirit of the Constitution of 1946 which provides equal treatment of private capital, whatever its origin. By intention, this type of discrimination was supposed to have been avoided: de facto, many national firms were disadvantaged.

The public in Brazil probably has little more than latent prejudice against foreign business investments. In fact, as recently as 1958, public opinion in that country apparently regarded private foreign investment favorably.[51] During times of great social tensions, however, the latent public prejudice can be activated as it was in the early sixties in Brazil:

49. Reynold Carlson, "The Economic Picture," in Herbert L. Matthews (ed.), *The United States and Latin America* (Englewood Cliffs, N.J.: Prentice Hall, Inc., 1963.), p. 123.

50. See Lincoln Gordon and Engelbert Grommers, *op. cit.*, pp. 41–44.

51. A poll in twelve countries taken in 1958 regarding the opinions on foreign private investment which included two countries in Asia, Brazil and another Latin American country, Canada, and seven European countries showed that the responses in Brazil indicated the lowest level (14 percent) of opinion which regarded private foreign investment as "bad" for the country; and the ratio of favorable to unfavorable attitudes on private foreign investment was the highest of any country included. (See Brazilian Embassy, *Survey of the Brazilian Economy 1958*, Washington, D.C., p. 63) .

The majority of the Brazilian population is obviously not well versed in economic theory and analysis. It is thus quite willing to accept an emotionally satisfying explanation of the causes of underdevelopment, since it is not capable to verify the theoretical soundness of the arguments or to test their empirical validity. There results a great demand by opportunistic politicians for scapegoats, and there exists none better than foreign capital. Moreover, quite a number of noncynical politicians sincerely believe in this explanation created by their colleagues.[52]

Ranged against the anti-foreign investment coalition is a different group of men of diverse backgrounds and interests whom I shall call the "constructive nationalists." Within this category it is possible to identify the following groups: the more progressive leaders of the indigenous business community, especially the *paulistas,* some of whom are associated with foreign capital in joint ventures; a large group of professional men; some high-level government officials, many of whom, at one time or another, have held positions of responsibility in the Bank of Brazil, the National Development Bank, the National Economy Council,[53] the ministry of finance, and in planning agencies of several of the Brazilian states; and a group of economists, many of whom have been trained in American universities, and more recently, in the Getúlio Vargas Foundation. Although these groups may disagree on specific issues (for example, the desirability and degree of financial stabilization), they share a common philosophy with regard to the strategy of modernizing Brazil. They would regard government action as complementing and strengthening rather than replacing the market mechanism. They are reformists in that they favor progressive income taxes, land reform, and rural development and conceive of government as an effective instrument for expanding the nation's economic infra-structure—e.g., transportation and power—and in providing social capital—low-cost housing, education, health and sanitation. They favor the participation of foreign investment as an additional source of savings,

52. Werner Baer and Mario Henrique Simonsen, "American Capital and Brazilian Nationalism" (mimeographed manuscript).

53. *Conselho Nacional de Economia* was created by the Constitution of 1946 to study the country's economic life and needs and to suggest appropriate measures to the competent government agencies. It is a constitutional organ affiliated with the Brazilian Congress.

foreign exchange, and technical and managerial skills, all of which have been notably scarce in Brazil. Over the long view, they contend that Brazil will grow away from its dependence on foreign assistance through the growth and diversification of its economy and the cumulative capabilities of its people. Because the constructive nationalists favor the participation of private capital from abroad, they have been labeled *entreguistas,* the leftist epithet for the act of opening Brazil to foreign-capital investment. Speaking on television in Rio de Janeiro in early April of 1964, economist Roberto Campos, who resigned in late 1963 as Brazilian ambassador to Washington, described the climate for Brazilian moderates under President Goulart:

> We were intimidated with slogans. We were made to feel guilty about advocating co-operation with our traditional friends. . . . If we did not go along with expulsion of foreign capital, we were called sellouts.[54]

Briefly stated, the extreme leftist group in the anti-foreign investment coalition argues that foreign direct investment exploits Brazil. The argument may assume a scholarly tone as in the publications of such economists[55] as Caio Prado, Jr., and Aristóteles Moura; at another level, it may take on the form of pure diatribe, as in the attacks on foreign capital of Leonel Brizola and Sylvio Monteiro.[56] Brizola even manages to blame Brazil's inflation on "imperialist plundering." Asked how to explain inflation, he states: "It is as if imperialism had attached a large pump to our body in order to suck out our blood. Since we cannot resist, they remove the blood and inject water in its place." [57] The leftist group claims that the foreign companies operating in Brazil earn exorbitant profits and that these in turn have become a major cause of Brazil's persistent deficits on international account. Put another way, these arguments claim that the operations of the foreign subsidiaries drain the country of precious exchange—a

54. *Business Week,* April 11, 1964, p. 72.

55. See, for examples, Prado's *op. cit.,* and Moura's *Capitais estrangeiros no Brasil,* Editôria Brasilense, 1960.

56. See Monteiro's *Como atua o imperialismo ianque* (Rio: Ed. Civilizacão Brasileira S. A., 1963).

57. Victor Rico Galan, "The Brazilian Crisis," *Monthly Review,* Vol. 15, No. 12 (April, 1964), p. 673.

leakage which can only be repaired by a law limiting profit remittances, or better still, by keeping private foreign investment out. The popular phrases *sangria de divisas* and *sangria de nossa economia* (bleeding of foreign exchange: bleeding of our economy) convey the notion of an economic octopus (especially the United States variety) whose tentacles are attached to Brazil. Where the mineral sector is concerned, the leftist arguments become especially crude: foreign investors are accused of depleting exhaustible resources and offering nothing in return. *O petróleo é nosso* (the oil is ours) and *o ferro é nosso* (the iron ore is ours) reflect this notion and have become useful political slogans to justify the inefficient operation of Petrobras[58] and Brazil's failure to become one of the world's major exporters of iron ore.[59]

"INVESTMENT CLIMATE" AND CAPITAL FLOW

We have noted that foreign capital, private and official, was an indispensable element sustaining Brazil's industrial growth after 1954 when the coffee boom came to an end and the international terms of trade moved against the country. The very substantial inflow of private loan and venture capital was the consequence of policies designed to attract investment from abroad.

In response to Brazil's deteriorating international payments position in the latter forties, quantitative restrictions were imposed on capital outflow and service payments. By SUMOC Instruction 25 of June 3, 1947, profit remittances were limited to 8 percent of registered capital, while amortization transfers were restricted to 20 percent per year. At the same time, the official exchange rate of 18.50 cruzeiros per dollar became progressively overvalued as prices in Brazil continued their upward climb. By freezing the exchange rate at an increasingly unrealistic value, foreign investors were in effect subsidized when remitting profits

58. Petrobras, especially during the Goulart administration, was the home of thousands of political jobs. According to the U. S. Consulate in Salvador, private oil-drilling companies contracted by Petrobras were able to drill holes at less than half the cost of the government firm.

59. With more than one-third of the world's estimated iron ore reserves—most of it is of the highest quality—Brazil has lost an excellent opportunity to become a major world exporter of the mineral. The country currently supplies only about 2 percent of the world market.

(dollars were artificially cheap) and penalized when making new investments (cruzeiros were artificially expensive).

After 1953, the market for foreign exchange became increasingly more free, and quantitative restrictions on profit and amortization transfers were eliminated. An important innovation, SUMOC Instruction 113, introduced in early 1955, enabled foreign investors, under prescribed conditions, to import equipment without exchange cover in return for a cruzeiro capital participation in the enterprise by which the capital equipment was to be used. The "law of similars" (see Werner Baer's discussion of this measure) was invoked, offering the incentive of direct investment in an expanding protected market coupled with the threat of complete exclusion for the unventuresome latecomer. The flow of private loan capital to Brazil was greatly expanded after preferential exchange treatment was authorized to finance medium-term credits covering imports of equipment registered with SUMOC as being of "special interest to a national economy." The interdependence of external loan and venture capital was cited by the president of Brazil's National Economy Council:[60]

With the increase of venture capital, there was an increase in loan capital. In large measure this is explained by the fact that the new foreign investors which came to Brazil brought their own capital and also their connections with international financial institutions. In this way, the modification of the legal treatment of foreign capital stimulated and increased its inflow: directly, in the area of venture capital; indirectly, in loan capital.

In the seven years between 1947 and 1953, the inflow of venture capital averaged only 15 million dollars per year, while profit remittances averaged 47 million dollars; in the following eight years, 1954 to 1961, when no restrictions on profit remittances were in effect, new venture capital (not including reinvested profits) averaged 91 million dollars annually, while profit remittances fell to an average of 33 million dollars. The movement of private autonomous loan capital to Brazil followed an even more dramatic pattern: new medium and long-term loans from private

60. Humberto Bastos, *O problema dos capitais extrangeiros no Brasil*, Centro de Cultura Economica, 1962, p. 13.

sources abroad were negligible in the first period, then surged to an average of 180 million dollars per year in the second.[61]

The year 1961 marked the close of a sustained period of rapid industrialization and economic growth in Brazil. The new economic climate was characterized by increasing hostility toward private capital, especially foreign direct investment, as reflected in the Profit Remittance Law of September 1962. The deteriorating economic picture was also reflected in an accelerated rate of inflation; increasing government control of the private sector through the formation of additional "autarchias"; an alarming expansion of Brazil's external short-term debt; paralysis of the major ports, especially of the strategic port of Santos; and extreme leftist infiltration of the power structure of the nation: key labor unions, the armed forces, student federations, and, most important, the agencies of government.[62]

The Profit Remittance Law placed a limit of 10 percent of registered capital on the annual remittance of profits of a foreign-owned enterprise. Profits reinvested by foreign subsidiaries in Brazil were treated as foreign-owned "national capital" which could not be transferred. The law thus created a specious distinction between capital accumulation as a result of a foreign-currency investment (via the balance-of-payments mechanism) and capital accumulated from profits reinvested in the host country by the foreign subsidiary. The latter provision had an especially discriminatory effect on enterprises whose activities produce highly variable earnings. For example, if a given firm in a three-year period earned profits of 7 percent, 0 percent, and 23 percent on registered capital (an annual average of 10 percent) , it would have the right to remit 7 percent the first year but only 10 percent the third year; the extra 13 percent, if reinvested, could not be registered as capital for purposes of calculating annual remit-

61. SUMOC, *Relatorio do exercicio de 1961*, table 19.

62. Negotiations involving about 400 million dollars of U. S. public assistance to Brazil were disturbed on March 14, 1963, by the release of a statement made by Ambassador Lincoln Gordon to the effect that Communists had infiltrated the Brazilian labor unions, the government, and the National Student Union. However, the ambassador's untimely remarks were later "clarified" by the U. S. State Department. See *Hispanic American Report*, XVI, No. 3 (May, 1963) for an elaboration of U. S.–Brazilian credit negotiations.

tances in the future. Technical assistance and licensing arrangements were also affected by the law. Remittance of royalties and technical fees were limited to 2 percent of the annual gross receipts for goods manufactured or sold. Moreover, royalty payments by a subsidiary in Brazil to its parent company abroad were forbidden by the law.[63]

Prior to the passage of the Profits Remittance Law, numerous groups and official bodies in Brazil came out strongly opposed to the negative features of the bill. The Vargas Foundation and the National Economy Council cited the country's unhappy experience with an earlier law which had arbitrarily restricted profit remittances and predicted that another dose of restrictive legislation would deter further entry of private investment and hasten the repatriation of foreign venture capital previously accumulated in Brazil. The National Economy Council published a lengthy report on its analysis of the profits remittance issue.[64] The council's most important recommendations were twofold: to permit revaluation of investments for inflation and incorporate all reinvested profits in the base upon which profit remittance limitation would be applied and to attack the problem of excessive profits through an antitrust law and income tax laws, which would control excessive profits and encourage reinvestment of profits.

Most foreign companies were not bothered particularly by the 10 percent limit, since few of them were earning that much; more important, they were disturbed by the provision of reinvestment of profits and by what the law revealed about the attitude of Brazil's politicians toward foreign investment.

The law on profit remittances should be viewed against a background of specific acts of hostility to foreign investors in Brazil. Among these were the expropriation without compensation of the subsidiaries of American and Foreign Power Company in the States of Rio Grande do Sul and Pernambuco; the threatened military intervention and subsequent shutdown of the

63. Economist Intelligence Unit, *Quarterly Economic Review: Brazil*, No. 49 (February 1964), p. 4.

64. A good summary article of the Council's reasoning and conclusions was published in its *Revista do Conselho Nacional de Economia* IX, No. 6.

Swift and Company plant in the city of Rio Grande; the refusal by government regulating agencies to grant the foreign-owned telephone and electric power companies adjustments in their rates in the face of chronic inflation;[65] a moratorium on all profit remittances abroad, including payments for licensing and technical assistance agreements, between September 1962 and the overthrow of the Goulart regime; the credible prospect of expropriation of the foreign petroleum distribution facilities; and the Goulart administration's failure to honor the "memorandum of understanding" which was signed between the Brazilian Embassy in the United States and the American Foreign Power Company, outlining the bases for the purchase by Brazil of the several utility plants. Finally, President Goulart's real views on the role of foreign private investment in Brazil were made explicit during the inauguration of the government-owned Victoria Steel and Iron Company in Espírito Santo when he accused the foreign companies of "plundering" the economy.[66]

As predicted by the most competent authorities in Brazil, the entry of new venture investment from abroad declined and then ceased altogether. In the 1956–1961 period, coinciding with the Kubitschek administration, the annual inflow of venture capital (not including reinvested earnings) averaged 112 million dollars; in 1962 it was 71 million dollars; in 1963 it fell to 31 million dollars; and in the first half of 1964 no additional investment took place.

THE CASTELO BRANCO ADMINISTRATION AND THE INTERNATIONAL FINANCIAL COMMUNITY: IMPLICATIONS AND PROSPECTS

When the new administration assumed power on April 1, 1964, as a consequence of a popular military-civilian coup, it inherited a stagnating economy. The Brazilian industrial growth rate, for example, dropped from an average 9.6 percent per annum during

65. At the end of 1963 there were more than one million unfilled requests for telephones throughout Brazil, almost as many as the actual number of installed phones. (See *Conjunctura Economica*, February 1964, p. 143.) The writer recalls that in 1963 the monthly rate for the use of a phone in the city of São Paulo was equivalent to 25 U. S. cents and a call by public telephone cost less than half a penny!

66. *New York Times*, Sunday, Nov. 3, 1963.

the 1947–1961 period, to 6 percent in 1962 and less than one percent in 1963.[67] The country's international credit position was gravely impaired. Brazil's external debt of nearly four billion dollars both voluntary (autonomous loans) and involuntary (deficit financing), pushed the country to the edge of insolvency. There was a growing fear of a unilateral moratorium as 1,300 million dollars in foreign debts were scheduled to mature in 1964 and 1965.[68] The country's gold and foreign exchange reserves at the end of 1963 were the lowest year-end total in more than a decade, and a large share of the gold was already pledged as guarantee for loans from the United States. Moreover, foreign private investment, as already mentioned, came to an abrupt halt toward the end of the Goulart regime.

The new administration[69] set out to get the Brazilian economy moving again. Under the leadership of Minister of Planning Roberto Campos, an outstanding economist and former ambassador to Washington, the government had laid down three basic economic objectives: stabilization, development and reform. With respect to Brazil's critical international economic position, it became necessary for the new administration to regain the confidence of the international financial community to reschedule the nation's external debts and reactivate the inflow of long-term private capital. The government took some dramatic steps to stimulate the flow of foreign venture capital to Brazil. Undoubtedly the most important single measure designed to restore the confidence of foreign investors was the amending of the Profit Remittance Law of 1962. The amendments essentially incorporated the earlier recommendations made by the National Economy Council. The 10 percent annual limit on profit remittances was repealed; the "capital investment" base could now be adjusted for reinvested profits and for inflation; and earnings could be re-

---

67. *The 1964/1966 Action Program of the Brazilian Government* (Analytical summary prepared for the Ministry of Planning by Benjamin Higgins.), p. X-2.

68. Economic Intelligence Unit, *Quarterly Economic Review: Brazil*, No. 49 (February, 1964), p. 4.

69. It is interesting to mention that Brazil's celebrated social philosopher Gilberto Freyre believes that the cabinet of President Castelo Branco may well be the most competent in the history of the republic. (See "When Executives Turned Revolutionaries," *Fortune*, September, 1964, p. 147.)

invested in the enterprise originating the profit or in any other national activity. Another significant amendment to the law established "a progressive tax on dividends and/or profit actually remitted in excess of a 12 percent average covering a period of three years—a provision which could prove relatively expensive for investors who remitted too much." [70]

Another important step indicating Brazil's serious intent to re-establish good international economic relations was the passage of a bill, in early October 1964, to purchase American and Foreign Power Company's ten subsidiaries for 135 million dollars, substantially within the terms outlined in the "memorandum of understanding" signed more than a year and a half earlier.[71] One of the conditions of the transaction stipulated that the company was to invest 75 percent of the proceeds from the sale within Brazil. Finally, in early 1965, Brazil and the United States signed an investment guarantee agreement which should further stimulate the flow of private United States investment to Brazil.

A number of American firms were responding favorably to Brazil's new investment climate.[72] The ranks of companies which in the fall of 1964 were once more increasing their Brazilian investments included Johnson and Johnson Company, International Telephone and Telegraph Corporation, Kaiser Industries Corporation, and Willys Overland do Brazil which embarked on a 32 million-dollar expansion program, including a new assembly plant at Recife. Other American enterprises seriously considering additional investments in Brazil were the Hanna Mining Company of Cleveland, which holds important iron-ore properties; Bethlehem Steel Corporation; Aluminum Company of America, which owns Bauxite reserves in Minas Gerais state; Union Carbide Corporation; General Motors Corporation, and Ford Motor Company. Alcoa was considering making substantial investments in a processing complex, including an alumina plant, fabricating mills and a primary smelter.

Brazil's prospects for diversifying and expanding exports have been significantly raised by the government's new iron-ore export

70. *Hispanic American Report*, XVII, No. 8 (October, 1964), 760.
71. *New York Times*, October 12, 1964, pp. 45–46 C.
72. "Back into Brazil," *Wall Street Journal*, October 7, 1964, p. 1.

policy. A Presidential decree, signed on December 23, 1964, with the support of the National Security Council, called for private competitive development of the country's vast iron-ore reserves.[73] President Castelo Branco's decision reversed a trend toward state monopoly set by leftists, some nationalists and the late President Getúlio Vargas. The decree aimed at increasing Brazil's share of world iron-ore trade, thereby raising the country's foreign exchange earnings and national income. Both the Hanna Mining Company and the Antunes Mining group, a joint Brazilian–United States venture in which Bethlehem Steel Corporation has an interest, were laying plans to expand their mining operations in Brazil, including the construction of shipping port facilities south of Rio de Janeiro. Hanna, which had been mining about 400,000 tons of ore annually, was contemplating raising its production to three million tons initially and later to six million.[74]

The World Bank sent a twenty-man Mission to Brazil in late 1964. The task of the mission, one of the largest study teams ever assembled by the bank, was to make a comprehensive study of the Brazilian economy and recommend long-term development and investment plans. Because of the country's size and complexity, the bank is approaching Brazilian problems on the basis of "integrated" development. A concerted and sustained financial effort involving investments by international lending agencies, the United States, Western Europe, Canada, Japan and others is the logical outcome of the bank's mission.[75]

As an initial step, the World Bank granted a credit to Brazil in early 1965 for 80 million dollars to help finance hydroelectric installations for Brazil's populous south-central region. The loan, the first extended by the World Bank to that country in nearly six years, was widely interpreted as a mark of renewed confidence in Brazil. Significantly, the United States government announced that it would make available under the Alliance for Progress public resources amounting to about 450 million dollars in 1965

73. "Brazil Decrees Private Development of Iron Ore," New York Times, Thursday, December 24, 1964, p. 27 C.

74. New York Times, Monday, December 21, 1964, p. 49.

75. New York Times, Friday, October 2, 1964, p. 51 C.

to Brazil. During the last nine months of the Goulart regime, United States Government assistance to Brazil amounted to only 30 million dollars: American officials felt that meaningful assistance was impractical for both economic and political reasons. The International Monetary Fund granted Brazil a 125 million dollar standby credit in February 1965. The IMF noted that the Brazilian economic program submitted to it toward the end of 1964 included important institutional reforms. Among those which the fund cited were the organization of a central bank, new tax measures and restraint on expenditures, the wider role given to the price mechanism in order to eliminate existing distortions gradually, a vigorous stimulus to exports, liquidation of commercial arrears, and measures designed to encourage an inflow of official and private foreign capital from abroad.[76]

The analysis presented in this chapter leads us to the conclusion that foreign private investment, particularly when associated with entrepreneurship, can continue to exercise a dynamic role in the economic and social transformation of Brazil—a transformation leading ultimately to better living conditions with freedom for all Brazilians.

76. *Brazilian Bulletin,* XXI, No. 459 (February 1965), p. 3.

5/ SOCIO-ECONOMIC IMBALANCES IN BRAZIL
BY WERNER BAER

> *Editor's Note: This chapter is based on a lecture delivered at Vanderbilt University under the auspices of the Graduate Center for Latin American Studies and the Graduate Program in Economic Development. The material is drawn from the author's monograph,* Industrialization and Economic Development in Brazil *(Homewood, Illinois: Richard D. Irwin, Inc., 1965).*

BRAZIL'S rapid industrialization atfer World War II created some basic socio-economic imbalances. This chapter will provide evidence to support the claim that the spring 1964 political crisis was a reflection of those imbalances.

INDUSTRIALIZATION AND GROWTH SINCE WORLD WAR II

Before the Second World War Brazil did not pursue a systematic industrialization policy. The industries which did develop in the first four decades of the twentieth century were stimulated through the automatic protection offered by the effects of the two world wars and the world depression of the thirties. These events drastically cut imports of manufactured goods, as a result of shipping difficulties in the case of the wars and the drastic decline of foreign exchange earnings in the case of the world depression. These import cuts spurred the development of the textile industry, certain food industries, and other light manufacturing industries. The government, however, was never inclined to support the new industries formally, and after each world crisis a serious setback occurred as more competitive manufactured imports found their way back into the Brazilian market.[1]

In the first years after the Second World War, Brazil was still primarily an agricultural country, heavily dependent on its traditional exports, mainly coffee, cocoa, cotton, and sugar. Although Brazil came out of the war with substantial amounts of foreign exchange reserves, these vanished within one year as a result of an import spurt, largely in consumer goods. This led to the institution of direct controls over imports, consisting principally of exchange controls, which have continued in one form or another up to the present time.[2]

In the late forties and early fifties, Brazilian policy-makers gradually realized that by retaining its traditional economic structure the country would not be able to attain high levels of economic growth. A high rate of economic growth had become of prime concern for two reasons. First, as in many underdeveloped countries in the post–World War II era, Brazil experienced the revolution of rising expectations of the masses, which meant that policy-makers were under pressure to establish policies which would raise the standard of living in a fairly short period. Second, the problem of raising the standard of living was complicated by the population explosion. The rate of population increase rose from 2.4 percent per year in the nineteen forties to more than 3.1 percent in the fifties, one of the highest in the world.[3]

From long-term trends of its principal exports, it gradually

1. For a more detailed survey of the period see Celso Furtado, *The Economic Growth of Brazil: A Survey from Colonial to Modern Times* (Berkeley: University of California Press, 1963).

2. The most authoritative work to date on Brazil's postwar foreign exchange control system is a doctoral dissertation by Donald Huddle, which was written for Vanderbilt University.

3. Werner Baer and Isaac Kerstenetzky, "Import Substitution and Industrialization in Brazil," *American Economic Review*, May 1964.

became clear that Brazil could not hope to attain the desired growth rates by keeping its economy geared to the export of its traditional crops. Ever since the second decade of the twentieth century, the share of food and agricultural raw materials in world trade has declined. The prices of these commodities have fluctuated substantially, reaching high levels during the Korean War; but they have declined ever since. Since the early fifties, the prices of many of these primary products in relation to prices of manufactured goods imported by underdeveloped countries have declined too. The reasons for these trends are twofold: the developed countries consume a smaller proportion of foodstuffs as their income continues to increase, while production of these foodstuffs in underdeveloped countries continues to grow rapidly, and the relative amounts of raw materials consumed in the production process of developed countries also declines, and these raw materials are often replaced by synthetics.

Table 1 shows that these trends have also applied to Brazil. Since 1954, the country's terms of trade have steadily declined. Although they did not fall to the immediate postwar level by the early sixties, one should consider that the export quantum has not increased much and is still below the early postwar level. Most important, the country's foreign exchange requirements are much greater because of its development efforts.[4]

With continuous balance-of-payments difficulties, the policy-makers became aware of these trends and gradually concluded that a massive import-substitution program was the only way out. Thus, the exchange-rate policies were slowly altered from being simply instruments of balance-of-payments protection into instruments designed to promote actively the development of an industrial base.

The prospects of a large protected market acted as a great stimulus to both domestic and foreign capital. But other actions taken by Brazilian authorities further strengthened this stimulus. In the early fifties a development bank was organized to finance both government and private enterprises in key developmental

4. For a discussion of the declining terms of trade and their relation to Latin American economic development see Werner Baer, "The Economics of Prebisch and ECLA," *Economic Development and Cultural Change*, January 1962.

sectors. The foreign-exchange authorities made it possible for foreign investors to import capital goods without the need for exchange cover, if the investment was deemed desirable for the development of the country.

In order not to wind up with a simple "last-stage" industrialization, Brazilian authorities made use of an old law, "the law of similars." Before the First World War, Brazilian manufacturers who were already producing or intended to produce goods similar to the ones imported could apply for protection. In the fifties the registration of a product as a "similar" became the basis for a substantial amount of tariff protection and for placing goods in a high and protective exchange-rate category. This law was applied in such a way as to encourage a substantial amount of vertical integration, either within firms, i.e., having firms incorporate earlier stages of production within their activities, or even later ones, or within the country by the emergence of supplying or customer firms. It could thus be stated that, even if the protective devices used by the government initially stimulated industries of a "non-essential" nature, especially consumer goods industries instead of heavier types of industries, complementary policies provided substantial incentives for vertical integration and thus for the ultimate establishment of a "productive base" for the country.[5]

Other complementary activities of the government included the establishment of directly productive firms, such as the big steel enterprise at Volta Redonda, and major infra-structure projects, such as the large hydroelectric installations at Tres Marias, in the state of Minas Gerais, Furnas, Urubupunga in the south, and others.

These policies brought about a drastic change in the structure of Brazil's economy between the early postwar years and the early sixties. For example, as measured in 1947 constant prices, the share of agriculture in the gross domestic product declined from 27 percent in 1947 to 22 percent in 1961, while the share of industry increased during the same period from 21 percent to 34

5. For an excellent discussion of these policies see Lincoln Gordon and Engelbert L. Grommers, *United States Manufacturing Investment in Brazil: The Impact of Brazilian Government Policies, 1946–1960* (Boston: Division of Research, Graduate School of Business Administration, Harvard University, 1962).

percent. During that period Brazil experienced one of the highest real growth rates in Latin America, the growth of the real gross domestic product averaging almost 6 percent per year, reaching 7.7 percent in 1961. At the end of 1961, the crisis which lasted until 1964 began, bringing a sharp downturn in the real growth rate.

GROWING IMBALANCES

A concomitant of the Brazilian policy-makers' choice of rapid and massive import-substitution industrialization was a concentration of resources in the industrial sector at the expense of other sectors. By the early sixties the neglect of agriculture, education, regions outside of the dynamic center-south of the country, certain infra-structure investment, and the diversification of exports, were producing economic and social strains which were endangering the further growth of the economy. Let us examine some of these strains.

Agriculture. Agriculture has been among the most obviously neglected sectors. This is reflected, for example, in the small proportion of funds which were allocated to agriculture by the development bank in the first decade of its existence; 4 percent of the bank's local currency loans went to the agricultural sector, and only 1.7 percent of its foreign exchange loans went into that direction.[6]

Most striking is the lagging growth rate of agriculture. During the period from 1957 to 1961, for example, while industrial production increased at a yearly rate of 12.7 percent and while the population was increasing at a yearly rate of 3.1 percent, agricultural production for domestic consumption was increasing at a rate of only 4.5 percent. These over-all growth rates, however, hide a more basic disequilibrium. One must consider that because of internal migration the agricultural population was increasing at only 1.6 percent per year, while the urban population was growing at an annual rate of 5.4 percent. More agricultural products thus had to find their way into urban centers. Unfortunately, the agricultural distribution system of the country has remained in a very backward state. Little investment occurred

6. *XI Exposicao Sobre o Programa de Reaparelhamento Economico,* Exercicio de 1962, Banco Nacional do Desenvolvimento Economico, Rio de Janeiro, Brasil.

in storage facilities, and some economists have estimated that about 20 percent of the food destined for urban centers is lost in the distribution process.[7]

Viewed more closely, it also becomes obvious that the agricultural output has not adapted itself to urban requirements. For example, the urban population's diet, especially as its income increases, tends to change. Such items as meat and wheat become more important than previously. In the period from 1954 to 1961 the rate of increase in production of these products noticeably lagged behind the urban population growth. For example, during that period the slaughter of cattle herds increased at a yearly rate of only 2.2 percent, that of pigs by only 3.4 percent, and wheat production remained unchanged.

Agricultural production is carried on in a most inefficient manner. Productivity per acre has hardly changed for most major crops (see Table 2). The structure of land holdings in the traditional areas around the cities has not changed to conform to requirements of modern agriculture, and in most areas there has been little attempt to change the technique of agricultural production through more intensive use of the land, the use of fertilizers, better seed selection, and the use of more modern machinery. The existence of vast agricultural frontiers has given the country the opportunity to increase agricultural output without making substantial investments in new techniques for increasing the productivity of traditional areas, or without having to resort to drastic agrarian reforms in those areas.[8]

Increasing agricultural output by expanding into new areas has involved substantially increasing costs. The newly cultivated areas are farther away from the consuming centers, which means that increased agricultural production involves higher transportation costs. Also, given the already inefficient marketing system, the development of more remote agricultural frontiers further complicates the distribution problem. And there can be no doubt that the inefficient way of increasing agricultural production in

7. For an excellent review of Brazil's agricultural problems, see Julian Chacel, "Precos e custos na agricultura brasileira," *Revista Brasileira de Economia*, Setembro de 1963.

8. See *Ibid.*

Brazil has been a substantial and unnecessary contributing factor to the inflationary pressures.

A large part of the difficulty in agriculture has been the structure of landholdings. An overall examination of census data reveals a high degree of inequality of landholding, with larger properties having a relatively larger proportion of their lands uncultivated than the smaller ones.[9] However, in a country of continental proportions, the landholding structure of a number of subregions has to be examined in order to come to some conclusion concerning the relation between landholdings and agricultural productivity. In many parts of Northeast Brazil one finds the typical difficulties of a latifundio–absentee ownership type of agriculture, which includes, not only the problem of production, but also the explosive problem of social inequities existing within such a system. In the extreme south of the country, one finds the opposite type of problem, the area being dominated by small European-type farms, where continuous subdivisions have taken place in line with the inheritance pattern. These minifundios are often of quite uneconomical size.

In such areas as Minas Gerais, Western São Paulo, and Mato Grosso, where cattle farming takes place or where soils are poor (unless they can be artificially treated), and where the population is scarce, the latifundio system is not necessarily as inefficient and socially explosive as in the northeast. In other words, it is impossible to generalize about what would be the ideal landholding pattern in the country as a whole. Methods of dealing with the problem vary from region to region.

Because of extensive uncultivated areas, Brazil did not encounter agriculture as a bottleneck during its initial industrial spurt. It is, however, generally recognized that further industrial growth would be severely hampered if no breakthrough were made in agricultural productivity near the principal consuming centers. The rise of food prices relative to other goods not only creates social tensions in the urban centers, but it also contributes

9. William H. Nicholls, "Perspectiva estatistica da estrutura agraria do Brasil," *Revista Brasileira de Economia*, Junho de 1963. This is an excellent survey of the 1950 agricultural census. At this writing, only preliminary data for the 1960 agricultural census are available.

unnecessarily to inflationary pressures. One should also consider that since increased prices are absorbed by the middlemen,[10]
the rising terms of trade in favor of agriculture does not result
in increased profits for the producer, who might in consequence
be stimulated to increase his output and his efficiency. Finally,
with the increased strength of the labor unions, having increasing
success in demanding higher real wages for industrial workers,
continuously rising food prices will increase the real cost of industry. This might result either in a slowdown of industrial expansion, lower profits leading to diminished investments, or in an
incentive to continue industrial expansion in a capital-intensive
direction, increasing the difficulty the country faces in absorbing
the rising urban population.

A Brazilian economist has recently pointed out that, unlike
other countries where an agrarian reform was a prerequisite for
industrialization, Brazil could industrialize for a long time without any drastic agrarian change.[11] This is especially true because
the country's vast agricultural frontier provides it with considerable flexibility. The initial industrialization spurt has, however, focused attention on the backwardness of the agrarian sector, since continued industrial growth will depend to a large extent on agrarian reform. In a sense, one could say that given the
social pattern prevailing in Brazil prior to the Second World War,
an industrial spurt was needed to attain or make possible a
drastic change in the socio-economic relationships of the country-
side.

Education. All evidence indicates that education has lagged
behind the general development of the country. It has been es-

10. The faster rise of food prices relative to other goods is reflected in the higher
rise of the food component of the cost of living index relative to the index itself.
For example, for Guanabara, where Rio de Janeiro is located, taking 1953 as 100,
the cost of living stood at 1,507 in 1963, while the food component had risen to
1,680. An indication that the middleman absorbs a large portion of the price is a
comparison between the food component of the cost of living which reflects retail
prices and the wholesale price of food. In 1963, the former stood at 1,680, while
the latter stood at 1,342 (all these food data exclude coffee). See any issue of *Conjuntura economica*.

11. Dr. Chacel of the Fundacão Getulio Vargas made these remarks in a talk
given to the Latin American Economic Seminar of Yale University on March 19,
1964.

timated that in 1962 the illiteracy rate between the ages of ten and nineteen was 51 percent for the entire country.[12] For men over the age of twenty in urban areas the rate was 14 percent and in rural areas 40 percent; while for women in urban areas the rate was 15 percent and in rural areas 61 percent. These rates alone, however, do not indicate the dimensions of the problem. The level of education of the population is very low in proportion to the requirements of a modernizing society, and little had been done up through the early sixties to remedy the deficiencies.

The lag in education should be made quite clear by mention of a few statistics. In the decade of the fifties, with a population growth rate of 3.1 percent, the yearly increase in the rate of students finishing elementary schools was 2.6 percent, and the rate of increase in the number of students matriculated in elementary schools was 3.6 percent. In 1962 only 30 percent of the men employed in tertiary economic activities had finished elementary school, 20 percent employed in secondary economic activities and 5 percent employed in primary activities.[13] On the secondary-school level, the rate of increase in students being graduated from industrial schools was only 2.5 percent per year, commercial schools 6.1 percent, and university preparatory schools 7.2 percent. In examining the secondary-school situation, one should remember that the growth rate of the urban population was 5.4 percent per year. On the level of higher education, the rate of graduation of medical students was 3.7 percent, of engineers 4.9 percent and of agronomists 6.9 percent (the absolute number of the latter was 171 in 1950 and 332 in 1960).[14]

The low priority of education in the fifties is obvious when one considers that only 9.5 percent of the total central government expenditures went into education and research in 1950, and in 1960 this total was down to 6.1 percent. Local and state governments spent about 11 to 12 percent on education in the

12. Paulo de Assis Ribeiro, "A Educacao e o Planejamento," *Revista Brasileira de Economia,* Dezembro de 1962.

13. *Ibid.*

14. These data were made available to the author by the Brazilian Ministry of Education.

period examined. Thus expenditures on education on all levels of government as a proportion of total expenditures was no more than 10 percent. In 1963 the United States devoted roughly 20 percent of total governmental expenditures (on all levels of government) to education.

So far, only the quantitative lags in the educational system have been presented here. Unfortunately I am equipped to make only a few remarks about the qualitative aspect of the educational system from the point of view of the university system. The first thing that strikes the foreigner is that there is a dearth of secondary schools, that the majority of children wanting to go on to the higher educational levels have to go through private schools; but once admitted to the university, the education is free. This means, in effect, that the majority of students reaching the university level come from middle- and upper-class backgrounds, and the Brazilian society completely subsidizes the education on the university level.

The admissions examinations to the university are very competitive, and it is considered an achievement to have reached the university level. But once the student enters the university, especially if he wishes to concentrate in law, economics, or the humanities, he finds himself in a completely inadequate system. In most universities classes are held at night. The pay of professors is so low that they have to hold three or four other jobs to earn an adequate living. This means that professors are usually not prepared when entering the classroom, they have no time to keep up with their profession, and, needless to say, research activities are completely neglected. The system does not encourage full-time students. Most students have jobs with private firms or have already entered the army of government functionaries. The idealistic student soon finds that there is no premium put on hard work. Usually he is not taught how to work. Preparation for examinations consists of memorizing the professor's lectures or some second-rate text. The student discovers that the merit system really does not work. He does not develop study and research habits—only methods of beating the system. He will either become cynical and resign himself to the system, or he will in disgust join some radical groups.

Although I have given only a few impressions, it should be obvious that the quality of the higher educational system is rather inadequate to cope with the demands of a modern society for well-trained leaders. The situation is not quite as grim in medicine and engineering, although the traditional stress on theory rather than practical work (laboratory and field work) has in many cases produced difficulties.[15]

No prolonged explanation is needed to show that education is a bottleneck to the further smooth development of the country. It will result in severe shortages of trained manpower in the growing industrial sector, possibly leading to reductions in the potential growth rate; and it will also result in higher costs to industry, which will have to spend resources in teaching unskilled and unschooled labor or badly prepared professionals, and suffer lower labor efficiency for years.

Regional Imbalances. Brazil's phenomenal development in the fifties was concentrated principally in the south-central portion of the country. It should not be surprising that in a country of continental proportions the development process should have been concentrated in one region. Once a certain region begins to develop more rapidly than others, it tends to maintain its lead. New firms will tend to settle in the already growing region because external economies will make investment in that region more remunerative. Such external economies consist of a more readily available source of skilled labor (hence less spent on extra training by the firm), a wide variety of already available auxiliary goods and services which do not have to be imported (for example, if power supply is adequate, the individual firm will not have to build its own generators; if the roads are well paved, less merchandise will be destroyed on its way to the market), sources of supply might be easily within easy reach of the firm, or financial

15. The author has personal knowledge of cases wherein first-rate blueprints were made by engineers for development projects which were based on outdated material and which were therefore unusable. Such mistakes could have been avoided by a greater tradition of field work. It has been claimed that in an underdeveloped country good laboratory and field training is often too expensive, and that this explains the stress on theory. This is rather unconvincing when one sees the inordinate expenditures being made on luxurious university buildings in many Brazilian and other Latin American universities.

institutions will be more numerous and experienced in the developed region, hence the availability of adequate finance both for running current activities of a firm and for expansion.

Though differential rates of regional growth might be a "natural" phenomenon in a large country, the Brazilian northeast has presented the country with an explosive situation.[16] The northeast has for a long time been the less favored region of Brazil. It is periodically plagued by droughts, its more fertile parts are dominated by a backward latifundio system of agriculture, and while it contains 25 percent of the country's population, it contributes only 10 percent to the national product. Some of the states in the area have a per capita income of only 30 to 40 percent of the national average. On the other hand, the per capita income of the city of Rio de Janeiro or metropolitan São Paulo is about 300 percent of the national average (in dollar terms the average per capita income in Brazil was roughly 350 dollars in 1963). The illiteracy rate of the northeast is more than 70 percent, compared with the national average of about 50 percent.[17]

It has been claimed with good evidence that the industrialization of the country, most of it being located in the central-south, increased the problems of the northeast. The latter has been drained of its resources in a number of ways. There is a tendency for northeastern capital to flow south because of the greater opportunities for earning higher returns. The best northeastern manpower also tends to move to the more dynamic region. It is also important to remember that the industrialization of Brazil was an import-substitution industrialization. This meant that new industries were stimulated behind a protective wall. The protection was needed, since these industries were of a higher cost nature than the foreign competitors. Prior to the industrialization drive in the post–World War II era, the northeast of Brazil imported its manufactured goods from abroad, since it was a primary

16. For an excellent survey of the history of the northeast's problems see Albert O. Hirschman, *Journeys Toward Progress: Studies of Economic Policy-Making in Latin America* (New York: The Twentieth Century Fund, 1963) Ch. 1.; see also Stefan H. Robock, *Brazil's Developing Northeast: A Study of Regional Planning and Foreign Aid* (Washington, D.C.: The Brookings Institution, 1963).

17. Werner Baer, "Regional Inequality and Economic Growth in Brazil," *Economic Development and Cultural Change*, April, 1964.

producer. The industrialization program, however, forced the region to buy its manufactured goods from the higher cost central-south of Brazil. This meant that in exchange for its products, the northeast was not able to obtain as many manufactured goods as before. Using economic parlance, the terms of trade turned against the northeast of Brazil because of the industrialization procedures, and this can be regarded as an additional drain on that section of the country.

Since the late fifties the central government has attempted to counter some of these trends systematically. It created an agency to co-ordinate all the activities of the federal government in the northeast, called SUDENE.[18] The latter engaged in an elaborate plan to build infrastructure, making use of the great dam at Paulo Afonso, to change the structure of agriculture, and to attract industries. One of the agency's principal obstacles has been the antiquated landholding structure of the northeast, and it remains to be seen whether the government which took over in April 1964 is willing to deal forcefully with that problem.

Other Imbalances. I have by no means exhausted the disequilibria which appeared or made themselves felt more severely in the postwar industrialization process. For example, the whole stress in the industrialization period up to the sixties has been on import substitution, and very little was done to change drastically the structure of exports. It became fairly obvious by the early sixties that, with the dim outlook for Brazil's traditional exports, this would become a vital matter, because import substitution could not be carried beyond a certain point and the country would have to rely on the import of petroleum and capital goods for which foreign exchange would have to be earned. Also, by the end of 1962 the country's outstanding external debt amounted to more than 3.5 billion United States dollars, half of which was due by the end of 1965. With export earnings amounting to 1.4 billion dollars in 1961, imports 1.3 billion dollars, a service deficit of .4 billion dollars, and debt repayments due, it is obvious that the country would have to make an effort to develop new sources of foreign exchange earnings.[19]

18. SUDENE stands for Superintendency for the Development of the Northeast.
19. The year 1961 was chosen because the last full balance of payments figures

A review of economic imbalances in Brazil would not be complete, even in an impressionistic survey, without mentioning the problem of inflation. The curious thing is that Brazil up to 1961 experienced high rates of inflation and high rates of growth simultaneously. My researches have led me to the conclusion that inflation had a positive role to play in the decade of the fifties.[20] It acted as a mechanism which transferred resources from the consuming sector to the investing sector. This does not mean that inflation produced development at the absolute expense of the laboring classes, but it means that a large proportion of the *increment* in the national output was redistributed in favor of the nonconsuming classes. This process occurred mainly through a lag of wages behind prices. Enough data exist to make a good case for this hypothesis.

It is clear that the redistributive function of the Brazilian inflation was able to work because the wage-earning sector was not strong enough to insure the constancy of its share in the national product. The labor sector has been weakened partially by the stern control the government had over labor unions in the fifties. One could also venture the hypothesis that in a newly industrializing country, with a large reservoir of rural labor of which a large number arrives for the first time in the urban sector each year, there exists greater possibility of inflationary redistribution of income. It takes new arrivals from rural areas time to become relatively sophisticated in the ways of a purely monetary economy and understand the relation of general price increases to their wage increases, which are lagging. However, the much more frequent readjustment since 1961 of the minimum wage, the more frequent strikes, and the greater independence of the labor movement from government control (João Goulart having lost control over the labor leaders he formerly led), would seem to indicate that events of the fifties might not repeat themselves.

---

were available for that year. It does, however, represent the typical long-run situation.

20. Werner Baer, "Inflation and Economic Growth: An Interpretation of the Brazilian Case," *Economic Development and Cultural Change,* October, 1962; Werner Baer, "Brazil: Inflation and Economic Efficiency," same journal, July, 1963; the most thorough documentation is in Chapter Five of my recently published book.

I am not trying to imply that inflation is the best method of allocating resources in an underdeveloped country. Given a backward fiscal mechanism and generally weak economic policy instruments, the government will have difficulties in tapping outside savings. Thus, under certain conditions, inflation can perform a positive role through the forced savings mechanism. It isn't the ideal solution and can only be a temporary instrument, since most income groups will understand the system sooner or later and will make sure to keep their share of the national income. When this happens, inflation's positive role will have come to an end.

CONCLUSION: THE CRISIS OF 1964 AND THE IMBALANCES

The main argument I have been trying to make is that the political and economic crisis of Brazil of the early sixties is in part the result of the success of the industrialization efforts of the fifties. The growth of the modern industrial sector has put into bold relief the backwardness of agriculture, education, and the government's administrative machinery. The backwardness of these sectors is at present threatening the continued growth of the country. The success of the industrialization has made many social groups aware of existing inequities in the country's socio-economic system, and demands for redistribution of incomes both through agrarian reform and through the protection of the wage-earning groups' real income in the inflationary process are increasingly powerful politically.

Brazil's leaders are clearly in a dilemma. On the one hand, many socio-economic reforms are needed in order not to impede the further growth of the country. On the other hand, many reforms are needed for equity purposes but might endanger further growth. This is especially true of the insistence of wage-earning groups upon higher shares in the country's gross domestic product.

Goulart's two years in the presidency served only to sharpen the conflicts. He ruled by agitation, constantly dramatizing in a very demagogic way the need for reforms without ever presenting the country with concrete and feasible programs. His weakness resulted in his giving in to the demands of both the unions and the business community, ending in no change in the shares of the gross domestic product of any income group, but in an unproductive runaway inflation, reaching 80 percent in 1963. The politically uncertain climate, the agitation against foreign capital, and the passage of a stringent profit-remittance law in 1962 combined to make investors wary of the future; and investment activities fell drastically in 1962 and 1963. The rate of growth of the gross domestic product in real terms fell from 7.7 percent in 1961 to 3.7 percent in 1962, to 2.1 percent in 1963. Thus, with a population growth rate of 3.1 percent, the per capita income actually fell in 1963.[21]

Goulart's successors were still faced with the need for many basic socio-economic reforms. By the middle of 1965 little progress had been made toward meeting these problems due to the government's preoccupation in controlling inflation. The distributive dilemma—the need for *both* high rates of economic growth and a greater equity in the distribution of income—can be met in the next decade by substantial inflows of foreign capital and by a massive aid program of the United States and other advanced countries. I would not be surprised if within a decade and a half, assuming that this external aid will be forthcoming, assuming the achievement of basic socio-economic reforms, Brazil will have built itself a large enough industrial base to permit it to achieve both high rates of economic growth and social justice.

21. Preliminary data for 1962 and 1963 come from *Conjuntura Economica,* Fevereiro 1964.

TABLE 1/ BRAZIL: GROWTH, TRADE AND INFLATION

Year	Terms of Trade (1953 = 100)	Export Quantum	Real Rate of Growth[a]	Rate of Inflation[b]
1947	45	127	1.8	6
1948	44	131	9.5	4
1949	53	117	5.6	6
1950	93	102	5.0	11
1951	95	109	5.1	11
1952	90	90	5.6	21
1953	100	100	3.2	17
1954	134	86	7.7	26
1955	118	100	6.8	19
1956	113	108	1.9	22
1957	117	100	6.9	13
1958	119	96	6.6	17
1959	109	117	7.3	52
1960	101	118	6.3	24
1961	97	128	7.7	43
1962	84	114	3.7	52
1963	82[c]	131[c]	2.1[c]	80[c]

[a] Rate of growth of gross domestic product.
[b] Rate of increase of cost of living of Guanabara state.
[c] Preliminary data.

Sources: *Conjuntura Economica* and *Revista Brasileira de Economia*, Marco de 1962.

TABLE 2/ AGRICULTURAL PRODUCTIVITY IN BRAZIL
Yield per hectare of Selected Crops (kg per ha)

	1950	1951	1955	1956	1959	1960
Cotton	443	400	490	448	510	549
Rice	1,638	1,618	1,488	1,366	1,529	1,617
Wheat	816	584	921	967	515	625
Black Beans	690	692	662	611	651	676
Corn	1,287	1,309	1,190	1,167	1,258	1,298
Sugar (tons/ha.)	39	38	38	39	41	42
Coffee	402	394	419	287	495	436
Potatoes	4,787	4,827	5,029	5,413	5,454	5,398
Cocoa	554	416	429	420	381	347

Source: Servico de Estatistica Da Producão do Ministerio da Agricultura.

TABLE 3/ REGIONAL INEQUALITY IN BRAZIL
Regional Distribution of the Brazilian Population (in percentages).

	1947	1949	1957	1959	1960
North	4	4	3	3	3
Northeast	25	24	24	25	24
East	36	36	35	35	34
South	32	33	34	34	35
Middle West	3	3	4	3	4
Total	100	100	100	100	100

Source: computed from *Anuario Estatistico do Brasil*, 1961.

Regional Distribution of National Income (in percentages).

North	2	2	2	2	2
Northeast	11	11	10	10	11
East	37	37	36	36	34
South	48	48	50	50	51
Middle West	2	2	2	2	2
Total	100	100	100	100	100

Source: computed from data of the Fundacão Getulio Vargas.

6/ CHANGES IN THE GEOGRAPHIC DISTRIBUTION OF POPULATION IN BRAZIL, 1950–1960

BY ROLAND E. CHARDON

AMONG the more dynamic of the many changes which Brazil has been experiencing recently are those involving her population. Especially interesting from a geographer's point of view are the variations which have taken place in the spatial distribution of her people on the land. Changes in distribution of population are by no means new or unique in Brazil, but this chapter will restrict itself principally to an examination of recent ones. For convenience, discussion will be generally limited to population changes which occurred between the nationwide census years of 1950 and 1960.[1]

POPULATION DISTRIBUTION AND GROWTH IN BRAZIL AS A WHOLE

Brazil, with its 3.3 million square miles, is the world's fifth largest country, exceeded only by the Soviet Union, China, the United States, and Canada. Estimates indicate that there were about 80 million people in Brazil in 1964, making an average density of about twenty-four persons per square mile.

Settlement of Brazil, however, has not been uniform. Most Brazilians are essentially concentrated in clustered settlements,

1. Basic data for this chapter is provided by the following: Instituto Brasileiro de Geografia e Estatística (hereafter abbreviated to I.B.G.E.) , Serviço Nacional de Recenseamento, *VI Recenseamento Geral do Brasil, 1950: Brasil, Censo Demográfico* (hereafter abbreviated to *VI Censo*) , Rio de Janeiro, 1956; and *VII Recenseamento Geral do Brasil, 1960: Brasil, Sinopse Preliminar do Censo Demográfico* (hereafter abbreviated to *VII Censo*) , Rio de Janeiro, 1962. Two qualifications should be mentioned here: one is that many Brazilian and American demographers feel that, while the 1950 Census was the best ever taken in Brazil, the 1960 Census is far less reliable; the other is that preliminary data is being used here for the year 1960.

primarily in agricultural communities and small towns, but also including large cities. These settlements are found, as they historically have been, in the eastern part of Brazil, generally within some three hundred miles of the Atlantic Coast. In contrast, the northern and western parts of the nation are very sparsely populated, containing more than two-thirds of the country's area but less than 10 percent of its people. In certain sections of the interior, however, there are a few areas of relatively dense settlements, notably in southern Goiás and Mato Grosso, western São Paulo, and northwestern Paraná. This area has been the scene of recent colonization and includes the new national capital of Brasília, created largely to aid in the development of the "empty" but potentially productive interior.

Probably the most striking change in Brazil's population has been the tremendous recent over-all increase. During the period from 1950 to 1960, slightly more than 19 million people were added to the nation's population.[2] From a 1950 population base of roughly 52 million, this increase represents a 37 percent rise over the ten-year period, or approximately 3.1 percent annually. This rate of population growth is in line with that of many other nations in Latin America but is almost twice as high as the world average of about 1.8 per cent yearly.

This period also represents the decade during which Brazil's national population increased the fastest. In the previous decade (1940–1950), Brazil's population rose by some 11 million, a 27 percent increase, indicating that the 1950–1960 increment was nearly double that of the 1940–1950 period. Clearly, Brazil's population is not only growing rapidly, it is growing at an increasing rate. If the present rate continues, there will be very nearly 100 million persons in Brazil by 1970.

Population growth within any given area is a function of two variables: natural increase or decrease, or the difference between the number of persons born and those who die, and net external migration, or the net difference between the number of people moving into or out of that area. In the case of Brazil, as in most countries today, the former is by far the most

2. I.B.G.E., *VII Censo* (1960), *op. cit.*, p. 3.

important factor in accounting for the recent demographic expansion in the nation.

Brazil's precise rate of natural increase—that is, the difference between the birth rate and the death rate—is difficult to establish because the national data on births and deaths are scattered and poor. Such studies as have been made, however, indicate that the high rate of population growth evidenced in Brazil during the ten-year period results from the continuance of a very high birth rate coupled with a steadily decreasing death rate.[3] According to the best estimates available, the national birth rate appears to have dropped only slightly over the past sixty years (see Table 1). In the period from 1891 to 1900, the national birth rate is estimated to have been about 46 per thousand inhabitants;

TABLE 1/ ESTIMATED BIRTH AND DEATH RATES, AND RATE OF NATURAL INCREASE, BRAZIL, 1891–1960

Period	Birth Rate	Death Rate	Rate of Natural Increase
1891–1900	46.0	27.8	18.2
1901–1920	45.0	26.4	18.6
1920–1940	43.5	24.8	18.7
1940–1950	43.0	19.2	23.8
1950–1960	43.0	12.0	31.0

Source: I.B.G.E. *Contribuicões para o estudo da demografia do Brasil* (Rio, 1961); p. 28, for 1891–1950; 1950–1960 estimated.

1950 to 1960 the rate was about 43 per thousand. The death rate, meanwhile, decreased substantially during the same period—from about 28 to 12, or less than half. Subtracting the death rate from its corresponding birth rate indicates a rise in the rate of natural increase, from about 18 per thousand between 1891 and 1900 to about 31 per thousand between and 1950 and 1960.

The second factor affecting population changes in Brazil is net immigration or emigration. Once again, lack of certain data, especially concerning emigration, makes it impossible to ascertain precisely the effects this factor may have had on Brazil's population growth during the years 1950 to 1960. In the latter part of the nineteenth century and the early years of the twentieth,

3. T. Lynn Smith, *Brazil: Peoples and Institutions* (rev. ed., Baton Rouge, 1963), especially pp. 44–50.

immigration performed a very important function in the country's growth, numerically and otherwise. Since the 1930s, however, immigration has lost its relative significance as a contributor to the country's numerical population.

During the 1950–1960 period, approximately 600,000 immigrants were officially listed as having entered the country.[4] In addition to those immigrants so recorded, there seems to have been some unofficial or illegal "hidden" immigration, composed of persons who came into the country from neighboring nations.[5] Although no estimates of its dimensions exist, this immigration does not appear to have been large.

Brazil unfortunately does not keep official national emigration statistics, so it is not possible to know how many immigrants stayed in Brazil or how many Brazilian nationals moved away from their homeland. Net immigration or emigration as a factor in Brazilian population changes at the national level can therefore only be estimated very roughly. It may be reasonable to assume that about two-thirds of the immigrants remained in the country; but even if all of them had stayed during the 1950–1960 period, immigration would still total less than 5 percent of the national increase during that period. For the country as a whole, then, natural increase accounted for virtually all of Brazil's population increase between 1950 and 1960.

REGIONAL VARIATIONS IN POPULATION GROWTH

All sectors of Brazil have not shared equally in the country's population increase. Since regional differences in population growth are highly significant, not only to those areas with rapidly rising population but also to the sections of the nation which are either losing people or becoming stagnant, an examination of regional population growth differentials is in order.

In the most recent revision of his text, Professor T. Lynn Smith mentions that the greatest regional increase in population

4. I.B.G.E., Conselho Nacional de Estatística, *Contribuições para o estudo da demografia do Brasil*, Estudos se Estatística Teórica e Aplicada, Rio de Janeiro, 1961, p. 127 for the years 1950–1957; I.B.G.E., Conselho Nacional de Estatística, *Anuário Estatístico do Brasil, 1961*, Rio de Janeiro, 1961, for the years 1958–1960.
5. Smith, *op. cit.*, p. 138.

in Brazil occurred in the southern and southeastern parts of the country.[6] Table 2, which summarizes population changes by state in the years 1950 and 1960, shows this to be essentially the case. From this table it may be seen that the population of the eight southern and southeastern states increased by some 12.5 million, accounting for two-thirds (66 percent) of the national increase. This took place in an area representing only 18 percent of Brazil's total area. Table 2 also shows that, as a group, the southern and southeastern states had a relative increase of population higher than the national average, even though two of the largest states—Minas Gerais and Rio Grande do Sul—showed rates of growth lower than the national average. If these two states, which lie on the periphery of the south-southeast region, are excluded for a moment, the region underwent a 50 percent increase in population between 1950 and 1960.[7]

A number of factors help explain the population increase in the south-southeast region. This region in 1950 contained 30.4 million inhabitants, or almost 60 percent of the nation's people. Assuming a relatively equal rate of natural increase throughout the country,[8] the area having the greatest number of people would also tend to have the greatest increase in population, in absolute terms. Postulating from a 1950 base, a 37 percent population increase (the national average) for the south and southeast, one would expect to find 11.2 million more people in these two regions in 1960. As we have seen, the 1950–1960 increase was in fact 12.5 million—not much more than that which might have been expected solely on the basis of natural increase.

6. Smith, *op. cit.*, pp. 40–50.

7. The respective figures for the south and southeast regions, excluding Minas Gerais and Rio Grande do Sul, are as follows: 1950 population, 18,506,751; 1960 population, 27,682,224; absolute change in population, 1950–1960, 9,175,473; percent increase, 1950–1960, 49.5.

8. Which, of course, is not so. Such data as are available indicate significant regional differences in rates of natural increase, reflecting important local variations in birth rates and fertility ratios (generally somewhat lower in urban areas and a few rural districts) and death rates (also generally lower in cities and in the rural south and southeast) . See, for example, Smith, *op. cit.*, pp. 45, 97–117; also J.V.D. Saunders, *Differential Fertility in Brazil,* Gainesville, 1958, and especially I.B.G.E., *Contribuições, op. cit.,* pp. 59–123.

TABLE 2/ POPULATION CHANGES IN BRAZIL, BY STATE, 1950-1960

State	Population 1950	Population 1960	Population Increase, 1950–1960 Absolute	Population Increase, 1950–1960 Relative
North				
Rondonia	36,935	70,783	33,848	91.64%
Acre	114,755	160,208	45,453	39.61
Amazonas	514,099	721,215	207,116	40.29
Roraima	18,116	29,489	11,373	62.78
Pará	1,123,273	1,550,935	427,662	38.07
Amapá	37,477	68,889	31,412	83.82
	1,844,655	2,601,519	756,864	41.03
Northeast				
Maranhão	1,583,248	2,492,139	908,891	57.41
Piauí	1,045,696	1,263,368	217,672	20.82
Ceará	2,695,450	3,337,856	642,406	23.83
Rio Grande do Norte	967,921	1,157,258	189,337	19.56
Paraíba	1,713,259	2,018,023	304,764	17.79
Pernambuco	3,395,185	4,136,900	741,715	21.85
Alagoas	1,093,137	1,271,062	177,925	16.28
Sergipe	644,361	760,273	115,912	17.99
Bahia	4,834,575	5,990,605	1,156,030	23.91
Fernando de Noronha	581	1,389	808	139.07
	17,973,413	22,428,873	4,455,460	24.78
Southeast				
Minas Gerais	7,717,792	9,798,880	2,081,088	26.96
Serra dos Aimorés[a]	160,072	384,297	224,225	140.08
Espírito Santo	861,562	1,188,665	327,103	37.97
Rio de Janeiro	2,297,194	3,402,728	1,105,534	48.13
Guanabara	2,377,451	3,307,163	929,712	39.11
	13,414,071	18,081,733	4,667,662	34.79
South				
São Paulo	9,134,423	12,974,699	3,840,276	42.04
Paraná	2,115,547	4,277,763	2,162,216	102.21
Santa Catarina	1,560,502	2,146,909	586,407	37.58
Rio Grande do Sul	4,164,821	5,448,823	1,284,002	30.83
	16,975,293	24,848,194	7,872,901	46.38
Central-West				
Mato Grosso	522,044	910,262	388,218	74.36
Goiás	1,214,921	1,954,862	739,941	60.90
Federal District	—	141,742	141,742	—
	1,736,965	3,006,866	1,269,901	73.11
BRAZIL	51,944,397	70,967,185	19,022,788	36.62

a. Area under litigation between the states of Minas Gerais and Espírito Santo.

Source: I.B.G.E., Servicio Nacional de Recenseamento. *VII Recenseamento Geral do Brasil, 1960: Brasil—Sinopse Preliminar do Censo Demográfico* (Rio, 1962), pp. 2, 3, 6.

On the other hand, the fact that the south-southeast region, particularly the states of Guanabara, Rio de Janeiro, São Paulo, and Paraná, did gain more than the national average indicates some net in-migration from other parts of the country, or from overseas.[9] Some studies indicate, further, that considerable in-migration has taken place into this part of Brazil, accompanied or followed by out-migration to the central-west region, especially to Goiás and the new Federal District.[10]

Although many migrants coming into the south-southeast have moved on to the pioneer zones to the west, the southern and southeastern states obviously have a certain appeal to those arriving from other parts of the country or the world. The more familiar attractions include the fact that this part of the nation, particularly the area within the triangle Rio-Belo Horizonte-São Paulo, is and has been for a long time the traditional "core" or "heartland" of modern Brazil. As the national heartland, this part of the country has tended to have the best economic and social opportunities, the highest degree of urbanization and industrialization, the highest wages, the best medical, educational, and other facilities, and the national capital (until it was moved to Brasília in 1961).

It is, therefore, not surprising to find this "core triangle" exhibiting a high rate of growth. Also, most immigrants entering Brazil between 1950 and 1960 landed either at São Paulo or at Rio, attesting to the attraction of this part of the country to outsiders.

While the south and southeast of Brazil are obviously very important in terms of the nation's growth, other areas have increased their populations substantially—some, in fact, dramatically. These include the country's "fringe" areas, such as the pioneer zone of the central-west (on the western margins of present settlement), parts of the Amazon Valley, parts of Bahia, and certain smaller districts. Especially significant have been the population increases taking place in the country's urban areas, most of

9. On the assumption, probably valid as a generalization, that both birth and death rates are proportionately lower in this region than in the rest of Brazil; cf. I.B.G.E., *Contribuições, op. cit.,* p. 65, and Smith, *op. cit.,* p. 108.

10. José Fabio Barbosa-Dasilva, "A Sociological Analysis of Internal Migration in Brazil" (Unpublished Ph.D. dissertation, University of Florida, 1963).

which, as it happens, are located in the south and southeast regions.

URBAN POPULATION GROWTH

The census of 1960 indicates that Brazilian urban population growth between 1950 and 1960 was very impressive, reflecting largely a recent and very important migratory movement from rural to urban areas. This rural-urban migration, whose dimensions appear to be increasing steadily and rapidly, has been noted by a large number of scholars and travelers familiar with Brazil; and its effects on the cities, in terms of resulting pressures on housing, health, educational, employment, and other facilities, are the objects of intensive study today.

Forty-five percent of Brazil's population was listed as "urban" in the 1960 census, compared with 36 percent in 1950. The 1960 census also showed that the absolute increase in urban population between 1950 and 1960 was 13,208,047,[11] or roughly 70 percent of the total national increase for that decade. The relative increase in urban population was also about 70 percent for the period.

The figures provided by the Brazilian census may be used as an index of urban growth. They demonstrate clearly the importance of urbanization in Brazil. But the above census figures are, in fact, quite crude and tend to overstate the degree to which urbanization has actually taken place in the country between 1950 and 1960. The reason for this is that the term "urban" in the Brazilian census is used to include a large number of extremely small hamlets[12] and is therefore not as meaningful an index of urbanization as it might be, especially as the term is generally understood in the United States. Fortunately, there are several other ways of measuring urbanization in Brazil on a somewhat more refined basis.

The vision which perhaps comes to mind most quickly when one hears the term "urbanization" is that of people moving to a large, cosmopolitan city containing many thousands, if not mil-

11. I.B.G.E., *VII Censo, op. cit.*, pp. 10–11.
12. *Ibid.*, preface; see also Smith, *op. cit.*, pp. 76–77, 602, also Saunders, *op. cit.*, pp. 15–16.

lions, of inhabitants. Certainly the increase in population of such large cities provides a very valid measure of urbanization in a country and will be discussed below. But the concept of "urban" in Brazil can be broadened to include communities of much smaller size but containing within their "urbanized" areas a fairly large number of varied social and economic functions. In the author's opinion, a reasonably useful, quantitative, and yet readily accessible definition of "urban place" in Brazil is the community whose 1960 urban population (as listed in the Brazilian census of that year) was greater than 25,000. The 25,000-population limit is admittedly arbitrary, and no doubt some justification can be made for including as "urban places" towns containing fewer people. But the changes occurring in the population of urban places as defined here will provide a reasonable and probably more meaningful measure of urbanization than that provided by the summaries in the Brazilian census of 1960.

Using this measure, there were 145 urban places in Brazil, and the increase in population in those 145 communities between 1950 and 1960 was somewhat more than 9 million persons. This represents not quite half (48 per cent) of the total national increase of Brazil. The significance of the urban (as here defined) population rise becomes even more evident when one considers that in 1950 there were approximately 11.3 million persons living in urban places,[13] thus indicating that the 1950–1960 increase for this category was 80 percent—considerably higher than the 70 percent increase indicated by the "urban" category as defined in the Brazilian census.

Table 3 provides a summary of the changes in population in urban places by states, as well as the proportion of each state's population rise which was accounted for by urban places. Examination of this table shows wide variations in the latter figures. São Paulo and Rio de Janeiro-Guanabara exhibit the largest increases in urban population, and in the case of the latter almost all of the increment in the two combined states took place in urban places; this was largely due to the influence of the city of

13. Computed from I.B.G.E., *VI Censo* and *VII Censo, op. cit.,* for 1950 and 1960.

TABLE 3/ POPULATION CHANGES (1950-1960) IN BRAZILIAN
URBAN PLACES BY STATE

State	Number of Urban Places[a]	Population Change, 1950–1960	
		Absolute	Percent of Total State
North			
Amazonas	1	64,428	31
Pará	2	165,835	34
Amapá	1	19,097	61
	4	249,360	
Northeast			
Maranhão	1	59,344	7
Piauí	2	58,365	27
Ceará	4	306,819	48
Rio Grande do Norte	2	82,912	44
Paraíba	3	110,366	36
Pernambuco	6	505,572	68
Alagoas	1	62,775	35
Sergipe	1	44,977	39
Bahia	8	490,525	42
	28	1,721,655	
Southeast			
Minas Gerais	28	964,844	48
Espírito Santo	4	152,428	47
Rio de Janeiro-Guanabara	11	1,895,480	93
	43	3,012,752	
South			
São Paulo	35	2,551,105	67
Paraná	6	369,508	17
Santa Catarina	7	174,107	30
Rio Grande do Sul	16	719,045	56
	64	3,813,765	
Central-West			
Mato Grosso	3	75,472	19
Goiás	2	126,108	17
Federal District	1	89,698	—
	6	291,278	
BRAZIL	145	9,088,810	48

a. Urban places are defined here as communities whose 1960 urban population was greater than 25,000. In the case of several of the larger cities, the community includes the urbanized areas of adjacent municípios (see Table 4 below for specific urbanized areas).

Source: Compiled from I.B.G.E., Servicio Nacional de Recenseamento. *VII Recenseamento Geral do Brasil, 1960: Brasil, Sinopse Preliminar do Censo Demografico* (Rio, 1962), pp. 29–71, and *VI Recenseamento Geral do Brasil, 1950: Brasil, Censo Demografico* (Rio, 1956).

Rio de Janeiro. At the other extreme are the "pioneer states" of Paraná, Mato Grosso, Goiás, and Maranhão (described below), in which urban increases were minor compared with total population growth, with the exception of Brasília, the new federal capital.

Metropolitan cities in Brazil have undoubtedly had a tremendous influence on the urbanization process in that country. It is therefore interesting to separate the population changes occurring in the larger cities from those taking place in all urban areas.

For convenience, one may take the ten largest cities—that is, the top ten urban agglomerations—of the country, and find that in 1960 they contained almost 13 million inhabitants,[14] or roughly 18 percent of the total national population. In contrast, the combined population of these ten cities in 1950 was 7.6 million, or 15 per cent of the national population. More striking is the fact that in the 1950–1960 period the population of these cities increased by 5.3 million, or more than half (58 percent) of the urban increase as defined above and about 28 percent of the total national increase for that period. Table 4 provides a more detailed summary of the cities included among the ten largest in Brazil.

As may be seen from Table 4, the population of the ten largest cities in Brazil grew, between 1950 and 1960, at a rate far exceeding the national average, although not as fast, on a percentage basis, as the average for all urban places in Brazil. Nevertheless, the larger cities of Brazil are obviously highly significant areas of population growth in the country. Locally, they have often been dominant, as a comparison of Table 4 to sections of Tables 3 and 2 will show. For example, the urbanized area of Rio de Janeiro grew by more than one and a half million people between 1950 and 1960, accounting for 84 percent of the urban population increase in the combined states of Rio de Janeiro-Guanabara, and 79 percent of their total rise in population. Recife, in the state of Pernambuco, and Fortaleza, in Ceará, were equally dominant with regard to urban population growth in their states (account-

14. Computed from I.B.G.E., *VII Censo, op. cit.*, for 1960.

TABLE 4/ POPULATION GROWTH IN THE TEN LARGEST URBAN
AGGLOMERATIONSª IN BRAZIL, 1950-1960

Urban Agglomeration	Population in: 1950	Population in: 1960	Population change, 1950–1960 Absolute	Population change, 1950–1960 Relative
Rio de Janeiroᵇ	2,773,494	4,370,414	1,596,920	57.5%
São Pauloᶜ	2,208,361	3,815,062	1,606,701	73.0
Recifeᵈ	610,933	1,032,948	422,005	69.0
Belo Horizonteᵉ	367,181	723,286	356,105	97.1
Pôrto Alegreᶠ	394,201	721,534	327,333	83.0
Salvador	389,442	638,592	249,150	64.0
Fortaleza	205,052	470,778	265,726	129.0
Belém	233,386	380,667	147,281	63.2
Santosᵍ	235,371	370,025	134,654	57.3
Curitiba	138,178	351,259	213,081	154.0
Total top ten cities	7,575,433	12,874,565	5,308,966	70.3

a. Principal city plus urban population of adjoining *municípios*.

b. Includes urbanized area of Guanabara state and urban population of Niteroi,
São Goncalo, Duque de Caxias, Nilópolis, Nova Iguaçú, and São João de Meriti.

c. Includes Santo André, São Caetano do Sul, Guarulhas, São Bernardo do Campo,
and Barueri.

d. Includes Olinda, Jaboatão, Paulista, and São Lourenço da Mata.

e. Includes Contagem, Nova Lima, and Sabará.

f. Includes Canoas.

g. Includes São Vincente and Guarujá.

Source: Compiled from I.B.G.E., Servicio Nacional de Recenseamento. *VII Recenseamento
Geral do Brasil, 1960, op. cit.,* pp. 28–71.

ing for 84 and 87 percent respectively of their states' urban increases), but were far less so when compared with their states'
total rise in population.[15] Some large cities, such as Curitiba, in
Paraná, and Fortaleza more than doubled their population between 1950 and 1960, while Belo Horizonte, the capital of Minas
Gerais, came close to doing so.

Studies indicate that by far the most significant factor in the
spectacular growth of the large cities in Brazil has been rural-
urban migration; it is estimated that, of the total population
increase of these cities, in-migration accounts for some 70 percent.[16] The large cities are therefore receiving substantial num-

15. About 57 and 41 percent respectively.

16. José Francisco de Camargo, *Exodo rural no Brasil* (Rio de Janeiro, 1960),
p. 156, cites an estimate that, of the population increase of Brazil's eight largest
cities during the 1940–1950 decade, about 70 percent was in immigration. A recent

bers of migrants from other parts of Brazil. In the cases of Rio and São Paulo, the arrival of immigrants from abroad added even greater numbers to their populations. The reasons for rural-urban migration in Brazil, as in the rest of the world, are complex and not completely understood, although they undoubtedly include such factors as higher wages, dreams of greater opportunities and a better life in the cities, and difficult conditions in rural and small town areas. Many studies are now being undertaken to evaluate and measure the attitudes of persons who have migrated from rural to urban districts, especially to the large cities.

A further aspect of urbanization in Brazil may be noted here. This concerns the medium-sized cities—cities whose 1960 population was between 100,000 and 300,000 inhabitants, thereby excluding the ten urban agglomerations described above. There are fifteen such medium-sized towns,[17] most of which are regional trade centers and/or state capitals, and they also experienced very rapid population growth between 1950 and 1960. Their combined population increase was only one million persons,[18] but their percentage increase was a very high 88 percent. The growth of each city in this category exceeded the national average of population growth by a wide margin.

Although the author has not seen any studies of rural-urban migration to medium-sized cities, their rapid growth must reflect a fairly widespread rural-urban migration similar to that existing for the large cities. There may, however, be another factor of unknown significance, and that is a possible rise in the rates of natural increase of groups moving into medium-sized towns. If the death rate is substantially lower in these towns than in sur-

study of Recife indicates that migration accounts for more than three fourths of that city's population increase (Antonio C. Gonçalvez, *As migrações para o Recife: II. Aspectos do crescimento urbano*. Instituto Joaquim Nabuco de Pesquisas Sociais, Recife, 1961). See also I.B.G.E., *Contribuições, op. cit.*, p. 304, where estimates of the importance of migrants to cities are somewhat lower (around 60 percent).

17. Ranked by size, they are Campinas (São Paulo), Natal (Rio Grande dó Norte), Manaus (Amazonas), Maceió (Alagoas), João Pessoa (Paraíba), Goiânia (Goiás), Juiz de Fora (Minas Gerais), São Luis (Maranhão), Pelotas (Rio Grande do Sul), Campina Grande (Paraíba), Ribeirão Prêto (São Paulo), Aracajú (Sergipe), Sorocaba (São Paulo), Teresina (Piauí), and Campos (Rio de Janeiro).

18. Computed from I.B.G.E., *VI Censo* (1950) and *VII Censo* (1960), *op. cit.*

rounding rural areas, then it might be supposed that population increases in the towns could at least partially reflect a drop in death rates for those migrating from rural areas, coupled with continuing high birth rates arising from traditional rural values regarding family life and size.

In summary, urban population growth in Brazil, by whatever measure one chooses to use, has been significant in accounting for the nation's total population increase. Most of the urban growth took place in the south and southeast, where 108 of the 145 urban places in Brazil are located; there is consequently considerable overlap when one compares the population increase of the southern and southeastern states with the increase in towns with more than 25,000 inhabitants. In a sense, what we are saying is that a large proportion of the population increase in the south and southeast was in fact part of Brazil's rural-urban migration. On the other hand, urban places in other parts of the nation have also grown substantially; and, in some regions, in sharp contrast to the rural-urban generalization mentioned, a number of urban places have grown very rapidly in association with agricultural colonization and settlement in the newer and more sparsely populated parts of Brazil—the "pioneer fringe" extending along the western margins of more densely settled Brazil.

THE "PIONEER FRINGE"

To Brazilians, as well as to North Americans, the most dramatic and romantic of population changes in Brazil have been those involving the "pioneer" zones of the country. Indeed, the popular slogan *Marcha para o Oeste* represents the widespread optimism with which many Brazilians view this movement into their undeveloped lands.

Three major areas stand out as important areas of pioneer movement, but they are by no means the only ones. Locally significant colonization and settlement is going on in other sections of the country. All of the pioneer zones are being settled primarily on a spontaneous basis; but federal, state, and private assistance has been provided in many cases—the most glamorous (as well as expensive) of which has been, of course, the creation of Brasília, the new federal capital of the nation located far in the interior and very close to one of the more successful and significant of the recent colonization movements. Other public and private assistance has included the building of roads, clearing of land titles, and provision of credit and other facilities for the new settlers.

The most important "pioneer district" encompasses a zone fanning out from São Paulo to the north, the west, and the southwest of that state. This zone includes Goiás (and Brasília), southern Mato Grosso, and northwestern Paraná, as well as small sections of western São Paulo and Minas Gerais. It is not possible to determine without detailed analysis exactly how many people settled in this pioneer zone between 1950 and 1960, but two million would be a fairly accurate guess.

The settlement of this pioneer zone is partly associated with the continuation of the westward expansion of coffee cultivation, a feature of southeastern Brazilian economic life for much of the past century.[19] Coffee cultivation has recently been pushed westward in a semi-circle extending from Brasília to somewhat north of the Falls at Iguaçú (and even into Paraguay); but by far the greatest expansion in coffee plantings has taken place in northwestern Paraná, the state which now leads the nation in coffee production.

Other factors are significant. This region, almost entirely drained by the Paraná River system, is a geologically complex, generally gently rolling highland averaging between 500 and 4,000 feet in elevation. Many parts of this highland, particularly in São Paulo and northern Paraná, are underlain by diabase sheets which have weathered into some of the most fertile upland soils in the world—the famous *terra roxa,* or purple soils, of southern Brazil, so commonly associated with recent coffee production. The high natural fertility of these soils has proved a major attraction to settlers now moving into the pioneer zones of this area, especially to those wishing to make their fortunes by growing coffee.

One very important factor in the development of the northern

19. Ary Franca, *A marcha do café e as frentes pioneiras* (Rio de Janeiro, 1960) and Pierre Monbeig, *Pionniers et planteurs de São Paulo* (Paris, 1952). See also Preston James, *Latin America* (3d. ed.; New York: Odyssey Press, 1959), pp. 479-496, for a summary in English.

section of this pioneer zone was the creation of Brasília as the new national capital of Brazil. Now containing about 350,000 inhabitants, this city will provide a major urban nucleus and market for this area and thus will be a real impetus to settlement in south-central Goiás, although colonization in sectors to the south and west of the capital had been going on rapidly before the establishment of the new city. Other cities, expanding to keep up with the needs of surrounding rural areas, have grown rapidly from small, dusty pioneer villages to "boom" towns. Such names as Londrina, Paranavaí, and Maringá in Paraná, or Goiânia and Anapolis in Goiás, as well as Campo Grande in Mato Grosso, and, of course, Brasília itself, create an aura of excitement and dreams of wealth when they are mentioned in all parts of Brazil. The fantastic growth of some of these pioneer cities, along with the building of many roads and arterial highways throughout the area, reflects the relatively commercial nature of much of the agricultural settlement of this pioneer region.

A second, much less important pioneer zone includes the southwestern part of Paraná and smaller sections of Santa Catarina and Rio Grande do Sul. Again, detailed figures are not available, but it appears that this movement involved between half a million and a million persons in the period of 1950 to 1960. Colonization and settlement in this zone has generally been associated with small-scale diversified farming, including crop and livestock agriculture and dairy farming. This part of Brazil is subject to frequent and heavy frosts in winter; therefore commercial coffee cultivation cannot be practiced much to the south of the Rio Ivaí, in central Paraná.

In many parts of this pioneer area, and especially in southwestern Paraná, soils are very sandy and of low natural fertility. But there are districts in which soils are fairly productive, and locally there may be found excellent lands for agriculture. Population expansion in this zone has not occupied all land available, but settlement has pretty well "filled in" the unoccupied and available areas of much of the three states up to the borders of Argentina.

The third major zone of pioneer movement lies far to the north, in central Maranhão. Preliminary studies on a *município* basis indicate that close to 600,000 persons are involved in rural settlement and colonization in this area. It is difficult to establish accurately the reasons for this pioneer movement, but it is dramatic and clearly of great significance. It may well be associated with the flight of large numbers of people from farther east, from Brazil's Drought Polygon, an area characterized by high rainfall variability and frequent, prolonged, and very severe droughts. There was a particularly bad drought in 1958 from which many people are said to have fled to other parts of the country, and this may have been a major influence in the population expansion into central Maranhão.[20]

A number of state-directed colonization programs have also had some success; and the opening of new, previously unsettled (and untitled) land has allowed many farmers to move into this area. Again, it appears that by far the largest number of settlers have moved into central Maranhão on a spontaneous basis.

In this area, settlement is taking place in a climatic transition zone, with adequate, but not excessive, rainfall. Farther west, colonization is beginning to enter the great Amazonian tropical rainforest. Until very recently, by far the greatest number of settlers in central Maranhão were subsistence farmers, but some commercial farms have been established. Generally, however, colonization and pioneer expansion in this region contrasts sharply to that to the south, in that large numbers of farmers are engaged in subsistence agriculture. Few roads have been built into

20. Albert O. Hirschman, in his *Journeys Toward Progress* (New York: Twentieth Century Fund, 1963), states that this drought was ". . . one of the most severe ever experienced by the Northeast . . ." (p. 68), and that it ". . . brought in its wake a record exodus from the rural areas where crops were failing." Later Hirschman mentions emigration to Maranhão (p. 78). The Brazilian Drought Polygon has, due largely to its climatic vicissitudes, been an area from which many thousands and perhaps millions of persons have migrated, usually to coastal areas where rainfall is greater and more reliable, but especially to the south and southeast, as well as to the pioneer areas and, in earlier years, the Amazon Valley. Many of these migrations are permanent, but many others are seasonal; frequently large numbers of migrants leave the Drought Polygon during a bad period, only to return several years later upon hearing that the rains have returned. For a good summary discussion of internal migrations, and an excellent bibliography at the end of the book, see Smith, *op. cit.*, but especially pp. 144–198. See also James, *op. cit.*, and Hirschman, above.

this pioneer zone, and there have been no "boom towns" and talk of greath wealth, as in the south. Commercial crops have been limited largely to rice and food for travelers on the Belém-Brasília highway, on the western fringe of the pioneer zone. The pioneer district of central Maranhão, therefore, is of particular interest to those concerned with the settlement of new lands in Brazil.

We may now summarize from a population viewpoint the changes which have taken place in the four "pioneer" states of Brazil: Paraná, Mato Grosso, Goiás (including the Federal District), and Maranhão. Between 1950 and 1960 the combined population of these four states increased by 4.3 million, or almost one-fourth (23 percent) of Brazil's total national increase. In 1950, these four states had about 5.5 million inhabitants (see Table 2), or little more than 10 percent of the nation's people. In view of this, the population increase between 1950 and 1960 is quite spectacular—a 78 percent increase, in contrast to 37 percent for the nation as a whole. As mentioned above, very little (less than 18 percent) of this population growth is due to urbanization; in fact, such towns as have grown in these four states (including even Curitiba, the capital of Paraná) have done so almost entirely as a result of the rural expansion into the pioneer zones.

There are districts in Brazil in addition to the three major pioneer zones mentioned which can be considered "pioneer" areas, although some of these zones are not entirely agricultural. For example, industrialization in the middle and upper Rio Doce Valley, associated with the expansion of steel production and other manufacturing in southeastern Minas Gerais, has brought in large numbers of laborers to work in the steel plants and associated industries. Furthermore, the lower Rio Doce Valley has experienced a significant influx of agricultural pioneers, including cacao growers and subsistence farmers. In the far north, the territory of Amapá has had a proportionally large population increase because of the opening of manganese mines and associated developments. In Amapá there also have been established small nuclei of colonization along the northern bank of the Amazon estuary. Other limited areas in various parts of Brazil have experienced locally significant population increases, notably some of the towns along the Rio-Brasília highway.

SUMMARY AND CONCLUSIONS

The regional population changes in Brazil between the years 1950 and 1960 can be summarized as follows (see Table 5):

TABLE 5/ SUMMARY OF POPULATION CHANGES IN BRAZIL, 1950-1960

Category	Population Increase Absolute	Percent of Brazil
Urban places[a]	9,088,810	47.7
10 largest cities	5,308,906	
15 medium sized towns	1,006,748	
120 smaller towns	2,673,296	
Non-urban population in:		
4 "pioneer" states	3,620,878	19.1
7 South and Southeast states[b]	3,921,338	20.7
All other	2,391,762	12.5
	————	————
TOTAL BRAZIL	19,022,788	100.0
Total South and Southeast states	12,540,563	66.0
Total 3 "pioneer" States[b]	2,178,792	11.4
Urban population in rest of country	1,911,671	10.1
Non-urban population in rest of country	2,391,762	12.5
	————	————
TOTAL BRAZIL	19,022,788	100.0

a. Urban communities with over 25,000 inhabitants in 1960.
b. Excluding Paraná.

Of the 19 million increase, urban places[21] accounted for 9 million, or almost half of the total national increase. More than half of the urban increase took place in the ten largest cities of the nation. Six of these top ten cities are located in the south and southeastern parts of Brazil, and most of the cities containing more than 25,000 inhabitants are also located in the south and southeast. Consequently, a large increase resulting from urbanization also represents a large increase in the southern and southeastern states.

21. Defined as communities containing more than 25,000 inhabitants in 1960.

A substantial part of the remaining population increase can be accounted for in two ways: one involves 3.6 million persons, representing the population increase in the *nonurban* sectors of the four pioneer states; the second involves 3.9 million persons, representing the increase in the nonurban areas of the south and southeastern states not accounted for previously (that is, excluding Paraná). These three broad geographic categories absorbed 16.6 million of Brazil's total population increase of 19 million between 1950 and 1960—about 88 percent.

The geographic generalizations accounting for the population increase in Brazil can be restated in a slightly different manner. One may start by using T. Lynn Smith's statement that the south and southeastern parts of the country absorbed the greatest population increase, then add to those southern states the four pioneer states mentioned above. If this is done, we find that the 12.5 million persons representing the increase in the southern and southeastern states, plus the 2.2 million persons representing the increase in three pioneer states (excluding Paraná), total some 14.7 million persons out of a total population increase in Brazil of 19 million. These eleven states, therefore, account for approximately 77 percent of the total national increase between 1950 and 1960. To these figures, one may add the increase in those cities and towns with more than 25,000 inhabitants found in the remainder of Brazil, and having added these (1.9 million), we find that we have again accounted for somewhat more than 16.6 million persons, or 88 percent of Brazil's total population increase.

However the regional differences in population increase may be categorized, it is clear that the bulk of Brazil's population increase between 1950 and 1960 took place in a relatively small area. This could be—and undoubtedly will be—shown even more conclusively if one were to examine population increases on a *município* basis. For example, almost all of the significant population increase in the pioneer state of Maranhão took place in a relatively small part of the state: in its central portions. By the same token, a large part of the increase in population in Goiás, Mato Grosso, and western Paraná involved relatively small proportions of the total area of those states. Finally, the population increases in urban areas involved relatively large numbers of people on extremely small units of area.

The trend outlined above has been largely evident throughout the twentieth century, as T. Lynn Smith cogently points out in his recent text,[22] but the implications of the most recent figures are extremely interesting. Judging from the results just described, the rural population increase for the remainder of Brazil (largely the northeast and the Amazon Valley) appears to have been somewhat more than two million persons. This is less than the normal rate of natural increase, and the implication seems to be that these areas were areas of net emigration.

If this be so, placing it in context with the population increases occurring in other parts of Brazil, then one may state in an over-simplified way that, over-all, Brazilians between 1950 and 1960 generally moved away from the rural northeast (and especially the interior) to coastal cities, to the wealthier south and southeast, and to the "pioneer fringe."

Considering that the northeast has historically been the source of chronic emigration, primarily because of periodic severe droughts, and that Brazil seems to be participating in the world-wide trend toward urbanization, this generalization might be expected. Especially pertinent to this discussion, however, are two droughts that occurred in the interior of the northeast in the years 1951 to 1953, and again in 1958. The latter, a severe one, has already been mentioned, but it would have had a special distributional effect on a census taken only two years later. While widespread famines, which have commonly accompanied droughts in the northeast, were avoided by such emergency measures as food airlifts, there was nevertheless a mass exodus from the interior to other areas. Also, the 1951–1953 drought, while not as severe as that of 1958, probably influenced the distributional changes in population between 1950 and 1960, since it was the first severe drought to affect many parts of the northeast in nineteen years.

The timing of the 1950 and the 1960 censuses may account for some changes in the population distribution within this decade. But the fact remains that during this period and previ-

22. Smith, *op. cit.*, pp. 49–50.

ously the rural northeast was an area of persistent emigration. Thus it was a major source of immigration (and labor) for other parts of the nation. This emigration pattern reflects the hardships of the northeast, where marginal climatic conditions often mean poor crops and pastures. The average income of the rural *nordestino* is well under $100 a year.

The many and complex problems which have arisen from Brazil's substantial increase in urban population between 1950 and 1960 and the intensification of rural-urban migration are not restricted to Brazil. These problems are being faced by almost all countries undergoing rapid urbanization, although certain problems are even more pressing in Brazil than in other countries. With an economy whose basic production is largely agricultural, Brazil's urbanization has brought millions of persons to cities with industrial bases far too meager to provide adequate employment for their new residents. At the same time, an agricultural system with commercial production traditionally designed for export, but with domestic production tending to remain at the local subsistence level, has been seriously strained to meet the rising demands of the urban populations. A generally primitive, noncapitalized, and overwhelmingly slash-and-burn agricultural production system, transport bottlenecks, and many other difficulties have created food supply problems, often of a critical nature, for the cities. Finally, the more common problems arising from population pressures on urban facilities of all types have been felt by all cities in Brazil.

The rapid rate of urbanization in Brazil has meant an intensifying concentration of the country's population in clusters. In spite of its sophisticated cities, however, Brazil is still overwhelmingly a rural country by most standards, and there is the very definite expansion of rural settlement—the "pioneer" movement—to the west. Developments in Maranhão, as yet unstudied except in a few isolated cases,[23] are of paramount interest, since this movement involves small-scale farmers with very little capital or technical knowledge and since west-central Maranhão is

23. See, for example, Instituto Nacional de Imigração e Colonização, *Barra do Corda: uma experiência de colonizacão,* Rio de Janeiro, 1959.

the locale of the first large-scale attempt at spontaneous pioneer settlement into the great Amazonian tropical rainforest.

A spectacular pioneer movement (a continuation of the steady movement across São Paulo) of somewhat different dimensions is taking place to the south. The pioneer zone of Goiás, Mato Grosso, and Paraná gives every indication of becoming a permanent and lucrative agricultural area. Much of this movement is taking place in a boom atmosphere, enhanced by the glamor and economic importance of the new capital at Brasília.

The Paraná Basin of southern Brazil offers many opportunities to Brazilians and appears as one of the brightest spots in Brazil's social and economic future. It is blessed with a generally favorable natural environment and settled by people who frequently have access to technical knowledge and a little capital, if only because private land companies play an important role in the colonization of this zone. Federal and state agencies give assistance to the region, and roads to markets are being built. With the Paraná River as a major source of hydroelectric power, agricultural settlement will apparently be followed soon by industrial development.

Yet, a word of caution should be inserted even here. The fortunate occurrence of excellent soils has contributed greatly to the success of settlement in the Paraná Basin. But the widespread and continuing fame of the gently rolling and highly fertile *terra roxa* lands of this area has tended to obscure the fact that their extent is by no means limitless. Even in São Paulo and Paraná, where the purple soils predominate, they are interspersed with areas of very infertile, sandy soils. Farther north and west, in Mato Grosso and Goiás, areas of *terra roxa* are quite restricted, with most of this region containing lands of limited agricultural value. Extensive sandstone formations underlie vast parts of the western Brazilian highlands, while other areas are composed of dissected hill lands. The sandstone usually weathers into soils of extremely low natural fertility, and cropping of sloping lands increases the problem of erosion. While these poorer lands can certainly be utilized for agriculture, in the long run they usually require fairly high capital investments for increased fertilization, contour plowing, and other means of maintaining their productivity over the long term. Today, almost all available *terra roxa* lands in southern Brazil have been settled, leaving the less endowed areas for future colonization. Symptomatic of the situation is that only a few miles northwest of the new capital Brasília settlers are now attempting to colonize a region of rough land and very poor soils.

Both favorable and unfavorable regional developments have caused and accompanied the population changes which Brazil has seen between 1950 and 1960. Probably most serious, however, is that the population movements from the rural northeast to urban areas and into the pioneer zones indicate serious structural problems in Brazil's traditional agricultural posture—problems which must be resolved soon if the nation is to maintain progress in its economic, social, and political development. Virgin lands of high natural fertility are now sharply limited, and people who move to cities have not yet learned to produce their own food. It would appear that the key to Brazil's future success will be her ability to develop a new, more intensive and more productive system of agriculture, utilizing the best soils available to her farmers. These include not only the *terra roxa* soils of the southern part of the country, but also alluvial and other soils in other areas; later, when agricultural capital is sufficiently distributed, the extensive, flat, sandy soils covering so many sections of the nation may be cultivated.

In any case, recent changes in the geographic distribution of population in Brazil, while reflecting a *Marcha para o Oeste,* seem to indicate an even more dominant *Marcha para o Sudeste.*

7/ THE PLANNING AND CREATION OF BRASILIA: TOWARD A NEW AND UNIQUE REGIONAL ENVIRONMENT?
BY ARMIN K. LUDWIG

> *Editor's note: This chapter is based upon a lecture delivered May 13, 1965, at Vanderbilt University under the auspices of the Graduate Center for Latin American Studies.*

T HE creation of Brasília in 1956 engendered a variety of developments which have already begun to reshape parts of the surrounding landscape and which through extension and proliferation may well produce a new and different Brazilian regional landscape.

The principal purpose of this chapter[1] is to determine the probable nature and extent of this new environment. Because so many of the developments in the Brasília locale stem from past decisions relating to the nature and location of the capital, it is first necessary to place the "Brasília idea" in perspective—to establish just what was envisioned for it and how it came to be what and where it is today. Then, an analysis of the post-Brasília patterns and conditions in the region and an assessment of the

---

1. The field research on which much of this chapter is based was done by the author in Brasília in 1963 and 1964 under a grant from the Social Science Research Council.

179

actual and potential responses to them will allow us to sketch the characteristics and area coverage of the future functional organization of this part of Brazil.

THE PRE-BRASÍLIA CONDITIONS

The Significance of the Constitutional Fiats. As expressions of ideas held by Brazilian political leaders, however much they may or may not have represented widely held opinion, three of the last four Brazilian constitutions specified not only the move itself, but, with varying degrees of precision, the location of the new Distrito Federal.

Article Three of the document of 1891 reads:

A zone of 14,000 square kilometers (circa 5,600 square miles) on the *planalto central* of the Republic will be reserved to the Union and will be surveyed at the earliest opportunity so that within it can be established the future Federal Capital.[2]

In accordance with this Article the Commission for Exploration of the Planalto Central of Brazil, under the leadership of Luiz Cruls, was sent into the interior to gather information about the area and to demarcate the specified quadrangle.

The Constitution of 1934 stated that "The capital of the Union will be transferred to a central point in Brazil," [3] but the vagueness of the location was equaled by that of the mandate to move and nothing followed.

The Constitution of the *Estado Novo,* promulgated by Getúlio Vargas in 1937, while not prohibiting the move, gave no new impetus to it.

Not at all unclear was Article Four and its four sections in the Constitution of 1946:

Article Four The Capital of the Union will be transferred to the Planalto Central of the Country.

Section One With the promulgation of this act, within sixty days the President of the Republic will nominate a technical commission of qualified personnel to proceed with the study of the locality of the new Capital.

2. Herman G. James, *The Constitutional System of Brazil* (Washington: Carnegie Institution, 1923) , p. 221.

3. Horácio Mendes, "Brasília e seus antecedentes," *Brasília,* ano 4, número 40 (Abril de 1960) , p. 41.

Section Two The aforementioned study will be submitted to the National Congress which will deliberate same and will establish a time limit for initiation of the delimitation of the area to be incorporated in the domain of the Union.

Section Three Upon completion of the work of demarcation Congress will establish a date for the movement of the Capital.

Section Four Upon the transfer, the present Distrito Federal will become the State of Guanabara.[4]

All the constitutional directives, and particularly the last, played upon a growing national state of mind which imagined fulfillment of Brazil's centuries-old *Marcha para o Oeste,* or manifest destiny, through development of the mysterious, and supposedly rich, *sertão.*[5] Creation of the new capital was readily and easily linked by its proponents to the fulfillment of such a destiny, thus providing the move with a major rationale.

A second rationale held that a new and "antiseptic" environment to serve as the seat of federal power needed to be created. Through local land-use planning and its rigorous enforcement, the new urban environment could, according to this thinking, be maintained free of those pressures engendered by uncontrolled growth. Here, legislators could legislate and the executive execute far removed from the cosmopolitan atmosphere of congested, polyfunctional Rio de Janeiro, considered so deleterious to the processes of government since the early nineteenth century.

Note, then, that the new creation was to be an urban "colony," primarily political in function, and surrounded by controlled environs. It was not, therefore, to be multi-functional or labor-consumptive, but it *was* to be a catalyst for regional development.

Triângulo vs. Planalto. The status of the planned environment as the national capital together with the mono-functional and antiseptic qualities envisioned for it tended to conflict with its expected urban support requirements. Such a conflict was reflected in the results of two field investigations: one conducted, pursuant to Article Four of the 1946 Constitution, by the federal-

4. The Article Four referred to here is under the Transitory Provisions of the Constitution of 1946. See: Amos J. Peaslee, *Constitution of Nations* (Concord, New Hampshire: The Rumford Press, 1950), I, 220.

5. *Sertão* is effectively translated as "backlands."

ly established Coelho Commission, the other by geographers of the *Conselho Nacional de Geografia*. These studies were guided by three broad principles relative to the the selection of a site: a position near the demographic center of the country; the presence of available transportation facilities; a location on the borders of two or more states.[6]

The Coelho Commission returned a report in 1948 recommending the location of the new Distrito Federal within a rectangle of 77,000 square kilometers (circa 30,000 square miles) incorporating the old Cruls Quadrangle and extending into western Minas Gerais State (Fig. 1). The *Conselho* report deviated from the Planalto fixation and favored a site adjacent to the city of Tupaciguara, Minas Gerais. This location, in the Triângulo Mineiro[7] near the productive forested valley of the Paranaíba River, admirably satisfied the three requirements. In addition it held the urban support requirements paramount.

Nevertheless, in 1953 a commission of the Brazilian Chamber of Deputies accepted the majority report. Each of the twenty-two Brazilian states had an equal voice on the commission, thus giving the numerous, small northeastern states more weight to "pull" the site to the north. In this act, the traditional Brazilian historical-political patterns demonstrated their effect on the situation of Brasilia. Congress then authorized the executive to undertake site studies within the rectangle for which the Commission for Localization of the New Capital was created.

CONTRASTING REGIONAL LANDSCAPES
WITHIN THE RECTANGLE

The rectangle straddled the two distinctly different landscapes in this part of Goiás, thus offering further site and situation alternatives (Fig. 1). Its western one-fifth encompassed a portion of the moderately high population, agricultural, and infrastructural densities making up the Goiás axis, essentially recapitulating the Triângulo site conditions. The remainder of the rectangle en-

6. Preston E. James and Speridião Faissol, "The Problem of Brasil's Capital City," *The Geographical Review*, XLVI, No. 3 (July, 1956), 311.

7. Triângulo Mineiro refers to the western, triangular-shaped panhandle of Minas Gerais State, which separates Goiás and São Paulo States.

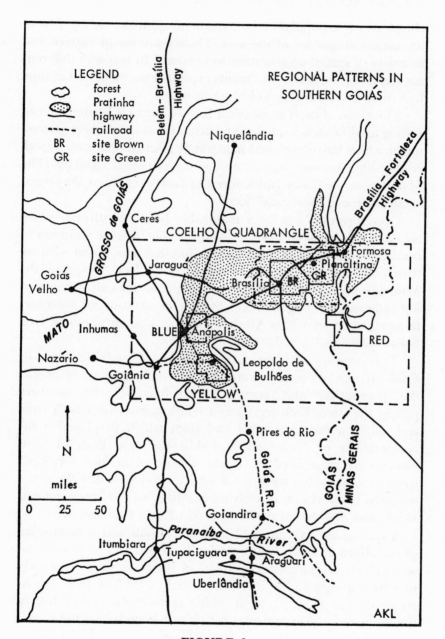

FIGURE 1

closed very low population and economic densities on the Pratinha surface to the east of the axis. These contrasts in pattern and intensity of spatial organization were rooted in two very different natural and physical environments exploited over a period of time by a common cultural-technical tradition.

The Goiás Axis. The physical base of the axis is composed of rolling to hilly surfaces covered by dense tracts of tall trees (mato) under which have developed moderately leached soils with a moderately high humus content and water retention capacity. The Mato Grosso de Goiás (thick forest of Goiás) contains the largest areal expanse of these conditions.

Opportunities here for a reasonably high agricultural return on a low capital input have resulted in a fairly dense accretion of rural population. Occupance of this forested area began with intensity in the forties, and continues today. By 1950, enough of the Mato Grosso de Goiás had been brought under cultivation that it contained the largest Goiás State concentration of sedentary farmers, many of whom produced marketable surpluses of rice, beans, coffee, cattle, and fruit.

The presence of a main road and the *Estrada de Ferro de Goiás* (Goiás Railroad) were instrumental in shaping axially the population and economic densities of the southern part of the state. Each served as a trunk along which both rural and urban populations grew and from which developed a net of secondary or feeder roads within the axis. Both of these routes were committed to, if not always maintained for, high-frequency, high-velocity flows of vehicles and provided the entire southern Goiás region its only surface links to the important economic and population densities of São Paulo City and State.

Capping the axis in 1950 were the urban and economic agglomerations of Goiânia and Anápolis (Fig. 2). The former, begun in 1935 as the planned capital of the state, grew in population from almost 15,000 in 1940 to nearly 40,000 in 1950 (an increase of 166 percent) as it added commercial and industrial functions to its governmental activities.[8] Founded in the 1850's,

8. The population figures were taken from: Instituto Brasileiro de Geografia e Estatística, Conselho Nacional de Estatística, Anuário Estatístico do Brasil, ano VIII (1947), 69, and ano XIII (1952), 53.

Anápolis became the railhead in 1935, thus usurping the role of entrepot envisioned for Goiânia, not served directly by the railroad until 1955. The railhead position of Anápolis combined with the agricultural productivity of the adjacent Mato Grosso de Goiás stimulated trade and food-processing activities. In 1940 the population of Anápolis was slightly more than 8,000, but by 1950 it had increased to more than 18,000, an increment of 126 percent.

The Pratinha. The predominant physical features to the east of the axis are the expansive remnants, or *chapadões,*[9] of the Pratinha erosion surface, highest and oldest level on the Planalto Central. The surfaces of these remnants, which truncate variously inclined Pre-Cambrian crystalline rocks, generally stand above the 1,000-meter contour level. Within the present Distrito Federal, however, the *chapadões* rise to the 1,100- and 1,200-meter level and make up most of the surface. This nearly flat landscape with long, low slopes occurs in areas with a vegetation association called campo cerrado, or tree savanna. This association is composed of vast tracts of scattered, short grasses studded at intervals by scattered shrubs and by open to dense blocs of low, scrubby trees. The soils which developed under the vegetation cover can be characterized as excessively permeable, leached and dispersed clays, low in humus content. They are underlain in places by iron oxide beds (called *canga* when massive and indurated, and *cascalho* when composed of nodules) which at intervals may be exposed at the surface.

A closer examination of this surface reveals a resource-use pattern in the mid-fifties typical of the Brazilian interior west of the Rio São Francisco in Bahia and Minas Gerais states. The principal economic units were the cattle *fazendas,*[10] the largest of which were marked out on the level, campo-covered *chapadões.* These fazendas were structured on a low-investment, low-return basis, so virtually none of the pasturage was improved to supplement the low carrying capacity of the natural grasses. At intervals, an agriculturally tractable soil occurred on the steeper slopes and

9. *Chapadões* are large, level-topped blocks, not unlike the mesas of the western United States.

10. *Fazenda* is equivalent to "ranch."

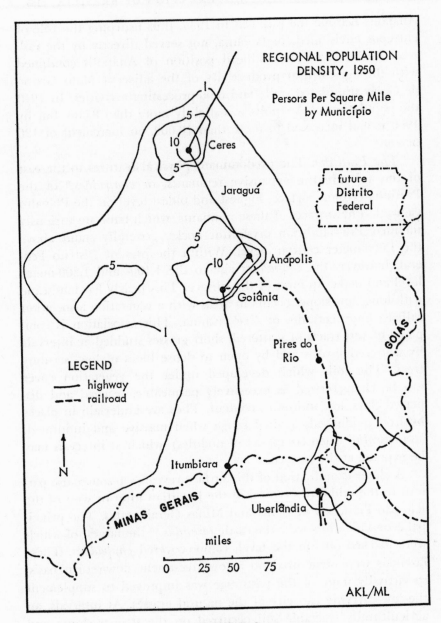

REGIONAL POPULATION
DENSITY, 1950

Persons Per Square Mile
by Município

future
Distrito
Federal

Ceres

Jaraguá

Anápolis

Goiânia

Pires do
Rio

GOIÁS

LEGEND

——— highway
----- railroad

N

Itumbiara

MINAS GERAIS

Uberlândia

miles

0   25   50   75

AKL/ML

FIGURE 2

forested bottoms created by streams incised into the surface. Its use by subsistence agriculturists and by a few small surplus-producing farmers gave rise to what little agricultural occupancy existed in this predominantly cattle-producing area.

Historically, the Pratinha surface was first utilized as a corridor. A level interfluve covered by *campo* (much preferred by the Portuguese to the forest), it was traversed by the famous Picada da Bahia (Bahia Pike) that linked the gold mines of Goiás to the west with the cattle ranches of the São Francisco Valley to the east. Along this route by the mid-1700s the colonial government has established a post to tax the eastward-moving gold. In the same period, a *pouso* (water, grazing, and rest stop) for cattle herds developed in the vicinity of this post. With the passage of cattle herds came the eventual spread of grazing activities onto the *campos* of the Pratinha and the ultimate division of the land into *fazendas*.

Predictably, the urban outgrowths of this cattle-based economy were few and small. The town of Formosa grew up near the *pouso* and fiscal post, straddling a narrow isthmus where streams to the north and south had cut deeply headward into the Pratinha. Formosa maintained itself as a cattle-exporting center and entre pot for a large *umland*,[11] but by 1950 it had attained a population of only 3,631. In the forties, Soares[12] reported the export of cattle on foot from Formosa to towns in southern Goiás and even to Barretos in São Paulo State, a distance of more than 250 miles. Webb[13] in 1957 recorded cattle moving from Formosa to Montes Claros in Minas Gerais, a walk of 300 miles requiring more than a month. After fattening in Montes Claros they were moved by rail to the Belo Horizonte market.

The only other even remotely urban place on this part of the Pratinha was the village of Planaltina, which, because it was

11. *Umland* is German for an area "around" or "about" a central place which is economically tributary to that place.

12. Lúcio de Castro Soares, "Função regional de Formosa," *Boletim da Secção Regional do Rio de Janeiro da Associação dos Geógrafos Brasileiros*, No. 2 (March 1948), p. 9.

13. Kempton E. Webb, *Geography of Food Supply in Central Minas Gerais* (Washington: National Academy of Sciences-National Research Council, 1959), p. 55.

situated near the center of the old Cruls Quadrangle, was the site of some early land speculation. Population had begun to agglomerate here in the early 1800s, possibly because of its locally famed arms craftsman and its position near the Picada da Bahia. But no sustained growth occurred, and by 1950 Planaltina had only 1,385 inhabitants. The town was subsequently incorporated into the Distrito Federal to be developed as an outlying urban nucleus.

The infrastructure of the Pratinha was weakly developed, but development was sufficient to support the low-level productivity of the small centers and dispersed population. The internal road net, even into the fifties, consisted primarily of unimproved, single-lane routes used most often by horsemen, *boiadas* (cattle drives), or oxcarts, and with less frequency but more difficulty by motor vehicles. All the major routes linking the Pratinha to distant regions, and whenever possible the local roads, traversed the flat *chapadões*. These surfaces where the *canga* or *cascalho* was exposed could support frequent and rapid movements of motor vehicles, but the clayey lower slopes and the stream crossings created serious bottlenecks. No paved roads were constructed on the Pratinha until the development of Brasília, but by the mid-fifties grading operations and distribution of the *cascalho* produced longer stretches of all-weather surface. Nevertheless, as late as 1956, between the railhead at Anápolis and the center of the present Distrito Federal, Carmin[14] found only limited portions of reasonably smooth, graded, and well-drained roads capable of supporting frequent movements of heavy loads in all seasons.

From the foregoing comments it is apparent that the cultural and economic patterns of this area based on cattle-grazing activities persisted practically unchanged during the 150 years preceding the creation of Brasília. Celso Furtardo's observation that "In a cattle-breeding region, the staple food being the export article itself, a reduction in exports has no effect whatsoever on domestic food supplies," explains in part the lack of pressure for

14. Robert L. Carmin, "Roads and the Advance of Settlement on the Goiás Frontier, the Region of Brazil's New Capital" (mimeographed report submitted to the Office of Quartermaster General, Civilian Expeditions Section, 1958), pp. 47–50.

structural changes in the economy of the Pratinha, or for abandonment of occupancy altogether.[15]

THE FINAL CHOICE OF THE SITE

Given these pre-existing patterns and conditions, the choice of the Brasília site tended to hinge on balancing off the need for an appropriate urban site against the need for a reasonable proximity to supply and support areas for the new urban complex. This balance is reflected in the eight final selection criteria which James and Faissol list according to priority assigned by Brazilian planners:

1. A gently sloping terrain—not too steep, not too flat.
2. A comfortable climate with no extremes of temperature or rainfall, and no violent winds, and at an elevation high enough to offer freedom from malaria.
3. A water supply adequate for a city of half a million inhabitants.
4. Nearby forested areas where agriculture can become established for the supply of vegetables and milk, and where wood can be procured for fuel.
5. A source of low-cost electric power located within 100 kilometers.
6. Locally available building materials, including lime for cement.
7. A subsoil suitable for building foundations and for excavation of sewers and subways.
8. An attractive landscape and nearby recreation areas.[16]

In 1954, the American firm of Belcher and Associates began a survey of the rectangle to determine at which places the largest number of criteria could be fulfilled. Five potentially acceptable sites were demarcated for the location of the new capital (Fig. 1). Each was given a color code, such as site Brown or site Green.

All five sites fulfilled within limits the eight criteria. The Pratinha surface and the level immediately below it admirably fit the terrain and elevation requirements, thus eliminating the malaria menace. All five sites were in the Aw, or savanna, climatic

15. Celso Furtado, "The Economic Growth of Brazil," trans. Ricardo W. de Aguiar and Eric C. Drysdale (Berkeley and Los Angeles: University of California Press, 1963), p. 70.

16. James and Faissol, p. 313. For additional criteria, and elaboration on the above criteria, see Departamento Administrativo do Serviço Publico, Servico de Documentacao, O relatório técnico sóbre a nova capital da republica (Rio de Janeiro: October, 1956), pp. 20–28.

region. This climate is marked here by a rainfall of 70 inches confined to the summer period from October through April, and by a bright, dry, and warm winter with daily maxima of about 85 degrees Fahrenheit. From time to time during the winter, however, the region is invaded by cool Antarctic air masses from the south which reduce nighttime temperatures. In June of 1964, for example, the temperature fell to 34 degrees Fahrenheit in Brasília, but this is extreme.

Many of the steams in the Pratinha region continue to discharge, albeit at reduced rates, during the dry season. Impounding could conceivably yield a constant supply of water for the half million users. But because the streams are incised, water has to be pumped up for distribution. Large forest tracts were not included in any of the sites. In this case, the criterion "nearby" left considerable room for interpretation. Relative to building materials and lime, the term "locally" also permitted a high degree of discretion.

The low-cost electric power criterion made mandatory a search for a power dam site. A suitable subsoil presumably meant avoidance of the indurated *canga,* or organic-alluvial soils in the valley bottoms. The attractiveness of the natural landscape is not enhanced by the scrubby *campo cerrado* and the flat Pratinha horizon, but the treeless *campo* areas and the "big sky" appeal to some.

Site Brown was chosen on the basis of the following combination of circumstances: first, its contiguity with another acceptable site (Green), permitting enlargement of the potential Distrito Federal around the capital city; second, its possession of an excellent reservoir-power dam site and an urban setting between the arms of the man-made lake; third, its location on the highest part of the Pratinha surface—an ideal setting for this symbol of Brazil's future.

As important as any of the above, however, was isolation of site Brown, reflected in its pre-Brasília patterns of occupancy and its distance from the Goiás axis. Proximity to the axis certainly militated against selection of sites Blue or Yellow. These latter were favored by Goiás residents, and rumors indeed persisted at the time that the site adjacent to Anápolis was the prime choice. Both Blue and Yellow, however, were traversed by either the infrastructural or population densities making up the Goiás axis. This fact conceivably raised fears of land expropriation problems. More importantly, the selection commission may have foreseen that nonpolitical developments would be difficult to control or, still worse, might subsequently overwhelm the political functions of the new environment. This would effectively nullify one of the basic arguments for the move from crowded, polyfunctional Rio de Janeiro.

The site for the new capital city was finally determined by a federal commission in April 1955, and the present Distrito Federal borders were drawn to incorporate both Brown and Green.

In September 1956, NOVACAP, the newly created, government Company for Urbanizing the New Capital, opened competition dedicated to the selection of a city plan. Information provided the contestants was limited to the terrain detail, size, and shape of the site between the arms of the lake and to the population of the city (500,000 inhabitants). That the capital provide for all the existing Brazilian federal functions and their necessary ancillary facilities was, of course, implicit in the instructions.

In March of 1957 the awards were made by a six-man jury composed of three Brazilians and three foreigners. Of the seven plans placing in the competition, six envisioned implementation from a point or nucleus outward. Only the airplane design of Lúcio Costa, incorporating a monumental axis (fuselage) of government buildings flanked by two wings of nongovernmental urban land uses, required no slow, organic growth.

The rapid completion of the entire Brasília project was given high priority by the early planners. They hoped to counteract vociferous critics and to convince those not wholly committed to the move. Above all, President Juscelino Kubitschek wanted to inaugurate this monument to his efforts before his term of office expired in January 1961. (This he did, incidentally.) These facts, together with the inclusion of the monumental axis, probably influenced the jury (to the degree they were subject to outside influences) in the choice of the Costa plan.

POST-BRASÍLIA LOCAL AND REGIONAL PATTERNS

Highways. Most of the post-Brasília changes in the organization of the Goiás region and the Pratinha surface resulted from the creation of a regional and extra-regional highway network (Fig. 3). Its construction was a part of President Kubitschek's drive to give Brazil fifty years of progress in five through the development of a modern infrastructure. Brasília was but one of the several major foci to and around which road building was concentrated. The new capital's large construction and support requirements made necessary strong links to the economic densities of the São Paulo–Belo Horizonte–Rio de Janeiro heartland and to the core of the productive Goiás axis. In addition, Brasília's position in the heart of a weakly developed locale, and on the margin of a much larger undeveloped interior, made it an ideal point from which to project multiuse routes with such high potential for triggering economic growth.

Several major Brasília-oriented highways were opened to traffic shortly after the construction of the capital began. By 1958, NOVACAP had completely asphalted the eighty miles of highway between Brasília and the railhead at Anápolis. This route was essentially the regional portion of the Brasília-Santos highway, extending from that port city six hundred miles to Anápolis. Except for a few minor sections it is now paved over its entire distance. By 1961, the federal government had asphalted the Brasília–Rio de Janeiro highway. The celebrated Belém-Brasília highway, which actually links the Amazon city with the Goiás axis at Anápolis, is presently considered negotiable, but the rainy season makes a quagmire of large sections in the north. Most of the Brasília-Fortaleza route is still under construction.

The State of Goiás has improved two roads from Goiânia into the agriculturally productive Mato Grosso de Goiás region. Routes have been extended north and west to Nazário and to Goiás Velho, the former state capital, until recently "lost in the *sertão.*" A thirty-mile section of this latter road, from Goiânia to Inhumas, are paved. This, in effect, links Brasília by pavement with this productive area.

In the western portion of the Pratinha, the State of Goiás has improved a route north from Anápolis toward Niquelândia,

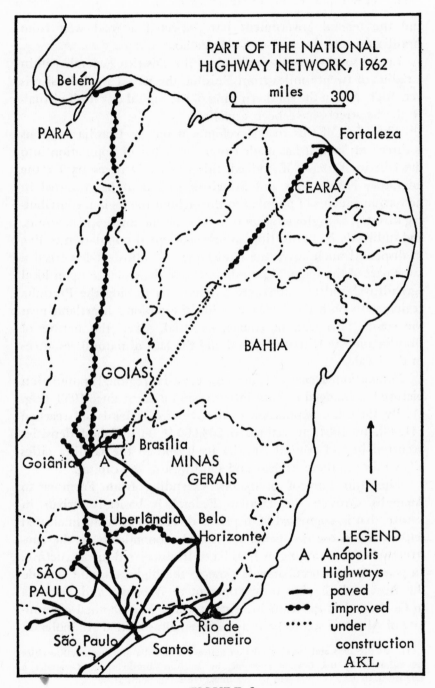

PART OF THE NATIONAL
HIGHWAY NETWORK, 1962

0   miles   300

Belém

PARÁ

Fortaleza

CEARÁ

BAHIA

GOIÁS

Brasília

Goiânia   A   MINAS
GERAIS

N

Uberlândia   Belo
Horizonte

LEGEND

A Anápolis
Highways
SÃO
PAULO   paved
improved
under
São Paulo   Rio de   construction
Santos   Janeiro   AKL

FIGURE 3

and the federal government has projected a road west from Brasília through Jaraguá to Goiás Velho.

In the southwestern quadrant of the Distrito Federal, within a radius of twenty miles from Brasília, the paved road density is very high, and in the southern wing of the capital city itself virtually all the streets have been asphalted.

The effect of this road development on the Brasília environs is threefold: first, it has made easier the influx of population into the Distrito Federal, if, indeed, this was really necessary for the migratory Nordestinos and Mineiros; second, it has resulted in new arrangements of population throughout the region, contributing directly, as agglomeration of road construction workers attests, and indirectly by permitting an urban-oriented population to live in dispersed nuclei over the landscape; and, third, it has freed a large part of the regional population from dependence upon local agricultural and manufactured products by linking the Pratinha region with both the Goiás axis and the nation's heartland near the coast. This was, of course, essential, given the nature of Brasília and the Distrito Federal and the lack of natural resources in the locale.

Population Density. The post-Brasília regional population picture has changed in both intensity and pattern since 1950 (Fig. 4). By 1960, the population of the Distrito Federal had reached 141,000; by 1964, an estimated 263,000.[17] The highest densities occurred in and around Brasília itself and in the satellite cities a few miles to the northeast and southwest of the capital.

The thin film of occupancy extending from Formosa to Anápolis through the Distrito Federal is basically urban in nature, that is, composed of dispersed dwellings or small nucleated settlements whose occupants are linked economically to the construction or functioning of Brasília or its associated infrastructure. In general, such occupancy is close to the highways, and outside the Distrito Federal is most apparent at Alexânia and Formosa in Goiás, and at Paracatú in Minas Gerais. The planned community of Alexânia stands halfway between Brasília and Anápolis on

17. All the 1963 and 1964 population figures for Brasília and the satellite cities are estimates by the Brasília office of the Instituto Brasileiro de Geografia e Estatística. In 1960 Goiania had 133,463 inhabitants: Anápolis, 51,169.

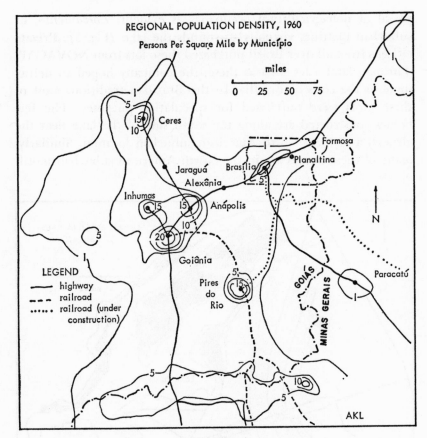

REGIONAL POPULATION DENSITY, 1960

Persons Per Square Mile by Município

FIGURE 4

the paved highway that links these two centers. Formosa has become a focus for Nordestino migrants moving toward the Distrito Federal down the Brasília-Fortaleza highway. A concentration of highway workers and their families has developed at Paracatú, where in 1960 the Brasília–Rio de Janeiro highway was still under construction.

The important thing to bear in mind is that virtually none of this population increase in the region is related to wealth-creating uses of the soil but is essentially urban-oriented. It is not an exaggeration, then, to say that Brasília is *in* Goiás but not *of* it.

Patterns of Occupancy. Within the Distrito Federal, beyond the concentrated urban residences of Brasília itself, a planned dispersal of nonagricultural occupancy is evident. *Loteamento*, or suburban platting, virtually surrounds the lake (Fig. 5). Private citizens from all over Brazil purchased these lots from NOVACAP, Through land sales such as these, the company hoped to defray some of the costs of Brasília. In the Brazilian tradition, most of these plots were purchased for speculative purposes. The few homes constructed are along the south side of the lake near the airport, a favorite North American suburban location. Similarly, many of these homes are in the North American suburban motif.

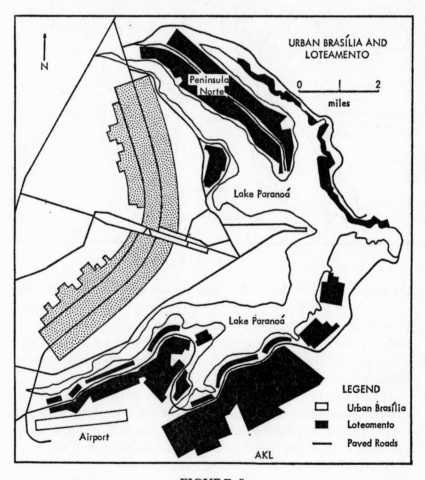

FIGURE 5

The peninsula north of the capital is devoid of residential occupancy.

At distances ranging from ten to twenty miles outside Brasília
lie the satellite cities (Fig. 6). The first of these, Taguatinga, to
the west, was created in 1959 to localize the burgeoning influx of
lower-class population which threatened to inundate Brasília
proper.[18] Subsequently, Sobradinho was constructed northeast of
the capital, and Gama was built to the south. Many people, however, remained in the shack villages on the vacant land in Brasília
in order to be close to potential employment. The recent revolutionary government has given Brasília shack-dwellers free lots
in Gama and has trucked both their dwellings and belongings to
the new sites. Many of the recent in-migrants to the Distrito
Federal have by choice, however, sought residence in the growing satellite cities.

By 1963 all the satellite cities had attained sizable populations
and two were showing signs of stability. Taguatinga had a population of more than 60,000. Its commercial core, containing many
permanent buildings, and the scattering of permanent residences
amid the sea of wooden shacks reflected a modicum of prosperity.
Gama had 20,000 inhabitants and almost as many permanent
buildings as Taguatinga. Sobradinho's 16,000 inhabitants lived in
an atmosphere of impermanence, since most were yet housed and
served in wooden buildings.

Town and suburban planning has become an accepted, indeed
a necessary, pattern in the vicinity of Brasília. There is no reason
to believe that such a pattern will not spread over the region as
more migrants divorce themselves from the soil and as those economically able become more willing to live in the very un-
Brazilian suburban homes surrounded by lawns.

18. Actually, Cidade Livre (now called Núcleo Bandeirante) was the first
"planned" urban development in the Distrito Federal. It served as the "base" supporting early construction of Brasília and housing most of the workers, was close to
the new capital, and lay within the Brasília watershed (composed of that area
drained by the short streams flowing to the lake). For these reasons it was to be
temporary. Attempts to stem its growth met with limited success. In 1961 and 1962,
for example, 3,000 of its inhabitants were moved to the satellite cities and the north
wing of Brasília. Subsequently, the government has given up the destruction of
Cidade Livre and has declared this "city" of 18,000 a permanent satellite.

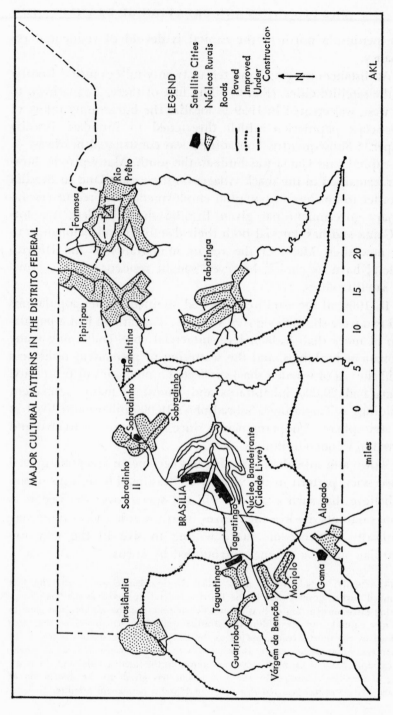

MAJOR CULTURAL PATTERNS IN THE DISTRITO FEDERAL

LEGEND

Satellite Cities

Núcleos Rurais

Roads

Paved

Improved

Under Construction

N

AKL

Formosa

Rio Prêto

Pipiripau

Planaltina

Tabatinga

Sobradinho

Sobradinho II

BRASÍLIA

Núcleo Bandeirante (Cidade Livre)

Taguatinga

Alagado

Braslândia

Guariroba

Várgem da Bençảo

Monjolo

Gama

miles

0   5   10   15   20

FIGURE 6

Agricultural Patterns. To compensate for the distance to sources of food supply, planners have tried to stimulate development of an urban-oriented agriculture within the Distrito Federal through creation of Núcleos Rurais (Figs. 6 and 7). Each Núcleo is composed of a group of contiguous small family farms. The farms range in size from 60 to 150 acres and extend in narrow strips away from the streams cut into the Pratinha surface. Laid out in this manner, each farm contains a part of the narrow forest belt in the valley bottom and a larger area on the slope. The soils on the slopes have a somewhat higher humus content and water retention capacity than the soils on the flat Pratinha surface above. As little as possible of this latter *campo cerrado* land is included in each farm.

The farms are leased on a "homestead" arrangement. A person must meet various criteria to qualify for the right to use the land, and he must subsequently demonstrate that he has made improvements on it.

Successful truck or fruit farming on these slopes, however, depends upon more than meeting some abstract qualifications. It depends, rather, upon a willingness or ability to make a high-labor, high-capital investment in the land, and upon access to a market. In the eastern part of the Distrito Federal neither of these conditions was fulfilled, thus forcing a reappraisal of land use here—still directed, nevertheless, to some kind of urban-oriented agriculture. The six Núcleos nearer Brasília have been at least partially occupied with varying degrees of success. The most successful is Taguatinga, to which the markets of both Brasília and Taguatinga city are proximal. The real key to its fulfillment, however, has been the well-organized and highly capitalized Japanese-Brazilian farmer's co-operative whose members occupy more than half of the thirty-nine farms here. The Brasília market is sufficiently strong to permit the Taguatinga farmers to import tremendous quantities of fertilizer from São Paulo. Another indication of the Núcleo's market orientation is the fact that at least one farmer specializes only in flowers.

The point to this discussion is that, given heavy inputs and access to markets, the myriad other slopes cut into the Pratinha might yield truck and fruit crops. Most Brazilians, however, are

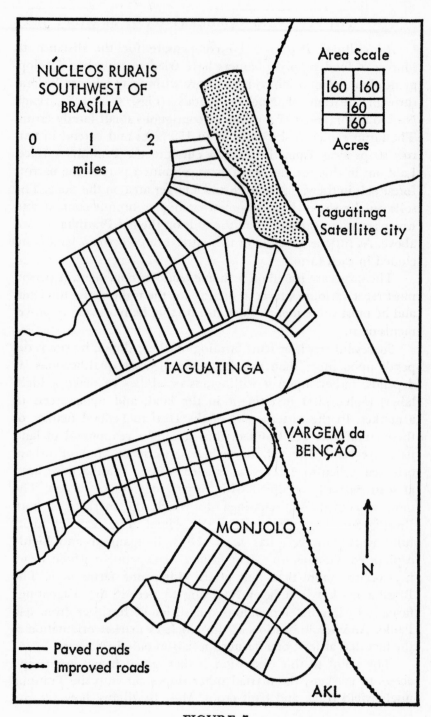

Area Scale

160	160
160	
160	

Acres

NÚCLEOS RURAIS
SOUTHWEST OF
BRASÍLIA

0   1   2
miles

Taguátinga
Satellite city

TAGUATINGA

VÁRGEM da
BENÇÃO

MONJOLO

N

—— Paved roads
••••• Improved roads

AKL

FIGURE 7

not yet interested in this kind of husbandry. This is in evidence, even in Taguatinga, where a lack of concern for the land results in unattended or unimproved farms. Farms in other Núcleos have become *chácaras* (week-end country places) for politicos, and some are even being occupied by tenants or subsistence agriculturists.

Potential Industrialized Agriculture on the Pratinha. The *campo cerrado* soils on the Pratinha surface have been largely ignored, chiefly because pressures for food and agricultural raw materials have not yet forced investments in research, technology, capital goods, and infrastructure necessary to bring these lands into production.

By mid–1964, however, the government agency charged with aiding production and distribution of commodities in Brasília had begun to allocate resources to the development of industries whose raw material requirements could stimulate regional agricultural growth.[19] In conjunction with private capital, this agency expects to construct mills to produce oils and feeds from soybeans, cotton seed, and corn; to build a plant to make alcohol from sugar cane; and to develop a rice-beneficiator and several cattle feed lots. Already under construction is a milk-processing plant.

A heavily capitalized complex of mills and associated activities in the Distrito Federal could conceivably trigger some investments in extensive industrialized agriculture on the Pratinha surface. Initially, it is true, these investments would probably have to be made under government aegis or at best involve but a small amount of private capital. And it is also true that this investment would have to be made in the face of somewhat cheaper inflows of commodities from the Mato Grosso de Goiás region.

Nevertheless, once these investments are initiated, assuming an increased demand for agricultural raw materials, both governmental and privately organized industrialized agriculture would find the vast, level surfaces of the Pratinha ideal for extensive operations. The proximity of these lands to the Brasília process-

19. Personal interview with Comandante Ivan Barcellos, head of Sociedade de Abastecimento de Brasília, Limitada, August 17, 1964.

ing plants could eventually more than compensate for the heavy inputs required for yields from these soils. It must be borne in mind, however, that such extensive agriculture is consumptive only of skills, not of labor.

CONCLUSION: TOWARD A NEW AND UNIQUE BRAZILIAN REGIONAL ENVIRONMENT?

The location of Brasília and its attendant urban-rural-infra-structural complex on the Pratinha surface combines two elements which will strongly influence the future patterns of occupancy and functional organization of this part of Brazil. The first of these elements is the Pratinha itself, a vast expanse of nearly level, un-occupied land, rare in Brazil. The second is Brasília. Dedicated in part to regional economic growth, Brasília is the seat of the federal bureaucracy, elements of which now seek to organize government and private capital and to channel this into the creation of plants for *processing* agricultural raw materials. This initial step may eventually lead to public/private investment in the research and technology necessary to bring the *campo cerrado* lands into *production*. Such a condition will radically alter the patterns and structure of limited areas inside the Distrito Federal and potentially larger areas outside. None of these developments, however, can be expected to compromise the capital's essentially political nature.

The results of initial government/private inputs will conceivably pave the way for less venturesome, strictly private investment in both the production and processing of agricultural raw materials. Owing to land planning in the Distrito Federal, any concentration of private investment will have to occur in the land beyond. Guided by the planned road net, the functional structures and patterns resulting from these inputs should spread to the limits of the Pratinha surface.

Given these conditions, we can picture three major patterns of occupancy and functional structures developing on the Pratinha surface.

Most of the land will be taken up by high-efficiency, indus-trialized agriculture supplying raw materials to processing plants concentrated initially in the Distrito Federal. As this land use spreads, however, new plants will be constructed at points along highways central to the producing areas. The limited labor requirements of this industrialized agriculture will tend to keep the total rural population low.

Small urban nuclei or suburban residential clusters will develop adjacent to the processing plants or along highways which provide rapid access to the capital. The flow of income to these population clusters from industrialized agriculture, processing plants, and Brasília itself will generate some employment in the service sector of the economy. The number of persons employed in the service sector could possibly rise to two or three times the number of income-earners in these other activities. In neither kind of employment, however, can we foresee many opportunities for the unskilled thousands even now flooding into Brasília. At places where their construction is possible, small dams will provide electric power and water supply for these settlements.

Proximal to these population clusters, an urban-oriented agriculture will be established on the slopes cut into the Pratinha. Such an activity requires only limited amounts of land, but it is characterized by high inputs of capital, fertilizer, and equipment. Neither the aggregate population directly engaged in this kind of farming nor the employment it generates in the service sector will be large.

The question arises at this point whether productive developments on the Pratinha could have come about without the staggering expenditures for Brasília. It would seem that, given the country's growing needs for agricultural raw materials and the level, unoccupied Pratinha surface, Brazil might sooner or later have had to develop an industrialized agriculture here. The infrastructural network could have been anchored at Anápolis, and doubtless some of the processing plants would have located on the Pratinha, bringing along their service employment opportunities.

It is possible that Brazil might yet be better advised to concentrate her attention on the "worn-out" lands nearer the large coastal cities. In their present state these lands are probably no less capable of agricultural production than are the virgin *campo cerrado* soils. Perhaps Brasília has stimulated an unwarranted interest in the development of these soils. Yet there is that element of levelness on the Pratinha, a critical factor in the success of extensive, mechanized agriculture.

Without Brasília there would, of course, be no planned towns or suburban developments and no focus for migratory, jobless, and unskilled populations. Nevertheless, Brasília *is*. And, as a result, developments on the Pratinha will increasingly reflect the sophisticated urban-technical characteristics associated with Brasília and less of the *sertão* in which they occur. We may soon have the new and unique Brazilian regional environment sought by many who would create the new Brazil.

8/ RELIGIOUS MASS MOVEMENTS AND SOCIAL CHANGE IN BRAZIL BY EMILIO WILLEMS

THE role of religious movements in the process of culture change in Latin America is almost entirely unexplored. Attention has been focused on such phenomena as economic underdevelopment, political radicalism, illiteracy, technological backwardness, rural-urban migrations, and the growth of shanty towns, rather than on religious movements whose links with the main stream of cultural transformations seem less obvious. Reports presumably dealing with "whole cultures" have chosen to ignore movements involving millions of people, as well as the emergence of organizational patterns which constitute, in some ways at least, a revolutionary break with the past.

The stereotype of a thoroughly Roman Catholic Latin America may have deflected the attention of some students from the rise of non-Catholic religions and the attendant changes of the traditional social structure. It is true, of course, that non-Catholic religious movements are only in their incipient stages in some countries; but they have reached the proportions of mass movements in others.

Nowhere, however, have they found more diversified expressions or attracted more people than in Brazil. The three largest and functionally the most significant non-Catholic movements of contemporary Brazil are Pentecostalism, Spiritualism, and Umbanda. The two major Pentecostal sects, the Assembly of God and the Christian Congregation, were founded in 1910 as an outgrowth of Protestant proselytism. Since the Pentecostals have shown a biblical reluctance in counting their followers, almost no figures on their early development are available, but for about two decades their proselytic effort seems to have caused little concern to the established Protestant churches. A survey published in 1932 [1] stated that only 9.5 percent of the Brazilian Protestants, excluding the communities of German origin, belonged to Pentecostal bodies. The movement has gained momentum especially since World War II, and according to the Evangelical Federation of Brazil, the Christian Congregation counted, in 1958, a total of 500,000 members, including minors. At the same time, the total membership of the Assembly of God was reported to be 1,000,000. Thus out of a total of 2,697,273 Brazilian Protestants, 1,500,000 or 55 percent belonged to the two principal Pentecostal bodies. Should the total of 4,071,643 Brazilian Protestants reported for 1961 be correct, the Pentecostal movement would have by now well over 2,000,000 followers. [2]

The beginnings of organized Spiritualism were traced back to 1873 when the Society for Spiritualist Studies of the Confucius Group was established in Rio de Janeiro. There are no reliable figures on the dissimination of the new faith, but it did not reach proportions of a mass movement until 1920. Umbanda, however, is much more recent. If the source quoted by Bastide is accurate, its formal detachment from the Macumba took place by 1930, but it did not acquire its present characteristics of widespread religious movement until well after World War II. [3]

The reliability and significance of membership figures concerning Spiritualism and Umbanda are difficult to ascertain. According to Camargo, the number of Spiritualists grew from 463,400 in 1940 to 824,553 in 1950. [4] Official figures are lower, as the following table shows.

1. Erasmo Braga and Kenneth G. Grubb, *The Republic of Brazil: A Survey of the Religious Situation* (London, New York, and Toronto: World Dominion Press, 1932), p. 71.

2. Prudencio Damboriena, *El protestantismo en America Latina* (Friburgo y Bogotá, Oficina Internacional de Investigaciones Sociales de FERES, 1963), I, 16.

3. Roger Bastide, *Les religions africaines au Brésil* (Paris: Presses Universitaires de France, 1960), p. 443.

4. Candido Procopio Ferreira de Camargo, *Kardecismo e Umbanda* (São Paulo: Livraria Pioneira Editôra, 1961), p. 176.

Growth of Spiritualism in Brazil

Year	Total
1953	488,017
1958	636,449
1959	673,318
1960	680,511

Source: Anuário Estatístico.

Both Camargo and Kloppenburg recognize that the relatively low degree of institutionalization of Spiritualism and Umbanda makes statistical accuracy virtually impossible. The State Department of Statistics in São Paulo enumerates only those Spiritualists who are affiliated with some center. Most Spiritualists, however, meet only in private homes and are thus not covered by statistical inquiries. [5] The Umbanda is neither recognized as a separate denomination by the census authorities, nor do the

Kardecist Spiritualists . . . permit or tolerate that the Umbanda Spiritualists . . . declare themselves as "Spiritualists." Therefore, in official classifications, the enormous proportion of Umbandistas and Philo-Spiritualists appears under the common denominator "Catholic" . . .[6]

Sheer numbers seem to justify the classification of Pentecostalists, Spiritualists and Umbandistas as mass movements, but there is the added fact that all three are concerned with the transformation of the surrounding society. Some aspects of the proposed changes are mystical or utopian, others are practical and are actually being carried out; but, as we shall see further on, the mere existence of these movements constitutes evidence of a major change of the traditional social structure. No matter how different they may seem at first glance, all three movements share at least five major characteristics: they are concerned with similar forms of supernaturalism; they were originated by cultural diffusion; their beliefs are compatible with certain traditions of Brazilian folk Catholicism and messianism; they are organized in sectarian

5. *Ibid.*, p. 17.
6. Buenaventura Kloppenburg, "Introducción Histórica" in Candido Procopio de Camargo, *Aspectos sociologicos del espiritismo en São Paulo* (Friburgo y Bogotá: Oficina Internacional de Investigaciones Sociales de FERES, 1961), p. 19.

structures; and they perform, competitively, similar or identical functions.

It is assumed that the rapid expansion of the three movements may be explained in terms of their functional adaptation to a changing society and culture. Thus the description of the first four characteristics is intended to lead to an analysis of those specific needs and wants of several million Brazilians these movements appear to fill.

SUPERNATURALISM

The main concern of the three movements is with spirit possession. The belief in the descent of supernatural beings and their temporary incarnation in human beings occurs in a large number of widely different societies, and in spite of formal and functional variations the anthropologist easily recognizes a common denominator in such beliefs and their manifestations. Following the biblical model, the Pentecostals believe that, under certain conditions, they may be possessed by the Holy Spirit. Although reports on the possession of isolated individuals are commonplace, most cases occur during collective cult performances whenever the eagerly sought emotional lift has reached a high pitch. The audience is shaken by laughter, weeping, shouting, or chanting; some individuals talk in tongues or have visions of "celestial beauty"; some fall down in ecstasy and feel removed to heaven or paradise. God or the angels speak to them, and many return from their trance "full of the spirit of worship, prayer, and love." [7] Thus the charismatic gifts of the Holy Spirit are bestowed upon the faithful through the act of *tomada,* or seizure.

Brazilian spiritualism, in its most sophisticated version, follows the teachings of Allan Kardec. The sessions are attended by groups of faithful who number from five to one hundred.[8] One or several of the participants are mediums who, at the ritual request of the session leader, receive disembodied spirits of various types. "Spirits of the Light" utter advice about a variety of personal problems; promises of help alternate with mild reprehen-

7. W. C. Hoover, *Historia del Avivamiento Pentecostal en Chile* (Valparaiso: Imprenta Excelsior, 1948) , p. 33.
8. Camargo, *op. cit.,* p. 18.

sions which are sometimes administered with "a surprising sense of humor." Unexpected spirits may visit upon a medium, often with the malicious intention of confusing and shocking the participants.[9] The more "enlightened" spirits may offer so-called "passes" through the body of a medium, whose hands, touching head, shoulders and arms of the patient, are believed to communicate "beneficial fluids" facilitating the solution of physical, psychological or moral problems. The therapeutic powers of a medium possessed by a spirit are comparable to those of a Pentecostalist who performs miraculous cures or is cured himself by temporarily partaking of the powers of the Holy Spirit.

Umbanda is to be considered a successful attempt to combine the Macumba, or Brazilian version of voodoo, with some of the basic teachings of Spiritualism.[10] "In the African tradition the *orixá* who is a god, seizes the *Filha do Santo* (daughter of the Saint) whereas the *cavalo* (medium) of the Umbanda is possessed by a disembodied spirit." [11] Each *orixá* commands a vast number of spirits, and the medium, while in trance, becomes the bearer of the spirit's wisdom. The *orixás* are identified with certain Catholic saints. This of course is in contrast to the doctrine of Spiritualism. Thus Umbanda is the outcome of a three-way syncretism associating African, Catholic and Spiritualist elements in one loosely knit body of doctrine which makes allowance for unlimited local variations. To the extent that Umbanda centers engage in purely magical practices, including sorcery, they are called Quimbanda.

THE ROLE OF CULTURED DIFFUSION

None of the three movements originated in Brazil. In spite of an overly indigenous or nativistic approach in doctrine, ritual, and behavior, particularly among the adherents of the Umbanda, there is nothing autochthonous about any of its aspects. African cult forms, variously named Macumba, Candomblé or Xangô, antedated Umbanda syncretism by more than a hundred years.

9. The spirits of Catholic priests belong to this category.

10. Roger Bastide, *Les religions africaines au Brésil* (Paris: Presses Universitaires de France, 1960) , p. 443 ff.

11. Camargo, *op. cit.*, p. 36.

They have been accurately defined as adaptations of African elements transferred to Brazil by slaves. Direct lineal affiliation with these Afro-Catholic phenomena seems restricted, however, to certain urban areas of northeastern and eastern Brazil. In São Paulo, Camargo failed to discover any indication of a cultural continuity between Macumba and Umbanda. Thus the latter is to be considered the result of secondary diffusion, not only in São Paulo, but in other parts of Brazil. Perhaps the most puzzling aspect of Umbanda is its Indian component which is also part and parcel of the Macumba inheritance. Since both Macumba and Umbanda are urban phenomena, it seems extremely unlikely that these "influences" result from contacts with any identifiable Indian culture, not to mention the watered down and highly distorted versions of such indigenous grafts. Again, their presence is attributable to diffusion, probably through the channels provided by the popularization of Brazilian Indianism, a literary movement of the nineteenth century.

The introduction of Spiritualism to Brazil has been traced to the middle of the past century,[12] when Europe was in the grip of a Spiritualist wave whose backwash was powerful enough to reach the Americas. Yet in contrast to most areas of diffusion where it was hardly more than a fad, Spiritualism almost immediately took roots in Brazil, and by 1873 it assumed at least some of the aspects of an organized religion.[13] Amalgamation of Spiritualists and African elements in the Umbanda is relatively recent. To shed some light upon its meaning we shall attempt to interpret it in terms of certain processes of social change.

The largest of the three mass movements, Pentecostalism, can clearly be traced to the proselytic endeavors of two foreign missionaries, Daniel Berg, a Swede who founded the Assembly of God in 1910, and Luis Francescon, an Italo-American who became a Presbyterian in Chicago. A few years later, he was, as he put it, "sealed with the gift of the Holy Spirit," and repeatedly received messages from the Lord who suggested that he dedicate his life

12. Zeus Wantuil, *Las mesas giratorias y el Espiritismo* (Rio de Janeiro, 1958), p. 57.
13. Kloppenburg, *op. cit.*, p. 12.

to missionary work. Under "divine guidance" he went to São Paulo whose large Italian population proved receptive to his preachings. At first his Christian Congregation, founded in 1910, was a sect for Italian immigrants, and all services were conducted in Italian. By 1930, however, it was quite obvious that the Italians were rapidly being assimilated by Brazilian society, and among the native-born generations there were very few who wished to be reminded of the cultural heritage of their parents and grand-parents. Thus guided by opportunity and divine revelation, as are all decisions in this sect, the elders decided in 1935 to drop the Italian language. This well-timed adjustment to a changing cultural situation not only assured survival of the sect but laid the foundations for an increasingly rapid expansion outside São Paulo City and the state of São Paulo.

Recent diffusion of Pentecostalism has been accompanied by a heavy proliferation of new sects, some of which can be traced to the proselytic efforts of American missionaries.

COMPATIBILITY OF THE THREE MOVEMENTS WITH BRAZILIAN FOLK RELIGION

On the surface, the emergence of the three religious movements may be regarded as a break with the Roman Catholic traditions of the country. At the level of Brazilian folk religion, however, their incompatibility with existing beliefs and practices seems open to considerable doubt. In fact, it is our contention that at least part of the surprising vitality of these movements stems from their affinity with certain folk traditions. Folk Catholicism, unlike church-controlled religion, is flexible and unorthodox. In spite of occasional outbreaks of fanaticism, it is basically tolerant and receptive to innovations. The miracle is probably the most frequent source of change within the framework of folk Catholicism. Christ or the Virgin appears to a person; the locale of the vision rapidly becomes a center of miracles and worship and the visionary a thaumaturge or new saint. Folk Catholicism stresses the belief in mystical experiences, in possessions, and in charismatic leadership. A rich historical tradition of messianic movements established numerous precedents for the second coming of Christ taught by many sects.[14] True enough, the Pentecostal sects do not ordinarily announce the second coming of Christ at some future date. Their message contains the far more appealing prospect of an immediate coming of the deity. The repentent believer may expect the descent of the Holy Spirit *here and now* rather than in a distant future. And he comes to the individual rather than dispersively to a group of people. Communion with or seizure by the Spirit is an everyday experience which may be observed whenever the members of congregation gather for religious services. There is nearly always somebody who has visions, speaks in tongues or prophetizes. In fact, we never encountered a practicing Pentecostalist who had not been "baptized" by the Holy Spirit. It would seem that converts who fail to have such an experience withdraw from the congregation after a certain time.

Thaumaturgy or the working of miracles is another powerful tradition of folk Catholicism which the Pentecostal sects incorporated in their body of belief and ritual. There are two ways in which miracles are performed. Seizure by the Spirit is often accompanied by a miracle, in the sense that the person who has been seized by the Spirit finds himself suddenly cured of some "incurable" ailment. Another person, preferably the pastor, who has previously been seized by the Spirit, performs the miracle by touching the patient's head with his hands, or by uttering a prayer over him. Finally, an almost medieval belief in evil spirits, witches and demons of European, Indian or African extraction has been reduced, by the Pentecostals, to possession by the devil. There are a variety of ways in folk Catholicism in which evil spirits including Satan may intervene in human affairs, possession being only one of these. The Pentecostalists admit in their preachings and writings that the devil sometimes seizes a member of the congregation and speaks and acts through his body. Prayer, rather than any specific exocistic ritual, seems to be the defense against such occurrences.

The cult of the Holy Spirit, as practiced by the Pentecostals,

14. For studies of Brazilian messianism see Maria Isaura Pereira de Queiroz, *La guerre sainte au Brésil: Le mouvement messianique du Contestado* (São Paulo: Universidade de São Paulo, Faculdáde de Filosofia, Ciências e Letras. Boletim No. 187, 1957) , p. 1958.

has, of course, a precedent in the *Festa do Divino Espirito Santo*, part of the Iberian heritage and one of high points of the annual round of religious festivals.[15] The rural migrant who joins a Pentecostal sect thus finds himself on familiar ground. Here, an element of his own cultural background is brought back to him in a new and most exciting form.

In contrast to Pentecostalism, Umbanda is, in fact, a folk religion. To the Afro-Catholic tradition of the Macumba were added some of the essentials of Spiritualism to make it more palatable to the slowly rising urban masses and their yearning for middle-class symbols.

Umbanda, as well as Spiritualism, share with the Brazilian folk religion belief in spirits, both good and evil, and the possibility of communicating with or of being possessed by them. And the performances of the mediums, especially their healing powers, suggests considerable affinity with the role of thaumaturgy in folk Catholicism. One could conceivably interpret the continuity of the three movements with Brazilian folk traditions in terms of a pervasive mysticism which seems to constitute a common ground for understanding and emotional involvement.

STRUCTURE

The statement was made initially that the emergence of the three movements generated organizational patterns implying a revolutionary break with the past. To substantiate this assertion, it ought to be emphasized that the Pentecostal sects, Umbanda, and the Spiritualists recruit the bulk of their adherents among the lower social strata. Such organizational spontaneity, however, is out of line with the feudal traditions of Brazilian society.

Within these traditions, the upper classes, supported by the Catholic Church, were supposed to provide, paternalistically, for the material and spiritual needs of the lower classes which were not believed to have the ability to engage in concerted action of their own. On the whole, the lower classes lived up to this expectation which conveniently helped maintain the status quo. Occasionally they demonstrated a surprising and uncalled-for

15. Emilio Willems, "Acculturative Aspects of the Feast of the Holy Ghost in Brazil," *American Anthropologist* (1949), 400–408.

capacity for rallying around a messianic leader and his promises of a better world, but such rebellious endeavors were consistently suppressed whenever they appeared.

Two of these messianic movements produced repercussions far beyond their strictly regional character. Of the two, the movement of Canudos in northeastern Brazil in 1897,[16] bore the marks of a rebellion which made eventual suppression inevitable. But preceding the military campaigns against the rebels, there was a circular letter of the archbishop of Bahia to the parish priests of the region where the new religion had found thousands of adherents. It advised the priests that their parishioners be forbidden to hear the preachings of Antonio Conselheiro, the leader of the rebels.

Seeing that in the Catholic Church the holy mission of indoctrinating the people belongs only to the ministers of religion, it follows that a layman, whoever he may be, and however well instructed and virtuous, does not have the authority to exercise that right.[17]

To understand the social implications of the present mass movements, one has to keep in mind such authoritarian attempts to reassert the religious monopoly of the established church.

The messianic movement of the Contestado in southern Brazil in 1912 might not have led to military intervention by the federal government had it not been for the reaction of a big landowner who felt his power monopoly threatened by the sect.[18]

True enough, the ruling classes of imperial and republican Brazil showed a relatively high degree of tolerance or indifference towards the many distortions and misinterpretations of folk Catholicism as long as these were not projected in organizational forms felt to be incompatible with the established order. Even the *terreiros* or cult centers of the Macumba, Candomblé, and Xangô have been sporadically harassed or suppressed by the police authorities of some Brazilian cities.[19]

16. Euclides da Cunha, *Rebellion in the Backlands* (Chicago: University of Chicago Press, 1944).

17. *Ibid.*, p. 137.

18. Queiroz, *op. cit.*, p. 23.

19. At this point one may raise the question why Protestantism was allowed to develop into ecclesiastical or sectarian structures obviously at variance with the

The Pentecostal sects emerged as "by-products" of the revival-istically oriented Protestant churches. I have presented evidence elsewhere that the rapid growth of these sects is related, in space and in time, to major socio-cultural changes of the last three or four decades. The fact that the occurrence of Spiritualism and Umbanda seems confined to urban centers, particularly to the metropolitan areas of Rio de Janeiro and São Paulo, suggests that these movements are even more closely related to cultural change than is Pentecostalism, which has numerous rural ramifications. At any rate, the rapid development of all three movements seems to proclaim the coming of age of social strata formerly known for their lack of organizational spontaneity. The movements have proved their ability to develop a supernaturalism adapted to their needs and to defy openly, by their mere existence as distinct and antagonistic social aggregates, the traditional social order. Yet the attitude of defiance finds an even stronger expression in the internal organization of the three movements.

Most Brazilian Pentecostal sects are characterized by a pre-carious equilibrium between egalitarianism and charismatic leadership. In the sharpest possible contrast to the Catholic church and the rigid class structure of Brazilian society, the structure of the sects is characterized by the absence of an ecclesiastical hier-archy and by a radical reduction of the social distance between clergy and laity. In principle, the ministry is open to anybody who has scored some success as a missionary, and everybody is expected and encouraged to participate in the proselytizing activities of

---

hierarchical and authoritarian principles of the traditional society. This question cannot be fully answered in the present context. It must suffice here to point out that in many localities Protestant missionaries and their incipient congregations encountered serious opposition, harassment, or even persecution. Toleration or ac-ceptance of Protestantism, particularly in the larger cities, was frequently determined by the fact that some churches had been able to safeguard their own position by winning over members of the middle and upper classes, mostly through the pioneer effort of the Protestant schools. These proved to be highly attractive to the more progressive elements in Brazilian society who were dissatisfied with the obsolescence of the existing school system. And there were also quite a few upper class families, members of which had joined one or two of the more prestige-carrying Protestant churches. Julio Andrade Ferreira, *Historia da Igreja Presbiteriana do Brasil*, (São Paulo: Casa Editôra Presbiteriana, 1959), I, 195–96, and Emile Léonard, "O Protestantismo Brasileiro," *Revista de História*, Ano III, No. 10–11 (São Paulo, 1952) 450–451.

the sect. There is little or no emphasis on theological training, but to have received the gifts of the Spirit, especially his healing powers, ranks high among the qualifications of an aspirant to the ministry. Possession by the Spirit, however, is considered a grace rather than a privilege.

No sect has carried social egalitarianism further than the Christian Congregation. Its position *sui generis* within the Pentecostal movement is characterized by the fact that it minimizes the distinction between laity and clergy almost to the point of obliteration. There are neither bishops nor pastors. The spiritual leadership of the sect is entrusted to a self-perpetuating board of elders "invested with the gifts of the Spirit," meaning that they must have been baptized by the Holy Spirit.

Three requisites are to be fulfilled before a novice may accede to the board. First of all, the choice made by the board must be confirmed by the Holy Spirit. The novice is presented to the assembly of elders who seek illumination by the Spirit in silent prayer. If the choice is confirmed, the novice is "ordained" by the oldest member of the board. Finally, there must be unanimous agreement of the congregation to which the new member belongs. Neither the elders nor their assistants, the deacons, and co-operators, receive salaries or any other form of remuneration. They must even defray the cost of travels which they may be called to make in the interest of the sect.

"Os profissionais da religião estragam tudo" (the professionals of religion ruin everything) , we were told when we asked an elder why there were no salaried pastors. When we remarked that the work of the elders was a full-time job and, consequently, ought to be remunerated to free them from the obligation of earning a living, our informants recoiled in horror, as if we had committed a sacrilege. All elders appeared to have some regular occupation. One was a plumber, another owned a small printing establishment, still others were bricklayers, porters, and railway employees. There was also the co-owner of a large industrial plant who, at the request of his family, seemed to devote most of his time to the sect.

All business affairs of the sect are transacted by a separate board of administrators, but decisions on any level require approval of the elders, deacons, and co-operators. But first of all, the matters to be decided upon "must be presented to the Lord in prayer." In fact, it turned out that, no matter how trifling a decision might appear to an outsider, it is only made after a formal invocation of the Holy Spirit. Even the choice of a biblical passage to be read and commented upon in church is only made after the presiding elder has prayed for inspiration, and no elder would assume pastoral functions during a service without first seeking confirmation by the Spirit.

Unlike other sects we had opportunity to investigate, the Christian Congregation repudiates the idea of a pastoral mandate instituted by ordination and based on the assumption of implicit validity. Much to the contrary, the functionaries of the sect, regardless of rank and merit, must seek divine validation for each individual act they are called to perform. In fact, only the Holy Spirit has the power to make decisions, and the sect's functionaries are mere executors of his revealed will. Thus the Spirit stands for group consensus, and reference to his decisions prevents dissent within the sect.

In the Assembly of God and in most smaller Pentecostal sects, however, there is a structural inconsistency causing the sort of strain and stress which produces cleavages and schisms. On the one hand, the sectarian character of these groups emphasizes, surely as a reaction against the Catholic tradition, egalitarianism and the primacy of the laity, especially in all aspects concerning missionary work. On the other hand, the successful leader who has received more than an ordinary share of graces from the Holy Spirit, is easily held in awe by the faithful. His voice is respected as the voice of God, and if he can add to his other endowments the reputation of a miracle worker—a successful healer, perhaps— there is no limit to the reverence he is accorded by his followers.

Two opposing principles are thus operative in the Pentecostal sects; one is "democratic" and the other "authoritarian." They clash as soon as rival leaders with similar divine endowments arise and accuse the ones in power of misusing their authority or, as they sometimes put it, of "antidemocratic behavior." If the rival is able to sway enough followers, the split occurs and a new sect is born. There is now the Pentecostal Church Brazil for

Christ, the Pentecostal Church of Biblical Revival, the Pentecostal Church Miracle of Jesus, and seven or eight other sects which are almost continuously subdividing or changing their names. The Pentecostals tend to interpret this as an indication of growth rather than of disintegration, and one informant invoked the image of cellular fission which, in fact, defines the process metaphorically. The mother sect, in spite of losing part of its membership, is ordinarily not weakened in the long run and usually continues to grow.

The Pentecostal movement could and did take advantage of certain organizational precedents set by the Protestant churches, but neither Spiritualism nor Umbanda were equipped to absorb the sudden influx of many thousands of new adherents. There was, of course, a proliferation of local centers; but if either movement was to become a sect or church, the development of a large number of small, disconnected cult centers was certainly not the way to achieve that objective. Some means of unification or centralization had to be devised to insure doctrinal and structural coherence.

This proved to be less a problem to the Spiritualists than to the Umbanda. Allan Kardec's interpretation of the Gospel and his numerous other writings provided a body of doctrine in which the Spiritualists found a common denominator. Furthermore, the Brazilian medium, Francisco Candido Xavier, receiving authoritative messages from reputable spirits, validated that doctrine by reinterpreting it in terms which were particularly meaningful and appealing to Brazilians.

Whereas in Europe the Spiritualist idea was only object of observations and laboratory research, or of great and sterile discussions in the field of philosophy, and this in spite of the moral excellency of Kardec's codification, Spiritualism penetrated Brazil with all its characteristics of a Christian revival lifting the souls to a new dawn of the faith. Here, all its institutions rested on love and charity. Even scientific associations which, now and then, appear to cultivate it (Spiritualism) under the label of metapsychology, are absorbed by the Christian program, under the invisible and indirect orientation of the Lord.[20]

20. Francisco Cândido Xavier, *Brasil, coracão do mundo, pátria do Evangelho* (Rio de Janeiro: Federacão Espírita Brasileira, 1938), pp. 177–78.

The book from which these lines were taken, bears the significant title, *Brazil, Heart of the World, Fatherland of the Gospel.* It suggests the pride the national apostle and reinterpreter of European Spiritualism took in converting into a true religion what had been an intellectual hobby in its area of origin.

The foundations were thus laid for a structure which was to congregate thousands of local centers into federations. In 1951 there were already twenty-one federations in different states of Brazil,[21] but they were neither streamlined nor unified, and some of them competed for membership. Most regional federations joined the Brazilian Spiritualist Federation, but some did not. Spiritualist youth organizations began to emerge in 1932, and in 1949 the Youth Department of the Brazilian Spiritualist Federation was established. Its main objective is indoctrination. In São Paulo City, the two largest regional federations maintain a center of social assistance and evangelization which is sought by approximately ten thousand persons every week.[22] Spiritualism's rapid expansion is largely because its effort to solve social problems by providing institutional assistance. The relative position of the Spiritualist movement in this respect may be gleaned from the following comparative table.[23]

Institutions in Brazil, 1958

	Catholic	Protestant	Spiritualists
Hospitals	45	3	25
Clinics	178	56	168
Asylums	56	24	64
Shelters	50	15	104
Schools	1,008	618	435
Others	659	318	919
Total	1,995	1,034	1,715

The structural problems facing the Umbanda are compounded by "its internal dynamics which leads to instability of conceptions and a tendency toward syncretism of all conceivable

21. Kloppenburg, *op. cit.*, p. 16.
22. Camargo, *op. cit.*, p. 28.
23. *Ibid.*, p. 137.

shades." [24] There is no doctrinal or ritual unity; each *terreiro* (cult center) has its own system, and each leader thinks he has the monopoly on the absolute truth. The fiercely defended ritual peculiarities of each *terreiro* seems even more significant if the proliferation of these cult centers is taken into account. In the major areas of Umbanda development—the state of Guanabara and Rio de Janeiro—thirty thousand centers were reported some years ago.[25]

Umbanda is usually referred to as an "African" religion, meaning that, in addition to the presence of African elements in belief and ritual, its membership is composed of colored Brazilians. Although Negro membership looms disproportionally large, Umbanda has attracted too many individuals of non-African background to be classified as a "Negro religion." In São Paulo at least "the whites attend, in large proportions, the *terreiros* and even descendants of Italians, Syrians, and Japanese seek in its practices the magic effectiveness which had not been unknown to them in their countries of origin." [26]

The nature of the leadership prevalent in the Umbanda centers does not easily reconcile itself to the transfer of power to federative associations. In the Umbanda, Bastide writes,

the leader of the session who speaks to the mediums, questions the spirits, drives them away, or commands them, assumes the role of a thaumaturge; in the new sect he takes the place which the *pagé* occupied in Amerindian society, or on the African continent. No longer are the disembodied spirits dominant; it is the magician who becomes the master of the spirits.[27]

Unlike his Spiritualist counterpart, the Umbanda leader appears to be a modern version of the shaman who competes with other shamans for control of the spirit world and those who believe in his powers. He is unlikely to surrender a fraction of his power to a federation, and if he does it is usually external pressure or the impossibility of providing certain expected services which induces him to agree on an uneasy and precarious alliance

24. *Ibid.,* p. 33.
25. Bastide, *op. cit.,* p. 443.
26. Camargo, *op. cit.,* p. 35.
27. Bastide, *op. cit.,* p. 438.

with his competitors. There may be a local chief of police who loses no opportunity to arrest Umbanda leaders for "practicing medicine without a license" or for "breach of the peace." Experiences of this kind may convince the less influential Umbanda leaders of the advisability of joining a federation which has legal ways and means to protect them against high-handed police authorities. Nor is a local *terreiro* in a position to institute the kind of medical and social assistance which larger organizations can and do provide. The most effective and probably the largest organization of this sort is the Spiritualist Federation of Umbanda which claims to control 260 *terreiros* in São Paulo alone.[28]

To understand the structural differences between Umbanda and Pentecostalism, one has to compare the ways in which they have been growing. Like its predecessor, the Macumba, Umbanda has developed by the proliferation of local centers which achieved autonomy long before any central organization existed.

Pentecostalism, however, started with the foundation of sects by schism or secession from established churches. The new sects then set about to win converts by organized missionizing. Successful missionaries would found new congregations which were, in the beginning at least, dependent upon the central organization of the sect. Thus whatever authority or power is located in the individual congregation obviously derived from the sect, whose leaders tend to maintain structural ties with the local congregations.

With its emphasis on local uniqueness, charismatic leadership, and structural priority, the Umbanda proceeded in exactly the opposite way: integration has been possible only to the extent that local leaders have been willing to delegate at least some power to a broader organization.

FUNCTIONS

Healing. To substantiate our contention that the growth of the three movements is explicable in terms of their structural and functional adaptability to the culture of the lower social strata, it must be made clear, in the first place, that the term

28. Camargo, *op. cit.*, p. 53.

"lower strata" is intended to cover, not just the working class, but also the many who have achieved a rather precarious position in the lower ranks of the middle class. They all are beset by a variety of problems caused by the turbulent fashion in which culture change has been taking place during the last three decades. The identification of the three movements with the lower strata does not, by any means, imply identical composition of their membership nor the absence of variations in the social composition of local subdivisions of each movement.

The extent to which the three sects concern themselves with the alleviation of what may broadly be subsumed under the rubric, "physical and mental troubles," clearly indicates one of the areas where certain otherwise unsatisfied needs of the lower strata are met. The traditions of folk medicine with its countless magic components are, of course, very much alive. A steady flow of rural migrants from different regions carries a store of therapeutical magic to the city where a kind of "cross-fertilization" of the medical lore belonging to various subcultures takes place. It is against this background that the people's receptivity to the therapeutics of the Pentecostals, Spiritualists, and Umbandistas should be weighed.

The general inclination to accept, or at least to try out, the prescriptions of a prescientific medicine should be considered with the fact that the masses cannot afford the services of scientific medicine, and the free medical care provided by public and private institutions is highly limited. The constant influx of thousands of rural migrants, many of whom are in need of medical assistance, tends to make even generously planned institutional facilities inadequate within a few years. It is not surprising, therefore, that the prospect of having one's maladies cured constitutes the most powerful attraction of the three movements.

Among the Pentecostals, any leader who demonstrates unusual skill as a miracle healer is likely to draw large crowds. One of the most successful healers, an American missionary of the International Church of the Four-Square Gospel, gained many followers in São Paulo, and when his sect sponsored the National Crusade of Evangelization in 1956, many Protestant groups joined this interdenominational movement. The revival tent was (and still is) used extensively for spontaneous gatherings of the crusade which invaded many regions of Brazil. It seems that the revivalistic atmosphere of the crusade caused many defections among the established churches, and a number of new Pentecostal sects primarily concerned with the mediation of divine healing emerged.

The most conspicuous of new sects is probably the Pentecostal Church Brazil for Christ under Manuel de Mello, a markedly personalistic movement of considerable fluidity. Located in downtown São Paulo, the headquarters of this sect are constantly beseiged by a ragged crowd waiting patiently in line for a prayer or a few words of solace from the thaumaturge. The aspect of the crowd leaves no doubt about the recent rural origin of its components.

The therapeutic functions of Pentecostalism are not limited to individual healing performances; they seem to play a significant role in the broader context of conversion and the radical change of personal habits. Many of our informants associated sickness with vice and conversion with health. The recurrent leitmotif of many life histories volunteered by converts ran like this: "Before my conversion I lived in vice and sin. I was always sick and no doctor could cure me. When I finally accepted the Spirit, my ailment miraculously disappeared and I have enjoyed excellent health ever since." The idea of "rebirth" which is so often associated with religious conversion thus appears to contain a physiological component.

In the Spiritualist and Umbandista centers, equal emphasis is put on healing. Camargo found that more than 60 percent of those who approach either sect are seeking relief from some ailment.[29] In fact, both sects use the therapeutic prospect as a proselytic device.

While the Pentecostal etiology of diseases emphasizes vice or sin as a probable determinant of diseases, Umbanda stresses the notion that nonfulfillment of sacred obligations may arouse the wrath of an *orixá* (African God), who punishes by inflicting illness upon the negligent. An alternative explanation ascribes

29. Camargo, *op. cit.*, p. 94.

physiological or mental troubles to acts of black magic. In either case, magical procedures are prescribed to placate the *orixá* or to undo the effects of sorcery.

The more sophisticated etiology of the Kardecists recognizes the possibility of disembodied spirits causing the symptoms of physical or mental maladies. Such "fluidic" actions are inspired by vengeance, mischief, or simple ignorance on the part of certain spirits. But an illness may also be interpreted as a Karmic tribulation, by means of which a person redeems himself of faults committed in a previous life. A third alternative recognizes inadequate development of mediumistic capabilities as a possible cause of mental perturbation or actual sickness. Negligence or ignorance prevents a person from developing his mediumistic potential; he becomes the victim of forces which he is unable to control, or even to identify.[30] Spiritualism, of course, provides therapeutical resources against such sufferings, but along with the supernatural approach the techniques of homeopathic medicine are available.

Reconstruction of the personal community. Since the lower strata of the metropolitan areas of Brazil are predominantly composed of migrants from rural regions or preindustrial towns, it may be assumed that their endeavor to find a niche in urban society involves adaptive changes of considerable magnitude. Back in his home town or village, the migrant was a member of a highly integrated group of kinsfolk and neighbors who constituted, in the terminology of Jules Henry, his "personal community," or "the group of people on whom he can rely for support and approval." [31]

Usually a man was born into his personal community; he took its structural implications for granted and was consequently unable to anticipate the problems arising from being deprived of its benefits. Although some migrants succeed in rebuilding at least a simulacrum of the lost personal community by joining relatives or people from the same town, most of them suffer from severe cultural shock, leading to such forms of anomic behavior

30. *Ibid.,* p. 100 ff.
31. Jules Henry, "The Personal Community and Its Invariant Properties," *American Anthropologist,* LX (1958), 827.

as are reflected in the life histories of numerous sect members.

The migrant reacts to the novel situation by seeking, mostly by trial and error, a group of people in whose midst he may find emotional affinity and recognition as a person. Among the various alternatives he may choose, the three religious movements rank among the most accessible ones, especially since they compete with each other for new members and actually use proselytic techniques designed to solve personal problems in need of immediate attention. In any of the three movements, particularly in the Pentecostal sects, a person encounters the opportunity to rebuild his personal community.

The typical Pentecostal congregation is a highly cohesive primary group which tends to absorb the newcomer to an extent unmatched by most established churches. No matter how humble, unskilled or uneducated, the individual convert immediately feels that he is needed and relied upon; he is respectfully addressed as "brother," his services are requested by people who speak his own language and share his tastes, worries, and interests, who work with him at the same tasks and share with him the certainty of belonging to the "People of God," as the Pentecostals often call themselves. Whether he belongs to a construction team erecting a new temple or to a group of singing and guitar playing missionaries walking the streets, hospitals, and prisons in search of new converts, the Pentecostalist soon realizes that he belongs, that he is understood, needed and recognized as an equal among equals.

In the mediumistic sects, the participant encounters similar opportunities to rebuild his personal community. But there is one significant difference. Each center, or *terreiro*, is believed to benefit from the regular presence of particular spirits knowledgeable in the affairs of each member, his aspirations, afflictions and hopes, and willing to assist, encourage, admonish or censure him and thus to assume functions which are typically performed by the more influential members of one's personal community. Since the mediumistic religions emphasize the oneness of the "natural" and "supernatural," it seems to make sense to include the spirits among the prominent members of one's personal community.

Symbolic subversion of the traditional power structure. It was previously pointed out that sects seem to rid themselves of those structural elements of Brazilian society which have acted as a source of frustration. By asserting their organizational spontaneity, they have rejected the paternalistic tutelage of the upper strata. They emphasize social equality and thus negate the traditional class structure. "The festive character of the Umbanda means confraternization. In its midst there are neither classes nor castes." [32] They chose a theology which dispenses with the salvation monopoly of the Roman Catholic Church and its priestly hierarchy, which is perceived—rightly or wrongly—as a rampart of the traditional society. Their religious beliefs put the supernatural within the immediate reach of anybody who embraces the new faith.[33]

Yet direct and personal access to the supernatural, either through possession or through contact with those possessed, and vicarious participation in the benefits bestowed upon these by a spirit sets the members of the sects apart from ordinary humanity. The Pentecostalists especially like to think of themselves as the "Chosen People" or the "People of God." Possession by the Holy Spirit is interpreted as a legitimization of such privileged status. The sect members are, without exception, actual or potential recipients of the "Powers of the Spirit." The first seizure of "baptism by the Spirit," which a Pentecostalist seeks as anxiously as a Plains Indian seeks his vision, puts a seal of divine approval on the individual. By renouncing "the world" through repentance and adoption of an ascetic way of life one merits these extraordinary powers, which obviously contrast to the situation of powerlessness in which the Pentecostalists find themselves, individually and as members of a social class. The prevalent criteria of class differentiation, such as wealth, family background, education, and occupation, are ignored and often deprecated as manifestations of sinful *mundanismo,* or worldliness. Since the Pentecostalists as a class are not allowed by the "world" to attain distinction in any of these aspects, their valid-

---

32. Emanuel Zespo, *Codificacão da lei de Umbanda* (2nd. ed.; Rio de Janeiro: Editôra Espititualista Ltda., 1950), p. 147.

33. Some of these traits the sects share with the established Protestant churches.

ity is altogether denied. In a sense, this is subversion of the traditional or emerging social order in the language of religious symbolism.

Exactly what are these "powers of the Spirit" which confer special status on the Pentecostalists? In addition to thaumaturgy, spiritual illumination, persuasion, prophetizing and glossolalia are the most treasured graces accessible to the convert. Illumination, variously called *discernimento* (discernment) or *alta percepção interior* (high internal perception), enables the Pentecostalist to recognize and understand the truth, and the power of *persuasão* transforms him into a fearless and convincing missionary who finds himself under an almost irresistible compulsion to disseminate the Word of God.

Speaking in tongues and prophetizing constitute perhaps the most respected and admired powers conferred by the Holy Spirit. To be sure, there is considerable confusion among the Pentecostal sects concerning the nature and intelligibility of the tongues spoken by a person who is being seized by the Spirit. The tongue is sometimes believed to be a foreign language unbeknownst to the speaker except during the seizure. More common, however, seems to be the belief that a "tongue" is no common language but a special idiom through which the Holy Spirit conveys messages to the congregation or certain of its members.

When the speaker in tongues proffers his message in a trance-like state, he may not remember his utterances or that he has said anything at all. In this case, a prophet who has heard the message may translate its content to the congregation, if it is believed to have some edifying value. The intimate association of the two powers—glossolalia and prophetizing—is also expressed by the fact that the prophet often uses tongues to communicate his inspirations which, in some sects at least, are believed to come directly from God.

The social significance of the powers of the Spirit thus relates to the internal structure of the Pentecostal sects as well as to their position in the society at large.

The unequal distribution of these powers among the members of a sect opens up avenues of social mobility ordinarily denied to the Pentecostalists as members of an underprivileged class. The larger the share of such powers, the more likely it seems that the recipient will make his way to the top of the sectarian structure.

Bestowal of the powers of the Spirit upon the members of the Pentecostal sects acts as a compensatory mechanism for the frustrations inflicted by being deprived of actual power within Brazilian society. Or, to repeat the interpretation by Walter Goldschmidt:

The appeal of the emotional religion and the asceticism for the disfranchised is this: It denies the existence of this world with its woes. *It denies the values in terms in which they are the underprivileged and sets up in their stead a putative society* in the kingdom of God, where, because of their special endowments (which we call emotionalism) they are the elite. It is the society of the saved. Milleniarism is of the essence, for it is thus that the putative society is created; asceticism is the denial of the world in which they have been denied; and emotional participation is public acclamation of their personal acceptance into this world of super-reality.[34]

Similarly, the mediumistic abilities of the Spiritualists and Umbandistas confer a sense of power and achievement on both the mediums and those who are allowed to enter into personal communication with the spirit world through their mediums. A compensatory mechanism is put into motion when "meek public employees and humble domestic servants are suddenly transformed in vehicles of illuminated spirits, bearers of sublime message."[35] It has been pointed out that Spiritualists have indeed a moral obligation to develop their mediumistic capabilities or face the supernatural sanctions threatening those who have been remiss of their duty to acquire firsthand contact with the spirit world. Such emphasis tends to make available spirit possession to the largest possible number of adherents.

The Spiritualists invoke spirits, often the spirits of famous departed that are believed to have reached superior levels of perfection. Contact with such reputable spirits, particularly the per-

34. Walter R. Goldschmidt, "Class Denominationalism in Rural California Churches," *American Journal of Sociology*, XLIX (1944), 354.
35. Camargo, *op. cit.*, p. 125.

sonal interest which these take in one's affairs, contributes to ego enhancement.

While the Kardecists unequivocally seek the association of spirits that during their lifetime had achieved distinction and high status, Umbanda doctrine embodies contradictory elements suggesting a more devious approach to the spirit world and its structural interpretation. As pointed out before, Macumba rid itself of its socially most undesirable associations with low-ranking African cult elements to the extent that it became Umbanda, i.e., by adopting certain elements of Spiritualism.

Spiritualism becomes the idiom into which the phenomena of mystic trance are translated, and this idiom, accepted by the savants, studied by metapsychology, gives the African the assurance that his experience is no longer an experience of barbarians, or primitives, but that this experience has human rather than racial value.[36]

Thus the integration of Spiritualist principles gained increased social recognition for Umbanda and doubtlessly enhanced the self-image of its colored membership. The fact that some Brazilians of higher social strata were attracted by its rituals meant, of course, protection from its enemies and implicit transfer of power to the leaders of major *terreiros* who were no longer at the mercy of police officers and local politicians eager to capitalize on the reactions of the sect's opponents. And

adherence of the white civil servant, business man, or industrialist to Umbanda assumes, in the eyes of the Negro, the meaning of a reversal of values; no longer is the Caboclo, the savage, nor the African the slave, subject to all kinds of whims of the whites; they have become the gods of the new religion and the former master bends his head humbly to them.[37]

To lend more credibility to this interpretation, it ought to be added that spirits of slaves as well as those of former masters often appear in sessions attended by colored people. Invariably, the audience learns that the spirits of the slaves have already reached the higher levels of perfection, while their masters are still tormented by the illusion of being incarnated. They carry

36. Bastide, *op. cit.*, p. 432.
37. Bastide, *op. cit.*, pp. 467–468.

heavy chains and need all the charity and patience of mediums and guides to take their first steps on the narrow path of spiritual ascent.[38]

The adherents of the Umbanda are derided by the Kardecists for invoking the "inferior" spirits of "Caboclos" and "old Negroes." But the Caboclos and old Negroes stand for the Indian and African ancestors of the Umbandistas, and the vindication of high status for such spirits seems quite consistent with the desire to subvert the traditional social order and its value system. Since this subversion cannot be carried out in reality, it is transferred to the spirit world, where the Indians and the Africans occupy higher levels of spiritual perfection, and the class of the "masters" is relegated to the lower levels. In a broader sense, Umbanda may be interpreted as a manifestation of Brazilian nationalism, inasmuch as it emphasizes and thus validates the Indian and African heritage of the lower social strata.[39]

The emphasis placed upon the therapeutical and social functions of the three religious movements is not intended to reduce their religious significance to the point of obliteration. Much on the contrary, the extraordinary degree to which the lifeways of these people are pervaded by religious representations and norms—quite in accord with the sacredness of their cultural tradition—provides the atmosphere of mystical belief in which the spirits associate with man in an effort to build a better society, without the inequities and maladies that afflict its actual counterpart. In a more secularized frame of mind, the sects would probably cease to perform the functions which now constitute their main attractions. The success story of the three movements makes sense only when related to the context of sacred folk traditions caught in the turmoil of profound and rapid cultural change.

SUMMARY

There are now between four and five million people involved in what may be considered the largest religious mass movement in the history of Brazil, perhaps of Latin America. In the first

38. Camargo, op. cit., p. 125.
39. Bastide, op. cit., p. 468.

place, there is the rapid growth of Protestantism; but within Protestantism the characteristics of a mass movement proper apply primarily to the Pentecostal sects, whose combined membership is now in the neighborhood of two million.

The second largest movement comprises the various sect-like organizations which embraced the creed and practice of Spiritualism. Partially overlapping with Spiritualism there are some large cult groups, for example the Umbanda, whose doctrinal contents feed upon African elements which have been perpetuated by institutions such as Macumba, Candomblé, and Xangô.

The concomitance of these movements with socio-cultural change is, of course, more than mere coincidence. This chapter is intended to examine the relationships between the general process of culture change and the role and functions of these movements.

BIBLIOGRAPHY

Anuário Estatístico do Brazil. Rio de Janeiro, Brasil: Conselho Nacional de Estatística, 1958.

Bastide, Roger. *Les religions africaines au Bresil.* Paris: Presses Universitaires de France, 1960.

Braga, Erasmo and Grubb, Kenneth G. *The Republic of Brazil: A Survey of the Religious Situation.* London, New York and Toronto: World Dominion Press, 1932.

Camargo, Candido Procopio Ferreira de. *Kardecismo e Umbanda.* São Paulo, Livraria Pioneira Editôra, 1961.

Cunha, Euclides de. *Rebellion in the Backlands.* Chicago: University of Chicago Press, 1944.

Damboriena, Prudencio. *El protestantismo en América Latina,* Vol. I. Friburgo y Bogotá: Oficina Internacional de Investigaciones Sociales de FERES, 1963.

Ferreira, Julio Andrade. *História da Igreja Presbiteriana do Brasil,* Vol. I. São Paulo: Casa Editôra Presbiteriana, 1959.

Goldschmidt, Walter R. "Class Denominationalism in Rural California Churches." *American Journal of Sociology,* XLIX (1944), 348–355.

Henry, Jules. "The Personal Community and Its Invariant Properties." *American Anthropologist,* 60 (1958), 827–831.

Hoover, W. C. *Historia del Avivamiento Pentecostal en Chile.* Valparaiso: Imprenta Excelsior, 1948.

KLOPPENBURG, BUENAVENTURA. "Introducción Histórica" in Candido Procopio de Camargo, *Aspectos sociológicos del espiritismo en São Paulo*. Friburgo y Bogotá: Oficina Internacional de Investigaciones Sociales de FERES, 1961.

LÉONARD, EMILE. "O Protestantismo Brasileiro," Revista de História, Ano III, No. 10-11 (1952), São Paulo.

QUEIROZ, MARIA ISAURA PEREIRA DE. *La guerre sainte au Brésil: Le mouvement messianique du Contestado*. São Paulo: Universidade de São Paulo, Faculdade de Filosofia, Ciências e Letras. Boletim No. 187.

WANTUIL, ZÊUS. *Las mesas giratórias y el Espiritismo*. Rio de Janeiro, 1958.

WILLEMS, EMILIO. "Acculturative Aspects of the Feast of the Holy Ghost in Brazil." *American Anthropologist* (1953), 400-408.

XAVIER, FRANCISCO CANDIDO. *Brasil, coracão do mundo, pátria do Evangelho*. Rio de Janeiro, Federacão Espírita Brasileira, 1938.

ZESPO, EMANUEL. *Codificacão da lei de Umbanda*. Second edition. Rio de Janeiro: Editôra Espititualista Ltda., 1960.

9/ A PSYCHOLOGIST REFLECTS ON BRAZIL AND BRAZILIANS BY JOHN F. SANTOS

Discussions of Brazil and Brazil's problems have been a rather popular undertaking in recent years. But such discussions tend to neglect a most important factor—the Brazilian himself.

Talking with Brazilians, one quickly realizes that they perceive the nature of the problems—and the solutions—quite differently from the way in which, for example, Americans perceive it. Also, opinions differ among the various regions of the country, even within a given family. Certainly the people of São Paulo, Belo Horizonte, Rio de Janeiro, Porto Alegre, or Salvador and those of the interior show sectional influences in their opinions and attitudes toward national problems, as well as in their temperaments, ways of life, and styles of behavior.

Presenting an analysis of any group in the short space of one chapter, with little more than impressions and opinions to rely upon, obviously leaves something to be desired. But relatively little quantitative data is available on the psychological characteristics of contemporary Brazilians.

A wealth of general observations is offered, however, in the writings of the great Brazilian social historian Gilberto Freyre and in the works of Fernando de Azevedo, Clodomir Vianna Moog, and Paulo Prado, to mention just a few (please see bibliography). Especially interesting is a book by Dante Moreira Leite, *Caráter nacional brasileiro,* in which he summarized much of the Brazilian literature on national character and also reported some of his findings on Brazilian opinions about themselves and other national groups.

Any attempt to "explain" a group of people as varied and complex as Brazilians poses the very practical problem of where to begin and which characteristics to discuss. Since all of the important characteristics cannot be covered, only the more obvious ones that usually impress the foreigner and are probably most responsible for his attitudes and opinions about Brazil and Brazilians will be considered. There are, of course, many more subtle factors and considerations that only the Brazilian or the "Brazilianized" foreigner can appreciate or even recognize.

In addition, it is difficult if not impossible to observe any phenomenon, any individual or group of people in an entirely objective manner. Cultural conditioning of the perceptual and thought processes undoubtedly produces unique distortions, selection, exaggerations and insensitivities that can at best be only partially overcome. Certain problems and characteristics regarded as very important within a given culture may be de-emphasized or completely ignored by another group. It is not at all uncommon to observe long and heated discussions between people of different socio-cultural backgrounds, the final outcome of which is that the "other" person is seen as failing to take into account the most important factors.

The comments, observations, and analyses that will follow do not intend to evaluate Brazilian characteristics as good or bad, superior or inferior, nor to indulge in point-by-point comparisons of Brazilian behavioral characteristics with those found in the United States or other Latin American countries. On the other hand, there was no great compulsion to *avoid* comparisons which might be useful or interesting, and admittedly some biases have probably crept in inadvertently. More critical opinions about Brazil were voiced by Brazilians to the writer than appear here, and stronger opinions about Americans were expressed than the writer has ventured here about Brazilians. At any rate, to imply that *we* are invariably right, effective and superior and that *they* are invariably wrong, ineffective and inferior is just as rigid and unrealistic as the opposite point of view. It might be said more realistically that they are more adept in coping with certain types of problems and that we are more successful in dealing with others. At least a partial explanation for the difference in effectiveness of the two groups may well be found in their characteristic perceptual and cognitive "styles," in their systems of attitudes and beliefs and in their methods of coping with problems. Beyond these differences there are, of course, many characteristics that Brazilians and Americans have in common, and perhaps these have been given insufficient attention in the past, as well as in this chapter.

An attempt will be made here to relate some aspects of Brazilian behavior to the social system and to speculate on why the system elicits this behavior, which in turn influences the system and other members of the group, both narrowly and broadly defined.

A WAY OF LIFE

The realities of life in Brazil certainly do not encourage confidence. They seem more likely to inspire a sense of helplessness. For the Brazilian, it becomes a necessary mode of adaptation to play the game, to accept the frustration and ambiguity of the system, and to hope for the best. Moog has proposed an interesting explanation of how this sense of helplessness has affected the Brazilian and conditioned his thinking in terms of the *jeito*.[1] Confronted as they were by the awesome obstacles of mountains, jungles, and vast distances, Moog suggests that the dominant reaction of Brazilians was that of terror—a cosmic terror that he feels has been passed down through generations and persists today. The tortuously slow progress—all that was possible against this awesome nature—certainly did not inspire any feelings of pantheistic order or immediate mastery; it was conducive, rather, to the acceptance of inevitable reversals and detours, and it encouraged general vigilance, distrust and opportunism. The *jeito* and the emphasis upon skills in the ways of life and the intricacies of the system may thus be explained as a carry-over from adapta-

1. Clodomir Vianna Moog, *Bandeirantes and Pioneers,* trans. L. L. Barrett (New York: George Braziller, 1964) , p. 223. Vianna Moog refers to the *jeito* as "the famous Brazilian 'way' (means, order, twist, skill, propensity, and so forth) of doing things —'Let's find a *jeito*,' or 'We have to find the *jeito*,' the best way of getting something done—which the foreigner never quite succeeds in comprehending, a sign that the word *jeito*, with no exactly corresponding term in the principal Western tongues, fills a necessity of expression peculiar only to Brazilians and not to other peoples."

tion patterns developed in the past to cope with the physical environment.

Perhaps the most important characteristics of the *jeito* is the subtle bypassing of the system through the mechanism of mere "formal" satisfaction of rules and regulations. The behavior that first arises from the need to deal with the system may, however, become self-reinforcing and undergo further development and elaboration at least partially independent of past or present needs. Mastery of the system and the satisfaction of accomplishment do not, therefore, ordinarily seem to necessitate dealing with the system directly or bringing about changes in its structure or function. The real problems may remain untouched, unchanged and forgotten.

The longer one copes with the demands of life in Brazil, the more he becomes aware of the rules of the game, and what first seems to be lost motion and unnecessary gestures eventually becomes a natural way of getting things done. In developing skill in the art of the *jeito,* the adept foreigner often begins to feel a certain amount of appreciation for, and even pleasure in, its execution. But foreigners are almost inevitably amazed and confused by the number and complexity of rituals that must be fulfilled before even relatively simple things can be accomplished. While Brazilians are quite helpful and eager to lead the way through the morass of rituals, they also seem to take more than a little delight and satisfaction in remaining calm while the foreigner fumes and despairs in the process. There are, however, undeniable limits to the Brazilian's great tolerance for frustration. Careful observation of his reactions in a variety of situations suggests that a great deal of the frustration is discharged in such behavior as aggressive driving and the mass emotional orgies of Carnaval and the football games. It is not at all strange that the latter two are so important to so many Brazilians, and it is probably well that they continue to provide the occasions for such outlets.

INVOLVEMENT IN THE SELF, THE COMMUNITY, AND THE COUNTRY

It is important to consider competitiveness in understanding Brazilian behavior. There is a casualness about work, responsibility, and ambition and a joy in personal contact and good fellowship, but there is also an obvious determination to take care of one's self because no one else will. The constant threat to financial security created by the inflation, combined with the lack of social agencies, may be largely responsible. This does not imply that Brazilians are devoid of co-operativeness and social consciousness, but in adjusting to difficult and unstable conditions they have become necessarily accustomed to depending upon few people and have been hardened to misfortune and poverty. Interestingly enough, they often use social agencies for the poor and needy in the United States as examples of the impersonal American way of life. Brazilians prefer to give personally. This attitude is probably somewhat related to the lack of effective programs of aid for the mentally and physically ill, orphans, and illiterates. The *Nordestinos* that flood into São Paulo day after day have created tremendous problems for the city, the police, and the few social agencies that do exist, but so far as it is possible to tell, relatively little has been done to help these people now or to plan for future solutions. Again, a circumvention of problems is suggested along with a lack of involvement in the difficulties of others. Implied is the hope that God and his favorite children, the Brazilians, will find a way, without need for excessive effort and sacrifice.

The Brazilian is, therefore, principally concerned with his own and his family's happiness and well-being, whereas Americans seem more concerned with the problems and welfare of larger groups. The Brazilian realizes that he cannot solve all of the problems, so he doesn't expend any appreciable amount of energy trying to do so. He accepts the reality of the situation as he sees it and goes about taking care of himself as best he can, while he overlooks, de-emphasizes or forgets the problems of others. The American, on the other hand, seems to think that he can solve all problems, or that he would certainly like to try. He therefore becomes indirectly involved in many problems, some of which he doesn't even understand. In the process of attacking insoluble problems, the American on occasions may increase somewhat the likelihood that changes will be made and progress will result, regardless of how naive or misguided his actions may be; he may also create problems that weren't there before he offered his "help," or he may make already bad problems worse than they were. The Brazilian often appears overwhelmed by the magnitude of the problem. He decides, without trying and without guilt feelings, that it can't be solved.

Everything said thus far might indicate that Brazilians are not self-critical people. This is not the case. Brazilians are most critical of themselves, their products, their government and just about anything Brazilian. To be sure, they have much to make them critical, but there has been progress even though slow, and much more can be expected in the future if care is taken to see that important things are done. Certainly products have improved both in quality and quantity, but even when real progress is made in Brazil, the Brazilians remain the most difficult people to convince.

This is a very self-defeating attitude, and even in proclaiming national pride Brazilians' boasts are not always convincing. Foreign goods and foreign lands, are obviously preferred, as indicated by the buying habits of Brazilians and their eagerness to visit foreign countries. The preference for foreign goods often causes them to overlook national products comparable in quality and workmanship. Much of this attitude has developed because products newly on the market have understandably been poor in quality and have not always improved as rapidly as they should have. But, for better or for worse, the opinion has been formed, and being strong and definite in their likes and dislikes, Brazilians tend to stick by their opinions regardless of changes or improvements. Probably because they have had access to so little power or pressure to use on government or producers, they have had to express their feelings of frustration and hostility solely through verbal criticism, stylistic noninvolvement and ritualistic distance.

The reluctance of Brazilians to invest financially in the future of their country might well be related to their limited range of involvement and concern and to their lack of confidence in the country and its destiny. This has probably led to an unawareness or disregard for opportunities in Brazil that have been recognized by some foreigners anxious to move in with the capital and initiative lacking within the country. Perhaps the lack of confidence is fostered by too much knowledge of the system and its difficulties and a fatalism toward the chances of doing anything with it. Despite (perhaps because of) their lack of complete familiarity with the intricacies of the system, some foreigners have occasionally overcome or outmanuevered it and have capitalized on their success in grand fashion. There are undoubtedly many other psychological and economic factors in this process, but it is interesting to speculate on those just mentioned as predisposing conditions for the large number of successful business enterprises in Brazil that have been initiated by foreigners.

THE INTERPERSONAL REALITY

A great deal has been written and said about the friendliness and hospitality of Brazilians. This description, however, is somewhat oversimplified. The friendliness of Brazilians is somewhat comparable to that of Southerners in the United States. It is at first extremely difficult to know just how deep it goes. There are also great regional variations.[2] Certainly the friendliness encountered in Rio, where much time and effort are devoted to good fellowship, is different from the relatively brusque treatment characteristic of the busy, bustling city of São Paulo. The description of Brazilians as joyous, happy, smiling souls is more appropriate to Rio during Carnaval than to Lapa during the Feast of Bom Jesus or to Pôrto Alegre. It is a very biased "view from the Copacabana" and does not represent a true picture of what can be expected in many parts of the country. There is warm friendliness in the interior, to be sure, but superimposed upon it is a shyness not immediately penetrable. Foreigners who have lived for some time in the interior almost invariably find friendliness and courtesy, even in the poorest homes, once the initial shyness has been overcome. Certainly better treatment and consideration

2. *Ibid.*, pp. 223–224. Vianna Moog proposes that Brazilian politeness and courtesy vary as a function of the relative degree of mastery of nature attained within any given region. In the states of Amazonas, Minas Gerais, and Para, where this mastery has been slight and cosmic terror is great, politeness and courtesy are the rule, whereas in Rio Grande do Sul and São Paulo, where nature has been dealt with more effectively, the cosmic terror has subsided or has been overcome and less sociability exists. While this explanation has many intriguing features, it would not seem to apply in such cases as the city of Rio, where a lack of cosmic terror and highly developed social graces go hand-in-hand.

can be expected in the outlying areas where foreigners are a novelty than in the large cities where they are not. Any indications of prestige will usually bring invitations that are difficult if not impossible to refuse from the local officials and other persons of importance.

With some regional variations, interpersonal contact is generally easy and warm. Beyond the initial contact, however, some difficulty is encountered in developing a close relationship with individuals—more so with whole families. The family is a very tightly knit unit, especially in the interior, and the center of activities, including entertainment. Having a close friendship with a member of a family is one thing; being invited into family activities and accepted therein is quite another thing. But while gaining entrance into the family group is certainly not easy, once the breach has been made and the circle has been entered, the warmth and acceptance found there are truly gratifying.

More than a fear of thieves probably prompts Brazilians to build high walls around their homes. The walls are indications of a strong desire to protect privacy and to maintain the separateness of family units. Much of Brazilian life takes place within those walls, and for the most part only the family knows about it. There is very much of the "I-you, we-they" attitude. In a very real sense, the extension of the self is narrowly confined, extending primarily to the immediate family and a core of close friends but dropping off sharply beyond this restricted range. This, of course, is not unique to Brazilians, but the sharpness of the separation is somewhat unusual. It is not to say that there is not an awareness of community or national affairs or a lack of knowledge about international affairs in the large cities. Rather, there is a sharp decrement in the investment of energy, emotion and concern beyond the self, the family and the close circle of friends. This is strikingly different from American society, where closer ties often seem to develop between neighbors and friends than among members of a family. Another indication of these differences in the strength of family ties is the greater tendency of Americans to move away from the family home and to live beyond the reach of family influence. It would be interesting to know how family members in the two cultures would react to the same magnitude of threat to the family group. While it would undoubtedly be a cause for concern in both cases, it might be expected that the emotion generated by the threat to the Brazilian family would be considerably greater than that for Americans, whereas this would be reversed in the case of a threat to the larger community.

There are other differences between Brazilians and Americans. Diaz-Guerrero makes an interesting comparison of Latin and North Americans.[3] He proposes that North Americans tend to view external reality as something to be subjected to their will. He suggests that the success of American technology, for example, is an indication of this orientation. Latin Americans, by contrast, take a more fatalistic attitude toward nature and feel subjected to it. They have thus done relatively little to bring external reality under their control. In dealing with interpersonal reality, however, North Americans assume a more static state of affairs than do Latin Americans. To the Latin American, the interpersonal situation is very attractive and extremely fluid because two individuals are involved and both may act upon it. Interpersonal interactions are evaluated on the basis of the immediate pleasure and satisfaction that they bring. Diaz-Guerrero points out that because of this the Latin American would rather lose an argument than a friend, whereas the North American prefers to win the arguments. Brazilians in particular seem to move into interpersonal contact with more ease and gusto than do Americans. Americans, in fact, are often somewhat uneasy and uncomfortable, at least initially, with the open and intense emotionality of Brazilians. It would be interesting, therefore, to compare the degree of involvement that is possible between friends in the two cultures in firmly established relationship.

Further, Americans seem to show a strong tendency to become involved in community problems, social movements, and in the rights and problems of the underdog. They are apparently much more comfortable helping groups of people at some emotional and geographic distance than individuals in some close

3. Rogelio Diaz-Guerrero, "Mexican Assumptions about Interpersonal Relations," address delivered to the International Conference on General Semantics Mexico City, August 24-27, 1958.

involvement or interaction. They are even capable of extending their concern to the general well-being of animals. Very little of this exists in Brazil; at least, it certainly is not in great evidence. Brazilians lack enthusiasm for involvement at a distance and probably because of this have great difficulty in understanding certain aspects of American behavior. To the Brazilian, involvement at a distance is simply not direct and meaningful enough. While this is obviously not an all-or-none matter on either side, it does represent a relevant dimension upon which the two groups may be compared and by which some of their differences in behavior may be better understood.

A discussion of human relations leads appropriately to a consideration of promises and their function in the interpersonal situation. Schlesinger has discussed the original nature of promising as an act of magic, complete in itself, which eventually should give way to an appreciation of promising as a prelude to a later act of keeping the promise. He points out that maturity in thinking is not always completely achieved, so that the remnants of childhood thinking are to be found in many adults. He further mentions the cultural variation of promising as an act of courtesy in which individuals will promise anything with no intention or capability of carrying it out.[4]

This is quite relevant to the situation in Brazil, where the promise is a quick, natural and easy gesture. It is often made in the fervor or stress of the moment, in an eagerness to say the polite thing at the right time; but these promises so easily made are just as easily forgotten. To say that the gesture is insincere or meaningless would do an injustice to the personal involvement that Brazilians experience in interpersonal contact. It is the gesture that is important, the warmth and friendliness generated in the interpersonal encounter, the joy and satisfaction derived by both of the parties playing the "let's-be-friends" game. The details of what is said, and their projection into the future, place the emphasis where it should not be and detract from an appreciation of the experience of the contact. Undoubtedly a sense of em-

4. Herbert Schlesinger, "A Contribution to a Theory of Promising: Primary and Secondary Promising," address delivered to Topeka Psychoanalytic Association, June 1960.

barrassment in not being able to help and an unwillingness to admit this are also involved. The promise thus serves to protect the self as well as the other person because it preserves the cordiality of the situation. The naive foreigner, operating on assumptions derived from another culture, who accepts the promise with the expectation of future action is usually disappointed. He may also lose considerable time and often his faith in the sincerity of Brazilians. However, just at the point when he concludes that they cannot be expected to keep a promise, they may do so and retain a consistent course of unpredictability. There are undoubtedly certain principles which govern this behavior, but to the uninitiated they seem very vague and ambiguous and present difficult problems in adapting to the culture and in coping with reality in the Brazilian context.

Brazilians rarely turn a beggar away from the house without food or money or fail to give alms when asked by beggars on the street. This constitutes another interesting facet of Brazilian behavior. If the master of the house is away or refuses for some reason to give to the beggar, one of the maids will usually dig into her own modest daily salary to give something. This behavior often seems to be accompanied by a fear that bad luck will follow if this is not done. In the case of an especially wretched, sick or wild-looking beggar, the giving of alms is often followed by considerable blessing of one's self and the reciting of appropriate prayers. The ritual of giving to beggars does not appear to be prompted primarily by feelings of guilt or charity, although it undoubtedly has some basis in the religious background of the people. It may be one symptom of the anxiety produced by the extremely competitive circumstances of life in Brazil and the uncertainty produced by inflation and crises. Should luck run out and misfortune and hardship result, it is nice to be able to expect alms from those who are more fortunate, since the system offers little else in the way of protection.

The response of Brazilians to persons in other types of dire circumstances is in many ways similar to the sort of thing that has caused a great deal of concern recently in large cities in the United States. For instance, people may become ill and die in public without receiving help from passersby. As in other Latin-American countries, of course, giving aid under such circumstances can create many problems with the authorities for the Good Samaritan. In Brazil this detachment is not peculiar to the big city but seems to be more widespread. The big-city dweller in the United States, intent upon his own problems and his own business, bustles about in such a way as to give an impression of disinterest in others, but the Brazilian's quick reaction to personal contact and social interaction suggests a greater warmth and concern for others. Common to both, however, is a highly competitive way of life which necessitates the development of self-oriented attitudes and a sense of responsibility extending to the self, the immediate family, and close friends, but little beyond this.

SEX ROLES AND THE FAMILY

The roles of men and women in Brazilian society are obviously undergoing some important changes. This is not to say that the position of women is equal to that of men, but compared with other Latin-American countries the situation is relatively equitable and is improving. It is generally quite acceptable for women to acquire an education, even though their intentions are questioned more severely than those of men and their interest and dedication to academic pursuits is often depreciated. It is also acceptable for women to aspire to professional degrees. It does not seem especially demoralizing to the male students in a class for a woman to make the highest grades, and the demonstration of excellence in academics does not necessarily brand the girl as masculine and prompt the questioning of her femininity to the degree that it does elsewhere in Latin America.[5]

There is not the degree of *machismo* that Diaz-Guerrero describes as so characteristic of Mexican males.[6] The typical Brazilian casualness thus prevails, even in "tests" of masculinity. The lack of deep concern for such matters is indicated by the joke about the man who was insulted by a stranger and was urged by a friend to defend his honor. He refused and when his friend asked,

5. Rogelio Diaz-Guerrero, "Neurosis and the American Family Structure," *American Journal of Psychiatry* (1955), 112, 411-417.
6. *Ibid.*

"You're a man, aren't you?" the man replied, "Yes, but not fanatically so."

There are undoubtedly some regional differences in the roles of men and women and also some between the large cities and the interior. In the interior it is not at all uncommon to be invited to dinner and, after brief introductions, for the wife to retire to the kitchen to supervise the serving of the meal and not to appear again to intrude on the men's affairs. It is also difficult to forget the experience of passing a family on a cold, rainy day in the southern part of Brazil and seeing the father and boy child riding on the family horse with a greatcoat covering them while the shoeless mother and girl children plodded along behind.

Certainly the freedom of women is much more restricted than that of men in the middle and upper classes. It is generally acceptable for men to be quite friendly with women, but the girl friend or wife is not expected to show even the slightest interest in other males. Among the university students, when a young man is rumored to be interested in a young lady other young men tend to avoid her, even in the most innocent and casual of contacts. It is also advisable to be cautious about joking with married women, even in a large group, because the aftermath may be unpleasant for her.

Brazilian women have developed the art of being feminine to a very high degree. They are attractive, they know it, and they want others to know it and appreciate it. They obviously know their role and seem to have relatively little ambivalence about accepting it. The Brazilian woman evidently wields her influence in much more subtle ways than does the American woman. There is apparently less mutual threat between men and women in Brazil than in the United States because of the negligible overlap of roles and the more clear-cut lines of both male and female authority. At the present time, Brazilian women are becoming more interested in equal rights, but they also seem somewhat unwilling to give up the security of their present feminine role. They do not understand nor do they seem to desire the American type of relationship between husband and wife in which they see the woman as overbearing and the man as ineffectual.

The success of Brazilian women as wives and mothers may

well be related to the high degree to which they have developed their femininity and accept the woman's role. They certainly seem tolerant, even appreciative, of masculine dominance and the man's need for attention and authority. Men are generally not regarded as the good-hearted but inept bumblers that they often are in this country. Wives seem to run rather well-organized homes without being overly obsessed with the need to be spick and span. Their housekeeping skills are difficult to assess, because Brazilian women usually have help in their household chores in the form of servants, relatives or children. They can tolerate a great deal of the noise, disorganization, and confusion inevitably generated by children's play without becoming upset or unnecessarily restrictive. Of course, the fact that they usually have help probably makes it easier for them to be more casual about this than the American woman who ordinarily can depend only upon her gadgets and household service agencies for aid. These are very helpful, but they do not solve the problem of coping with active, playful children. For the Brazilian woman (if she is able to pay) the solution comes in the form of a servant who may only take care of the children or do this in addition to part or all of the other household duties. In contrast to American women, who have learned to get along without maids and seem to feel uncomfortable, apologetic and guilty about having them, Brazilian women are more at ease with servants than with the gadgets which will eventually have to take their place. They cannot quite bring themselves to believe that American women could possibly prefer to handle most of the household chores with help only from gadgets and businesses that specialize in services to the housewife. In the large cities, at least, they are becoming aware of the fact that this will also happen to them, but they cannot yet bring themselves to look forward to the day.

So far as love and courtship are concerned, there is presently no Brazilian Kinsey Report, nor is there likely to be one for some time. It is somehow difficult to imagine Brazilians giving that kind of highly personal information to an interviewer, even for purposes of a scientific study. They seem to have no strong need or desire to discuss or expose their personal affairs, sins, or guilt feelings. One indication of romantic fervor, however, may be observed quite easily by walking along the beaches and the streets of Rio at night.

The public aspects actually show wide variation. In the interior there are highly ritualized procedures, such as walking around the *praça* in the evening, chaperoned dates and the implied threat that frequent dating indicates marital intent. This is in sharp contrast to those patterns that appear along the Copacabana and the streets of Rio under the magnificent tropical moon. It is difficult to appreciate how "out of place" one can feel in an elevator, for instance, in Rio with a couple carrying on passionate love without the slightest concern for the rest of the world. The complete unconcern of other passengers, who act as though this torrid affair were the most casual sort of conversation, is testimony to the Brazilian philosophy of live and let live, or, in this case, love and let love.

Child-rearing in Brazil is casual and permissive, yet unusually strict in certain respects. As might be expected, boys seem to have an easier time. Their rowdiness is not only tolerated but encouraged to a certain degree, whereas the pressure for girls to be little ladies is even more noticeable than in this country. Conditioning for sex roles in the family begins very early, and, as already mentioned, the results are clear-cut in the apparent strength of identity produced in males and females. Freyre gives a vivid picture of certain customs and practices employed in the past to encourage masculinity early in the young men and also indicates that they were in many ways greatly pampered and indulged.[7] They still appear to be pampered to a substantial degree, and the behavior of adolescent males certainly shows the effects of it. Brazilians seem to be quite wary of adolescent males and appear reluctant to invite strangers to their homes who have teenage sons if they themselves have teenage daughters. A stroll through the downtown section of São Paulo or Rio when the high school boys are on the loose tends to confirm the opinion that these young fellows are a wild lot who are intent on living up to their reputation. Even the servants tend to encourage these tendencies in young males. If allowed to

7. Gilberto Freyre, *The Masters and the Slaves*, trans. Samuel Putnam (New York: Alfred A. Knopf, 1959).

express themselves, female servants often comment that the adolescent boy is growing into a big strong man and often mention his size and good looks. Needless to say, this further inflates the already over-developed egos of the young men. In many ways, the over-all effect is quite similar to that of the American teenager, and perhaps American movies have played some part in the more recent patterns of juvenile behavior. Brazilians in São Paulo and Rio identify the especially wild and carefree youngsters with the American term "playboy" or "playgirl."

While children are pampered to a considerable degree, Brazilian family life is nevertheless apparently able to accomplish a great deal in developing love *and* respect for the parents. There seems to be little doubt as to where authority lies in the family, yet somehow they are able to achieve a rather delicate balance between their affection and their demand for respect. This is apparently possible even where children may eventually follow interests quite far removed from those desired by the parents. In other words, even with a strong affection for the child there is a tremendous amount of tolerance for individuality in the pursuit of life and happiness. Parents in general do not seem to be demanding or scolding but somehow temper their authority with understanding, tolerance, and support.

ATTITUDES TOWARD WORK

Attitudes toward work have often been considered as providing some important clues about people and their way of life. In the case of Brazilians, these attitudes may easily be related to a variety of past and present factors. In facing the challenges of the vast land and the complex demands of everyday life, the Brazilian, as already noted, has had to accept delays and setbacks and to devise ingenious ways of achieving his goals and fulfilling his needs. When certain needs are delayed or inhibited, some of the emotion generated by this frustration is likely to find an outlet in other channels and a lowered tolerance for the frustration of other needs. All of this, coupled with the uncertainties of life produced by the growing inflation, has probably done much to cause the modern Brazilian to emerge as a person who has little confidence in the unpredictable future. This is not conducive to "saving for a rainy day," nor does it engender a concern for problems that have not developed, because there are already too many problems to be handled here and now. It is likely to strengthen the preference for immediate satisfaction whenever possible. In addition, for Brazilians, careful and systematic planning and attention to dull details and organization seems to detract from the full appreciation of the moment and from the spontaneity of life itself. It places the emphasis on the wrong thing at the wrong time.

The importance of work in Brazilian life thus presents a contrast to the American tradition. As Diaz-Guerrero has pointed out, such typical American expressions, as "An idle mind is the devil's workshop" and "Hard work is good for you," appear in Mexico as "Idleness is the mother of a delightful life" and "Work is sacred, don't touch it." [8]

While it is not suggested that Mexico and Brazil are entirely comparable, the contrast that these attitudes present between people who are obsessed with the need to be active and efficient and those who are not is instructive and occasionally amusing, undoubtedly from both sides of the fence. The main point is that Americans impress not only Mexicans but also Brazilians as being overly compulsive about work, getting the job done, and as emphasizing efficiency too often as an end in itself. The American in turn often perceives the Brazilians as lacking in these "essential" qualities and predictably attributes many of their problems and misfortunes to this and nothing more. Anyone with a moderate appreciation of both ways of life is tempted to wish that we could be a bit more like them and that they could be somewhat like us.

As always, of course, there are considerable individual and regional variations in attitudes toward work in Brazil. Persons may be found who hold down several jobs and work hard at each, while others specialize in doing nothing. The latter behavior does not seem to be regarded as undesirable and is even appreciated as an indication of "talent" and perhaps a form of industriousness in itself. Such "deals" are not easily arranged, and

8. Rogelio Diaz-Guerrero, "Socio-Cultural Premises, Attitudes, and Cross-Cultural Research," invited address delivered to the Seventeenth International Congress of Psychology, Washington, D.C., August 1963.

their successful execution is certainly prized as accomplishment, which in fact it is. The degree of industriousness found in São Paulo, where there are more opportunities for work and a greater probability that hard work might lead to a better life, is an exception. The cities of Curitiba, Caxias do Sul, and Pôrto Alegre to the south also seems to have an unusual atmosphere of industriousness, possibly because of German and other European influences, the climate, or a combination of these and other factors. In Rio, on the other hand, the attitude toward work is certainly not one of enthusiasm. Perhaps the people themselves are different or perhaps the lush vegetation and lovely beaches with their beautiful mountain backdrop present an invitation to relax and enjoy the surroundings—certainly more tempting food for the senses and the imagination than work.

To the north, in the coastal cities of Victoria and Salvador, the pace is noticeably slow. Activity may not decrease from Salvador to the interior, but it certainly does not increase. In the interior, however, this is greatly complicated by a number of factors, including the scarcity of job opportunities and potential rewards, even for a considerable expenditure of effort. Possibilities for advancement and gain, for luxuries and comfort, for education and prestige are so minimal as to create a situation in which work has practically a negative reward value. In addition, there are many physical illnesses that continue to weaken or infirm a sizable portion of the population and contribute to the lack of vitality and enthusiasm.

In the interior itself, however, there are pockets of activity around certain cities where trade may be brisk and opportunities greater. These isolated phenomena are fascinating and certainly are worthy of careful study. It is unfortunate that Brazilian research potential in the social sciences is not now adequate in manpower or funds to carry out long-range, large-scale studies of these areas to determine the human and environmental factors responsible for their development. In this and many other respects, Brazil abounds in potential research information about people and institutions in the process of development and change. A great deal of this valuable information will certainly be lost if such luxuries as research must await the solution of more pressing economic problems.

A great deal is summarized in the opinions and attitudes of a number of young Brazilians about work. Their comments generally indicate that the most desirable state of affairs is to have a well-paying job or jobs with minimal obligations in actual work or effort. They seem to feel little or no guilt about such an arrangement, because it is not their problem that they are allowed to do little or nothing. Responsibility for the work that is done is seen as the concern of the employer, not the employee. The fewer demands a job makes in time and energy, the freer one is to enjoy life and the pursuit of happiness. The situation is similar in the interior, but the opportunities to operate in this manner are considerably fewer. Throughout Brazil, the hard-working, conscientious, ambitious person apparently receives little support and encouragement from the economic and social systems and from the family and friends. Such characteristics are more likely to be viewed with puzzlement and concern. Only strongheaded, strong-willed individuals could be expected to prevail against such rousing disinterest.

➤ While there is certainly something to be said for a casual attitude toward work and accomplishment, it nevertheless presents some crucial problems for Brazil and Brazilians. It seems highly unlikely, for example, that the enormous problems in Brazil's northeast, particularly those in the so-called "Polygon of the Drought," will easily yield even to vigorous, persistent and imaginative effort. In the face of the present half-hearted and ineffectual efforts, these problems are very likely to remain unsolved forever. There remain also the widespread health, sanitation, and disease problems which continue to plague the whole country, and to these must be added socio-economic problems which include almost unbelievable depths of poverty, lack of interest and motivation for progress, an educational program which fails to provide even basic schooling for many, and communication and transportation systems which, while developing, are still highly inadequate.

Agriculture is primitive in most sections of the country, and there are relatively few effective institutions to train and disseminate knowledge. In addition, those who most need to make changes strongly resist change in agricultural methods. In the San Francisco Valley, industrial development is so rare as to be of little importance. There are scattered indications of progress, but because stimulation and resources are lacking there is too little realistic planning for the future. On the positive side, Silva suggests that during the last ten years the San Francisco Region has made some progress. Successive governmental agencies have operated there, and these agencies have probably been at least partly responsible for a growing expectation of further progress.[9]

CHANGE AND PROGRESS

Brazilians living in the large urban areas have been conditioned to accept changes over the last ten or fiften years. In general, they appear to enjoy these changes and have certainly developed an expectation of further progress. This contrasts sharply to the interior, where many of the towns have an almost medieval atmosphere and customs to match. Statements about openness to change in Brazil would thus vary considerably as a function of the area or place being discussed. In the city of São Paulo, for instance, progress is taken in stride and can be easily detected over the short span of one year. The city grows rapidly, facilities are added, and the choice of consumer products increases almost as one watches. However, it is necessary to travel only a short distance outside of the city to find conditions that must have prevailed a hundred years ago. It is possible even within the city of São Paulo to find pockets of almost unbelievably poor living conditions. While the slum areas, or *favelas,* are not nearly so obvious as those on the hillsides of Rio, they do exist.

Other large urban areas in Brazil have become conditioned to change to a lesser degree and seem eager for more. As the future unfolds and successive changes are introduced, there would seem to be little cause for concern about how these changes will be accepted in most urban areas. In the rural districts, however, it may well be a different story.[10] After so many years of isolation and

9. Fernando Altenfelder Silva, Brazil II, Peace Corps Evaluation Project (Unpublished field report, University of Texas, 1964).

10. Diaz-Guerrero, "Socio-Cultural Premises, Attitudes, and Cross-Cultural Re-

near abandonment, it is hard to predict how the *Nordestinos* will react to the immense changes likely to be upon them soon. It is strange indeed to find a city such as Bom Jesus da Lapa on the San Francisco River whose inhabitants are familiar with the regular arrival and departure of modern aircraft, yet some of them must live in the crevices of the great rock that stands as a landmark on the edge of the river. In spite of the extreme depths of poverty in Lapa, an expensive, modern club was recently built within the compound of a federal agency there. The need for some facilities for entertainment and socializing in a town such as Lapa is easily understood from the point of view of the government employees who work there, but the many thousands of wretchedly poor, diseased, and undernourished inhabitants outside of the compound would also seem to require some consideration. An adequate water purification system alone would probably do much to decrease the high incidence of schistosomiasis and other diseases which debilitate a sizable proportion of the population, and the cost would very likely be less than that of the club.

Similar examples come to mind. During a visit of a former high government official to Lapa, money was suddenly made available to pave some streets, paint the fronts of some buildings, and plant palm trees along the parade route that he was to take. Unfortunately the official stayed only a few hours, after which everything returned to normal, the palm trees died and only the memory remained to fill conversations, if not empty stomachs, in the hard days ahead. The majority of people living in such towns as Lapa are not likely to form any real expectations for change based upon such brief incidents. Indeed, most towns in the interior are not so lucky as to have even such a short-lived familiarity with the magic offered by funds.

search." Some of the notions proposed here in comparing culturally related behavioral characteristics may be helpful in the present context. Diaz-Guerrero suggests that cultures may be roughly classified as encouraging active or passive endurance of stress in coping with realities and problems of life by means of certain values inherent in the cultures. He indicated the importance of these psychological characteristics for economic development and social change and predicts that "underdeveloped" countries will be found to be mostly passive endurers of stress. Active endurers of stress may be expected to value socio-change with reservation and suspicion.

In many parts of the interior, change and progress undoubtedly have been retarded by those who gain the most by maintaining the status quo. It is naive to assume, however, that all of those responsible for frustrating or inhibiting progress do so because they wish to punish or exploit the poor and wretched peasants. Many of them see themselves as the defenders of these people whom they feel must be led and looked after like simple, uneducated children. Their rationalizations are every bit as firmly entrenched as those who take the opposite point of view. Both feel that they have the support of logic, facts, ethics, and even the Almighty. The truth is that they have been fighting a losing battle. Some progress has already taken place and more is inevitable. The exploited peasants already seem to know to some degree that they have been neglected and misused, although the extent of the injustices cannot be fully comprehended because of their limited scope of information and knowledge. Their perception, both of themselves and the system, precludes any favorable prognosis for organized and effective action on their part without considerable help and leadership from other elements within the country. The determination of *which* elements will ultimately provide the required impetus and organization will have obvious and far-reaching effects for the country and the hemisphere. But regardless of who fills the role of "Protector" or "Savior" of these masses, the danger is that the already grim facts will be made to seem even grimmer for emphasis, and when the last vestiges of power slip from the weakened grasp of the *fazendeiros,* the new elite will develop their own rationalizations for exploiting these people. Without considerably more education, organization and solidarity than they now have, it is doubtful that after the sound and the fury of any uprising or revolution have subsided the plight of the underprivileged masses who are the pawns in all of this will be greatly improved.

It may be difficult to understand why the Brazilian peasant has not demanded more in the past or does not exert more influence at the present time. Demands and expectations for a better life, however, presuppose some knowledge, conception or even fantasy about what is in the realm of possibility, which somehow must combine with the motivation, will and energy to achieve this goal. The depths of poverty and illiteracy in the interior, combined with the malnutrition and disease, the difficulties of travel and communication, all tend to focus attention on the here and now, on the fulfillment of basic needs and on the problems of simple survival rather than on fanciful thoughts about a practically unattainable "good life." To assume that unrest and pressure without proper leadership and organization is likely to do more than increase the confusion is equivalent to assuming that God is Brazilian and everything will eventually work out. Raw activity without co-ordination or direction may be as pathological a symptom as inertia and lethargy.

While most Brazilian revolutions have been relatively mild and isolated, there are some current factors which could change this. Other factors will surely tend to maintain the tradition. If successive attempts at solutions are tried and fail and if conditions continue to worsen, more drastic solutions may begin to seem, not only acceptable, but even appealing as the only way out of an impossible situation. But always working against violent and widespread upheaval is the amazing patience and tolerance of the Brazilian, combined with his strong commitment to the self and the family rather than the cause which might transcend these in importance.

When sizable numbers of Brazilians have occasionally acted in unity for a cause, the impetus has often been provided by a strong, almost fanatical single personality. This suggests that extremely strong pressures and incentives are required to break through the self-family barrier. If and when a leader or national figure is able to penetrate this barrier, he will undoubtedly find a great deal of potential strength and motivation to tap because of the readiness to help those who are accepted as "one of us." In a restricted and regional sense, Janio Quadros, and perhaps in some ways even Ademar de Barros, evidently were able to achieve a degree of penetration, although their acceptance may have varied considerably on the different levels of Brazilian society.

TOLERANCE AS A STRENGTH AND A WEAKNESS

Brazilians are justly famous for their great tolerance and patience. This tolerance has led to conditions which by any standard would have to be regarded as good, but it has also led to clearly self-defeating conditions. There is an undeniable openness to and acceptance of differences in people, as well as in ideas. This is not to say that Brazilians have no prejudices, in spite of their claims to the contrary, but they typically invest so little emotion in them that they are not greatly disturbed when these prejudices are threatened. Such prejudice as does exist, therefore, is so casual that whatever solutions evolve will probably come about with a minimum of difficulty and violence.

Prejudice against Negroes is relatively mild in Brazil, and the Portuguese tradition of free interaction and intermarriage with colored people, which has produced a highly mixed population in most of the areas they have colonized, is frequently mentioned as being partially responsible for this. Some prejudice also seems to exist between individuals showing different degrees of coloration or different types of facial characteristics. In households where both light and dark-skinned Negroes work, a great deal of infighting often develops. It is not at all uncommon for mulattos to say that they are not at all surprised that so-and-so did such-and-such because "you can never trust a dark-skinned person." Pointing out some of the obvious implications of these statements does not help the situation and appears to elicit some antagonism. There is no strong desire to be identified with the Negro.

Negroes in Brazil can move about much as they please, but economically they rarely attain the advantages of their lighter-skinned countrymen. There is, therefore, considerable personal freedom regardless of race, creed, or color, but opportunities certainly are not equally distributed. People of any color can gain entrance to most if not all publicly and privately owned facilities, but relatively few Negroes are in fact seen in many places because of their lack of financial resources. The same is true of the universities. In São Paulo, for instance, there are very few Negroes in either the state or private universities.

As far as private social gatherings are concerned, the presence of Negroes probably would not create any special problems, but they are rarely seen on such occasions in the middle and upper strata of Brazilian society. Their presence is more common in the lower part of the social scale. Informal conversations with university students in São Paulo seemed to indicate that marriage, dating, or frequent association with Negroes does present some problems in the middle and upper classes. The consensus was that dating would not be accepted readily by the family or within most social groups, although it would be more acceptable in certain liberal groups. Indications were that a loss of prestige would likely be suffered by the non-Negro boy or girl, with decreased chances for marriage in the middle or upper social strata. None of the comments seemed to be accompanied by any dislike of the Negro per se but seemed rather to be prompted more by concern about the generally lower social position occupied by Negroes.

There also exists a slight but identifiable prejudice toward the Portuguese. This is probably a reaction to Portuguese prejudice toward Brazilians in the past. It frequently shows up in Brazilian jokes about the Portuguese, and vice versa. There is some mild prejudice against Jews and Italians in the city of São Paulo. The typical casualness of the Brazilian toward such matters, coupled with his low investment of energy and emotion in the problems of others, is not likely to produce civil rights demonstrations or violence such as has erupted in the United States.

It will, however, be interesting to note problems which may arise out of the rapid growth of the Japanese population in Brazil. Their farming operations in the State of São Paulo have certainly attained more success than those of other Brazilians in the area, and this seems to have generated some mild resentment as well as appreciation. The willingness of the Japanese to indulge in long and hard work and to sacrifice a great deal to get ahead, combined with their apparent lack of emotionality and their re- sistance to assimilation, probably makes them more conspicuous on the contemporary Brazilian scene than their physical character- istics. While some prejudice seems to be developing against them, it is unlikely that this will reach major proportions, although it may well develop into the most serious problem of this type with which Brazil has thus far had to cope. There are stories in the Northeast about Japanese having been forced out of certain areas because the local population did not want them as competitors in farming or business.

On the negative side of the ledger, Brazilian tolerance has

allowed an amazing degree of ambiguity, inconsistency, and confusion to develop in most aspects of daily life. Brazilian attitudes toward racial differences, individual freedom and individuality may be commendable, but their tolerance has also endured corrupt and erratic government. Brazilians do not readily rise up in indignation over such conditions but are prone to accept and even condone them until they reach proportions which threaten to bring about a national calamity.

THE RELIGIOUS INFLUENCE

Certainly no discussion of Brazil would be complete without some mention of the religious influence. The role of the Roman Catholic Church and the Catholic religion is, however, difficult to appraise. The fact that the country is almost entirely Catholic does not mean much, because many of the people who claim Catholicism as their religion have almost no firsthand contact with it nor any real knowledge of it. Brazilians characteristically wear their religion very lightly. The forms that it takes in some isolated areas of the country and in certain Macumba groups is strange indeed. In fact, the church seems to have been more successful in transmitting superficial aspects of Catholicism than the depth and substance of its system of beliefs. This undoubtedly is related to problems of illiteracy, but it probably goes far beyond that. From the point of view of sheer numbers there never have been enough priests to provide anything approaching adequate religious training in Brazil.

The Catholic Church seems at the present time to be having a more constructive influence than in the past, through the working clergy, which is becoming increasingly interested and active in social problems and social action. More and more priests are taking an active role in the defense of the rights of the working classes. Brazilians still, however, show a great deal of ambivalence toward the Church and the clergy. Religion is often mentioned as being good and essential, but there is also some suspicion directed toward the church as an institution and toward the clergy. There is an obvious intermingling of respect and fear. In spite of this, the impact of the church is undeniable in many of the customs, in the role of women, in the attitudes of patience and tolerance, and in the willingness to assign responsibility to God rather than to the self. It is certainly one of the identifiable fibers running through the culture. While it has not been the catalyst for change and progress that it might have been, it remains a source of potential good and an institution with considerable power and influence. What there are of the non-Catholic groups seem to be of good caliber so far as personnel is concerned, but while their work has been commendable their operations are relatively restricted and their impact remains negligible.

THE URBAN AND THE RURAL

Present-day Brazilians (as well as their ancestors) take an interesting attitude toward the interior of their country and its inhabitants. In São Paulo many people enjoy talking about the interior and identify with the *bandeirantes* (Brazilian equivalent of the pioneers) and their exploits, but relatively few of them ever travel far into the country. This undoubtedly is partly because of the quality of transportation and accommodations available in the interior. In fact, tourism is poorly developed throughout the country, despite the number and variety of sights that it has to offer. The city dwellers value comfort more than adventure, but more important seems to be their lack of interest in their own country. Brazilians are usually amazed at the foreigner who expresses a desire to see the various regions, and they are especially impressed by anyone who has actually visited many areas in the interior.

It is always interesting to listen to tales about life and experiences in the interior, then to learn that the place is only a hundred miles or so inland and the adventure is based upon a short visit during childhood. Inhabitants of the interior are often characterized as calm and gentle, yet in certain parts they are also described as carrying guns and large knives. While much of what is said is essentially true, though exaggerated, it is often based upon second-hand information. The city dwellers generally know very little about the interior and its problems. They are fascinated by the people but are fearful and suspicious of them. The way of life in the interior represents the simple, good life of the past, and yet it is not what one would want for oneself, since it offers relatively little comfort and convenience.

There is no great concern with the problems of the interior, although its plight is recognized and deplored to some degree. The shock that is produced by a description of disease, malnutrition, and poverty does not prompt many Brazilians to go into the interior to help alleviate the misery and suffering. The rural areas, in contrast to the cities, represent another world of realities and values, another way of life which should best remain in the past, to be talked about but not experienced. Nevertheless, they do represent the past, and at least some of Brazil's essence and uniqueness derive from those harsh but intriguing places with their sad but gay, simple but complex, gentle yet violent, timid but proud people. There is still a thrill in the mystery, danger, and adventure in the people and the places that fascinates the urban Brazilian from afar.

SUMMARY

The Brazilian way of life has worked amazingly well in developing close family relationships, a deep respect for individual freedom and a tolerance for all kinds of people and ideas. But while it has facilitated the solution of certain problems, it has also been somewhat responsible for the creation of other problems or has inhibited their effective solution. For instance, in producing a deep concern for the self and the family, it has also restricted the degree of involvement in people and events beyond these limits. Further, the uncertainties and complexities of life in Brazil have caused a strong emphasis to be placed upon the need to cope with the system itself rather than the solution of pressing problems which are often ignored, bypassed, or neglected.

There has undoubtedly been an increasing uneasiness in recent years about the future in Brazil, along with a mounting sense of frustration and resentment. It is difficult for many foreigners to understand how Brazilians have stood up under the demands and stresses of daily life yet managed to remain reasonably calm and even joke about conditions. Each new crisis seems to move an already difficult situation closer to the point of no return, yet somehow the inevitable never seems to happen. One social scientist who has been in Brazil for more than twelve years remarked that many years ago it seemed to him that something drastic had to happen, but it never did; and many times since then he has had the same feeling, but now he is beginning to wonder whether it ever will.

There are at least some indications that the crises which precipitated the recent revolution may have somewhat shaken Brazilian casualness and complacency. It is difficult to believe, however, that a real upheaval and revolution could possibly have taken place so quickly and easily and with so little bloodshed as it did in Brazil. This experience could possibly produce some badly needed re-evaluations and insights on the part of Brazilians. Ideally, it could help bring about a greater appreciation of the fact that the welfare of the nation largely affects the welfare of most, if not all, of those who are a part of it and that it is becoming increasingly difficult to insulate oneself and family from the problems of the community or the nation.

Brazilians and their way of life will apparently have to undergo some significant changes if they are to bring about the development and modernization of their country they desire. There appears to be a growing concern about progress and development, at least in a segment of the population. The interest and involvement in ideas and plans have, however, been much stronger than in the action that would have made progress and development a reality. Thus the strategy, the promise of a solution, the here and now have received considerable attention; but the implementation and actualization have been neglected and often forgotten. An obvious need also exists for the development of confidence in Brazil by Brazilians. In order to build confidence and self-respect there will, however, have to be an increasing measure of success and an expectation of substantial progress and development. Such expectations can only be healthy and lasting if they grow out of real accomplishments and the facing of some harsh realities. This may well require Brazilians to deal with their problems and stresses more actively than they have in the past. This will obviously be difficult and will require many years of careful reshaping of values, as well as behavior. Diaz-Guerrero suggests that Cervantes's

Don Quixote was a warning to the Spaniard that if he suddenly dared to deal with his problems and stresses in an active manner he would only succeed in creating much more stress than he would ultimately have to endure passively.[11]

There will undoubtedly be much resistance to change as demands are made that are perceived as infringing upon the self and the family. There should, however, be much potential and motivation to draw upon if a commitment to the common effort can come to be perceived as a way of realizing self-family goals and security. Great sacrifices have been made in the past; but they have been extracted through the growing inflation, the lack of progress and development, and through corrupt, inconsistent and inefficient leadership, rather than through the direct operation and demands of the government which has often been permissive and ineffectual. Under these circumstances, the delusion has developed that it was possible to accomplish that which needed to be done without paying the price in money or effort. Hopefully, changes in Brazil will follow careful and far-sighted preparation, so that Brazilians will be increasingly prepared to cope with their ever-growing problems in the future. While it would be foolish to anticipate great changes in a short period of time, perhaps it is not overly optimistic to hope for some indications in the years immediately ahead that a groundwork is being prepared for subsequent and more far-reaching developments.

11. *Ibid.*

BIBLIOGRAPHY

AZEVEDO, FERNANDO DE. Psicologia do povo brasileiro in *A cultura brasileira: Introdução ao estudo da cultura no Brasil.* São Paulo: Cia. Editôra Nacional, 1944.

DIAZ-GUERRERO, ROGELIO. Mexican Assumptions about Interpersonal Relations. Address delivered to International Conference on General Semantics. Mexico City, August 24–27, 1958.

———. Neurosis and the Mexican Structure: *American Journal of Psychiatry* (1955) 112, 411–417.

————. Socio-Cultural Premises, Attitudes and Cross-Cultural Research. Invited address delivered to the Seventeenth International Congress of Psychology. Washington, D.C., August, 1963.

FREYRE, GILBERTO. *Problemas brasileiros de antropologia.* Rio de Janeiro: Edições C. E. B., 1942.

————. *New World in the Tropics.* New York: Alfred A. Knopf, 1959.

————. *The Masters and the Slaves,* Translated by Samuel Putnam. New York: Alfred A. Knopf, 1953.

————. *The Mansions and the Shanties.* Translated and edited by Harriet de Onís, with an introduction by Frank Tannenbaum. New York: Alfred A. Knopf, 1963.

LEITE, DANTE MOREIRA. *Caráter nacional brasileiro* in Boletim No. 230, Psicologia No. 7, São Paulo: Faculdade de filosofia, ciências e letras da Universidade de São Paulo, 1954.

VIANNA MOOG, CLODOMIR. *Bandeirantes and Pioneers.* Translated by L. L. Barrett. New York: George Braziller, 1964.

PRADO, PAULO. *Retrato do Brasil; ensaio sobre a tristeza brasileira.* IV edição. Rio de Janeiro: F. Briguiet and Cia. Ed., 1931.

SCHLESINGER, HERBERT. A Contribution to a Theory of Promising: Primary and Secondary Promising. Address delivered to Topeka Psychoanalytic Association, June, 1960.

SILVA, FERNANDO ALTENFELDER. Unpublished Field Report. Brazil II Peace Corps Evaluation Project, University of Texas, 1964.

OLIVEIRA VIANNA, FRANCISCO JOSÉ DE. *Evolução do povo brasileiro.* 2a. ed. São Paulo: Cia. Editôra Nacional, 1933.

————. *Raça e assimila ção.* 2a. ed. augm. São Paulo: Cia. Editora Nacional, 1934.

————. *Pequenos estudos de psicologia social.* 3a. ed. augm. São Paulo: Cia. Editôra Nacional, 1942.

————. *Populações meridionais do Brasil.* 5a. ed. Rio de Janeiro: Livraria José Olympio Editôra, 1952. IIv.

10/ EMERGING PATTERNS OF
THE BRAZILIAN LANGUAGE
BY EARL THOMAS

PORTUGUESE is spoken by about 85 million people scattered widely over the earth. This places it about eighth in usage among the languages of the world. The same basic vocabulary and grammatical forms are used by nearly all speakers, and a considerable unity exists in the written language. There are, however, important differences in the spoken language among the various regions in which it is used.

By far the greater part of this number is found in Brazil, which has a present population of approximately 75 million. Speakers of other languages are found in Brazil in very limited numbers. Most of these are in two groups: the relatively few uncivilized Indians in more distant parts of the interior and a very few immigrants who have not yet learned the language. Many Indians speak Portuguese only; others are bilingual. Those who do not speak the language of the country number perhaps less than one-half of one percent of the total population.

Certain immigrants, notably the Germans, formerly maintained their own languages in communication and education, but this today is very limited. Spanish, as a language of Brazil, is non-existent.

Outside Brazil, Portuguese is spoken in Portugal by about ten million people and by smaller numbers in the present and former overseas territories of that country. These include Angola, Mozambique, several smaller African territories, and the Asiatic territories. In some regions where Portugal lost political control centuries ago the language is still in use.

In the United States there are perhaps 300,000 persons who use Portuguese habitually in the home. Most of these are immigrants from the Atlantic islands, and are concentrated principally in three regions: the New England coast, the coast of California, and in Hawaii.

A Brief Historical Sketch. The Portuguese language originated in the western part of the Iberian Peninsula as the local form of spoken Latin. This was, of course, not the language of educated Romans such as Virgil and Cicero but the speech of Roman soldiers, merchants, and minor officials. The Latin they spoke was rather general throughout the Roman Empire but was already different from the classical Latin of our textbooks. An American equivalent would be the speech of the person who says, "I ain't got none," or "Me and him done it."

The natives of what are now Galicia and Portugal spoke other languages, of which little is known. Some of them spoke Celtic (some of the ancestors of the Irish emigrated from there), others probably did not, but they all had to learn Latin after the Roman conquest, which was more or less completed in the second century B. C. Of course, the Romanization of the area took a long time, reaching first those people of the cities who had daily contact with their new masters and spreading to the country only after several generations. The final transfer from the native languages to Latin was probably brought about by the Christian church, which eventually reached every individual and taught each one the basic tenets of that religion—in Latin.

The destruction of the Roman Empire caused a general breakdown in communications from region to region. The church continued, however, to maintain some communication, and consequently linguistic unity, within each diocese. Thus, while spoken Latin continued to evolve as it had in the past, the changes were not so uniform. The regional differences became greater and greater. Educated persons still wrote in Latin as well as they were able, but most of the people had no written language. The changes continued, unchecked by education.

It is always difficult to determine why certain changes take place in a given language. Why, for example, do Portuguese and French have nasal vowels, while the other Romance languages do not? Some changes may be the result of speech habits existing in the pre-Latin languages—an accent so general in that area that it was unnoticed and became a part of normal speech. Other changes may have resulted from invasions by peoples who spoke other languages and carried over certain characteristics of their own languages when they adopted the speech of the country.

Williams believes that one important difference between Portuguese, on one hand, and French and Spanish on the other was brought about by the Germanic invaders.[1] These invaders are thought to have spoken Latin with the strong stress of the Germanic languages, causing the unstressed syllables to become weaker and finally to be lost. There were relatively few Germans in Portugal, hence the influence was weaker. As a result, many Portuguese words are longer than the corresponding Spanish ones. Compare the Portuguese *carregar, menino, dívida* with the Spanish *cargar, niño, deuda.* Perhaps a tendency to lose certain consonants (intervocalic *l, n,* and *d*) is also a result of more evenly distributed stress. In any case, very little influence of the Germanic languages is found in Portugal. Most of the words which were adopted are found in other countries and were used everywhere in Latin in the later years of the empire.

The differences between Portuguese and Galician were minimal in the Middle Ages. An extensive literature was written in the common language through the fourteenth century. In the twelfth century Portugal became an independent country, while Galicia remained united with León and Castile. In the eight centuries that have passed since then, the speech of the two regions has moved farther and farther apart. Galician has been reduced to a group of dialects largely spoken by the country people and rarely used today in writing.

In the sixteenth century, for reasons that are not clear, there were several important changes in Portuguese. Most basic was a strengthening of the stressed syllable, while the unstressed ones were greatly weakened. In the spoken language of Portugal today, many of these unstressed syllables have entirely lost their vowels,

1. Edwin B. Williams, *From Latin to Portuguese* (2nd ed., revised; Philadelphia: University of Pennsylvania Press, 1962).

although the various regions of Portugal differ somewhat in this respect. The written form of the words was already established and has continued essentially to the present. The modern speaker will usually omit the vowel given in parentheses in the following words: *árv (o) re, esp (e) rar, sáb (a) do, m (e) nino, p (e) ssoa, amizad (e), pouc (o)*. In addition, the vowels *a* and *o* are generally weakened in pronunciation when unstressed.

A tendency to weaken certain consonant sounds developed at this time or later. The *d* and the *b* (sometimes confused with *v*) are frequently heard in Portugal pronounced as in Castilian, without cutting off the current of air to make the "explosive" sound. A more general development is the palatalization of the *s* before a consonant to the equivalent of *sh* or *zh* in English.

These changes which took place in Portugal from the sixteenth century on were not carried to Brazil. Although examples of all of them may be heard there, some more than others, they nearly always can be traced to a local population containing a large proportion of modern immigration from Portugal. The palatalization of the *s* before a consonant thus is heard largely in such coastal cities as Rio de Janeiro and Belém, but rarely in the interior. Even in these cities it is far from universal, or even consistent in the speech of one person. While the quality of unstressed vowels may vary somewhat from one part of Brazil to another, they are, with few exceptions, pronounced clearly as full vowels everywhere.

These differences in pronunciation form the most obvious distinction between the speech of Brazil and that of Portugal. As we shall see, there are other important differences. These differences are concealed in the written language by the traditional spelling, which maintains most letters that represented sounds in the sixteenth century. It is much closer to the reality today in Brazil than in Portugal. Recent spelling reforms have tended to maintain these letters in an attempt to preserve, as far as possible, the unity of the language.

In 1500, Pedro Alvares Cabral, on his way to India, swung west off the coast of Africa and landed in Brazil. Verifying the fact that it lay to the east of the line of Tordesillas, he claimed the land for Portugal. Pero Vaz de Caminha, the fleet scribe, wrote a glowing account of the country which eventually got back to Portugal. Although at that moment India was more interesting to the crown, ships began touching on the coast irregularly, and a few sailors were shipwrecked or abandoned on the shore. Colonization followed soon after 1530.

During most of the sixteenth century the colonists were relatively few, and most of them were men. There were also many men in the colonies temporarily—sailors and merchants, government officials, troops, and missionaries. Lacking Portuguese women, these men found the native girls attractive. The permanent settlers established regular households; the transients found temporary solace for the loneliness of the New World. These women belonged to various tribes of the Tupi-Guarani family which occupied the coast from the mouth of the Amazon southward to a point below Rio de Janeiro. From there the area occupied by these tribes extended south and west to Paraguay.

The language of the Indians differed very little throughout this vast territory. The women naturally reverted to their native language in the absence of the men and taught it to their children. The children of mixed parentage thus became generally bilingual. Indeed, for a time, so much of the population consisted of these bilingual *mestiços* that the country came very near to losing the Portuguese language completely, or at least of remaining bilingual, as did Paraguay. The missionaries contributed to this situation by learning the native language, preaching in it, and composing songs and poems. For their convenience in making translations of religious material, they created a "general language," by ironing out the localisms and variant forms. The crown felt it necessary to forbid the use of Tupi in the colony in 1727.

But there were other forces working against Tupi. Immigration, both from Europe and from Africa, increased steadily. Portuguese won the battle. Tupi retreated toward the interior and eventually faded away. Today it exists only in restricted areas in the Amazon Valley and along the border of Paraguay. There were certain fields, however, in which it was indispensable; a great many words persist as names of plants, animals, natural features, and place names.

The Portuguese spoken by the colonists and their descendants was left in a situation very similar to that of spoken Latin during the time of the formation of the Romance languages. There were very few schools in colonial Brazil, and those that existed were elementary. The wealthier planters and officials (these last entirely Portuguese) sent their sons to Portugal to be educated. No schools of higher education existed in Brazil until after the arrival of the royal family in 1808.

The majority of the people were illiterate, almost entirely uninfluenced by literary standards. The literature of colonial Brazil was written by immigrants from Portugal or by Brazilians educated in Portugal. Their language was that of Lisbon and Coimbra and of the literary traditions of Europe. Through the eighteenth century, they wrote for limited numbers of readers in America and found most of their following in Portugal. So they did not write as those around them spoke, nor even as they themselves spoke; for the Portuguese would already have found a great part of their vocabulary unintelligible.

As happens in nearly all countries, this literary language was continued by tradition, modified only slowly by its constant contact with the vernacular. Political emancipation removed the constant influence of Portuguese schools, so that the pronunciation of the educated classes doubtless adjusted rapidly to the speech of the country. But the syntax of the literary language, and to a lesser extent the vocabulary, continued in the molds of Lusitanian Portuguese.

The Romantic movement took root in Brazil about the middle of the nineteenth century. Among its developments are the literary types known as *sertanismo* and *indianismo*. The first dealt with the Brazilian of the interior, with tropical nature, with the customs and mode of life of the backwoods Brazilian. The second was a romantic treatment of the Indian. Both types necessarily introduced a large vocabulary of regional terms. Their style also shifted noticeably in the direction of the spoken language, since the Romantics were writing mostly for their own countrymen.

Especially since the Modernist movement, which began in 1922, Brazilian literature has become an important national cultural expression. It is written by men educated in Brazil and deals with Brazilian topics, for Brazilian readers. By necessity, as well as through the conscious effort of many writers, the language in which it is written has changed more and more in the direction of the spoken language.

Accompanying this change, or possibly preceding it, is a change in the attitude of the Brazilian speaker toward his language. He takes pride in its national characteristics. He speaks it in most situations with little regard for theoretical correctness, invents words and colorful expressions, and sprinkles his conversation with slang. His language is a continual source of interest and amusement. He plays with it as with a complicated toy. He searches continually for new ways to express his thoughts. Where a more disciplined language tends to limit variety of expression on the theory that there is one best or correct way of saying anything, Brazilian creates ever new ways, piling synonym on synonym, form on form, idiom on idiom. The foreigner who learns it at all well is nearly always as fascinated with it as the native and enjoys speaking it on all possible occasions.

As always, the greatest resistance to linguistic change comes from the schools. Even today the Brazilian schools, like their counterparts in the United States, go on teaching forms and constructions which have not been used in speech in generations (some, in fact, have never been), which appear only rarely in modern literature, and which the teachers themselves are incapable of using with any facility. The result is linguistic confusion. Perhaps the best example is the placing of pronoun objects in relation to the verb. Here the spoken language (say, in the preschool speech of the children of educated families) is fairly regular and simple. But the rules taught in school are very different, since they are based on usage in Portugal, on literary works, and in some cases on traditional rules that never represented actual usage. The result, especially in writing, is such utter chaos that a professor of Portuguese in a Brazilian university once said to a class, "I give up. Put your pronouns anywhere you want to."

Modern Spoken Brazilian. Let us proceed to the characteristics of the spoken language of Brazil, contrasting it both to the language of Portugal and to the remaining elements of the literary language of other ages. But it is first necessary to establish what is meant by "spoken Brazilian." There are, of course, various levels of speech here, as in any other country. The speech of a man changes as he acquires more education. The speech of an individual changes with the social situation in which he finds himself. We cannot consider the language of the professor in the classroom, the orator addressing the public, the priest in the pulpit typical of the linguistic behavior of these same persons when they are chatting with family or friends. On the other hand, there are characteristics of the speech of the illiterate and of some regions of the country which cannot be taken as typical of the general population. We should take as the norm the speech of persons of some education, speaking informally among themselves, no matter whether they consider it "correct." They do not, of course, speak consistently in the type of language described below, even in the most informal circumstances; the influence of the schools, while not great enough to effect a drastic change, does affect certain aspects of daily speech and causes a great deal of the type of confusion so common in American English. Young children of educated families, before they have attended school too long, are largely free of this influence and give a very useful check in doubtful cases.

Portuguese in both countries has seven oral vowels. The *e* has two phonemic sounds, *é* (similar to the vowel of English "met,") and *ê* (similar to the vowel of "mate," but without the off-glide). Similarly, there are *ó* and *ô*, somewhat like the vowels of "ought" and "oat."

The weakening of unstressed vowels in Portugal has resulted in the most obvious difference between the two types of Portuguese. Practically all unstressed vowels are spoken clearly in Brazil, although the exact quality of the vowel often varies from region to region. Thus, some Brazilians pronounce the first vowel of *tocar* as *ô*, some as *ó*, and a few as *u*. Similarly, an unaccented *e* may be heard as *é*, as *ê*, or as *i*, but almost never does it weaken to the vague vowel so frequently heard in Portugal (similar to the *a* in English "sofa"). The vowel *a* may also be longer than the stressed one. After the accented syllable, however, some vowels do weaken. Some entirely disappear in the syllable between the stressed syllable and the final one. Brazilians omit the vowel in parentheses in the following words: *árv (o) re, sec (u) lo.*

In the last syllable, when unstressed, only three vowels are used: a weakened *a*, *i* (written *e*), and *u* (written *o*).

Another feature of spoken Brazilian is the nasalization of all stressed (and some unstressed) vowels which precede the nasal consonants (*m, n, nh*). In Portugal, the vowel is not generally nasalized if the consonant forms part of the following syllable; one may therefore pronounce any of the seven oral vowels in this position. But, since *é* and *ó* do not have nasal forms, they are replaced in Brazil by nasalized *ê* and *ô*. The nasal *a* sounds almost exactly like the vowel of colloquial American "hunh?". The Portuguese name *António* is pronounced (and written) *Antônio* in Brazil. Portuguese *viémos* is *viemos* (no accent written in either case) in Brazil.

The nasal sounds are more traditional in another respect in Brazil; the ending *em* still represents a nasal form of the diphthong *ei*. In Portugal it has become a nasal *ai*. The Portuguese poets thus have numerous rhymes for the word *mãe*, "mother." But for the Brazilian there is not a single rhyme in the language. In order to keep the orthography of both countries uniform, it has been agreed to write such words as *ninguém* with the acute accent, although it is not accurate in either country. The Portuguese says *ningãe*, the Brazilian *ninguêm*.

There are striking differences between the two countries among the consonant sounds. The Portuguese often pronounce *b, d,* and *g* with the weak spirant value familiar to all those who have studied Spanish. But the Brazilians almost never do so. The *b* especially varies a great deal in Portugal from one region to another. Along the Spanish border, many people confuse it with *v*. The Brazilian who hears this sound thinks that the Portuguese is reversing these two letters. One well-known anecdote has a Brazilian ask a Portuguese, "Why do all of you Portuguese say *b* for *v* and vice versa?" The reply is, "Not all of us do; just the *vurros*."

The value of the phoneme represented by initial *r* or double *r* between vowels is a peculiar development in Brazil. There is no confusion with the single *r* (a single stroke of the tip of the tongue, as in Spanish), except at the end of the syllable. But the double *r* varies enormously within Brazil. From Rio north, it is generally pronounced in the back of the mouth, or farther back, with the uvula. It may be voiced, but it is usually voiceless. It may have any of the sounds given to the letter *j* in Spanish, any value given to French *r,* or some variants not heard in either of those languages. In the single town of Belo Horizonte, nine pronunciations were heard, different enough to have been nine different phonemes. They vary, not only from region to region, but from person to person, and within the speech of the same person. The *carioca* often makes the sound so weak that it is difficult to distinguish it from English *h.* For him, the English words "red" and "head" are extremely difficult to tell apart. In São Paulo, a tongue-tip trill is used, but very little stronger than the single *r.* A *mineiro* (from Minas Gerais) and a *paulista* were talking one day, when the latter said, "Olha aquêle carinho." The mineiro looked around for some demonstration of affection, until he realized that his friend was saying *carrinho,* "little car."

In the three southernmost states, this phoneme has the value of the same phoneme in Spanish—the strongly rolled tongue-tip trill. This is also the sound in Portugal.

In Rio and in several east-central states, *t* and *d,* whenever they are followed by the sound of Portuguese *i,* become respectively equivalent to English *ch* and *j.* The prestige of Rio as a center of culture and as a point of broadcasting radio and television programs is spreading this pronunciation rapidly over other parts of the country. The name "Ruth" is spelled in modern orthography *Rute,* but sounds to the American ear like "hootchie."

As in Spanish, words in Portuguese do not begin with *s* followed by another consonant. They are preceded by the vowel *e.* Many Americans are familiar with the inability of Spanish speakers, even many of those who speak fluent English, to pronounce such words as "school" without prefixing the vowel. But Brazilians have no difficulty. They have taken the English word "smoking" for the meaning "tuxedo," and never need an initial vowel. When pronouncing native words of this type they very often omit it.

The letters *w* and *y* have been abolished in the official orthography, but the semiconsonant sounds they represent in English are of very common occurrence. The Brazilian does not need to prefix *g* to the former. However, if a man whose given name is "Wilson" wishes to pronounce it very clearly, he may say "oo-ilson."

The digraph *lh* represents the palatal *ll* of Castilian. The change of the sound *y* and its several variants, so widespread in the Spanish-speaking world, is found only among the lowest levels of culture, and even there to a limited extent. However, the sound is frequently replaced by a simple *l*—regularly when the following syllable begins with a palatal sound: *fil* (*h*) *inho, fol* (*h*) *inha, al* (*h*) *eio* and colloquially in many words when the following vowel is *e* or *i: velhice, mulher,* pronounced *vilice, mulé.*

Portuguese has a consonant not found in the better known European languages, represented in writing by the digraph *tl.* It is found in a number of words of Greek origin, and in certain onomatopoetic words. The sound is produced by placing the tongue against the upper teeth, in the position for pronouncing *t,* but releasing the air at the sides, rather than at the tip of the tongue. It occurs in *atlas, Atlântico,* and *tlintar.*

No final consonant is used except *s* in most areas of Brazil. Final *r* has been lost in the speech of most people. Final *l* has become a vowel, so that *mal* sounds exactly like *mau.* Neither a word nor a syllable can end in any of the stop consonants *b, d, g, p, t,* and *k.* They are always followed by a vowel, which official orthography recognizes very often at the end of the word but not within it. The same method is used to break up initial consonant groups consisting of *p* and certain other consonants in words borrowed from the Greek. The vowel written in parentheses is pronounced, but not written, in the following words: *ob* (*i*) *jeto, sob* (*i*), *ad* (*i*) *mira, dig* (*i*) *no, ap* (*i*) *to, arit* (*i*) *mética, chic* (*i*), *p* (*i*) *sicologia, p* (*i*) *neumonia.* The extra vowel has been recognized in the spelling in the following words: *Rute, chope* (*chopp*), *clube.* When the consonant concerned is *t* or *d,* the vowel has the usual effect of changing them to the values of English *ch* and *j.* No other consonants are affected. The main stress of the word is not affected, but the intrusive vowel bears a secondary stress if it falls in the second syllable preceding the main stress. Thus the vowel in parentheses in *ad* (*i*) *mirável* is often pronounced with a stronger stress than the preceding and following vowels.

In rapid speech, however, Brazilians often pronounce consonant groups at the beginning of a word which English speakers would consider difficult. The numbers sixteen through nineteen often lose the vowel of the first syllable and become *d'zesseis, d'zessete, d'zoito, d'zenove.* The imperative of the verb *desligar* comes out frequently as *d'zliga.*

The general character of Brazilian, in contrast to European Portuguese, is highly vocalic. A succession of five or six vowels is very easy to find on the printed page, and often all of them are pronounced. A native of the state of Piauí is called a *piauiense,* a word containing five consecutive vowels. And such combinations as the following can be invented without much difficulty: *Eu lhe disse que ou êle ia ao museu ou eu ia ao automóvel.* This sentence contains a sequence of twelve vowels. They are never separated by glottal stops, as in the Hawaiian language or frequently in English, but are pronounced in unbroken succession.

Perhaps the most difficult feature of Portuguese for the foreigner to master is the alternation of vowels in different forms of the same word, which is variously known as radical changes or as metaphony. Many nouns and adjectives have close *ô* in the masculine singular form, but open *ó* in the feminine and both plurals. This feature is usually predictable but much more complex in the verb. It involves both sounds of *o,* both sounds of *e,* and sometimes *i* and *u.* The foreigner who uses the wrong vowel in such a word may be saying something quite different from that which he intends.

DEVELOPMENTS IN SYNTAX

The internal structure of the sentence and the use of inflectional forms are as different from those of modern Portugal or of classical literature as is the pronunciation. Many of the older forms are, of course, quite familiar to all from the printed page, and some are used on occasion in speech.

Perhaps the most striking fact about the verb is the loss of the second person. The plural is so far lost that very few can use it, even if they try. It is largely limited to poetry and to religious services. Brazilian Catholics address God as *vós*, Protestants as *tu*. The fact that Brazilian Protestantism is largely based on German immigrants and on missions supported by the English and Americans probably explains this usage. Public speakers, too, often use the second person plural in formal speeches—sometimes with disastrous grammatical results.

The second person singular of the verb with the subject *tu* has largely disappeared, except in Rio Grande do Sul and in small areas of the northeast. One does hear the subject *tu* among the uneducated in other areas, but the verb is almost always in the third person.

The usual mode of address is *você* among friends, or even among strangers of the same age and rank, and *o senhor* to persons of higher category in age or rank. This last form has a feminine equivalent, *a senhora*, with which one addresses women, whether their titles be *senhora* or *senhorita*. All these words take the third person form of the verb. They all have regular plural forms. A notable feature, which reflects the increasing democratization of Brazilian society, is the steady extension of the use of *você*. *Vossa Excelência*, formerly much used as a mode of address, is now reserved for such dignitaries as the president and senators, and then only on formal occasions. It is quite likely that *o senhor* will follow it into oblivion in another generation.

Another feature of the verb, obligatory in speech, is the distinction between the simple verb form, such as "I speak," and the progressive form, "I am speaking." The literary language does not insist on this distinction, but one must keep the two forms separate in speech in order to be understood. The language has two alternative progressive forms, *estou falando* and *estou a falar*. The latter seems to be somewhat favored in Portugal, where neither is obligatory. But while Brazilian books make considerable use of *estou a falar*, its use in speech is ridiculed. Brazilian usage in this respect is amazingly similar to that found in English. The main difference is that certain verbs which do not use the progressive in English do so in Brazil. One says, "I am seeing," "I am hearing you," "I am not understanding you," in exactly the same circumstances as "I am talking."

The Brazilian has abandoned some of the traditional verb

tenses and has developed new ones or extended the scope of some already existing. The traditional future and conditional forms are rarely heard in speech, except the forms of those verbs whose future stem is monosyllabic. This includes, in addition to monosyllabic infinitives, three verbs which use a shortened infinitive—*trarei, farei,* and *direi*—and the verb *estar,* which often loses the first syllable in colloquial speech. To express futurity, one may use the simple present or either of two periphrastic futures: *vou falar, hei de falar.* The conditional is generally replaced by the imperfect tense or by verb phrases, as in the future, but with the auxiliary in the imperfect.

In addition, the auxiliary *ir* can be used in the future and conditional tenses, followed by an infinitive, to form two new constructions which indicate probability, previous arrangement, assumed obligation, or reported intent. Thus, *Êle irá proferir um discurso* means, "He is supposedly going to make a speech."

The auxiliary of the perfect tenses in the spoken language is always *ter,* never *haver. Ter* is also used widely, although not exclusively, as the impersonal verb "there is."

The synthetic past perfect tense *falara* is still used in expository literature, both with that meaning and, more rarely, as an imperfect subjunctive. But only two words are in common use in that form. One is *tomara,* used exactly as Spanish *ojalá,* "I wish," and the other is *pudera,* used as an exclamation roughly equivalent to "no wonder!"

The Portuguese has kept the original Latin meanings of the preterit tense, which have in other languages been divided between this tense and the compound present perfect. Thus, *falei* is equivalent to both "I spoke," and "I have spoken." The compound tense *tenho falado* is used in a very limited way, but for this meaning it has no alternative. It refers to action that was either continuous or continual in the recent past but is not thought of as still in progress. Thus, *Tenho falado com êle* means, "I have spoken to him continuously or repeatedly."

The subjunctive mood has survived more completely in Portuguese than in most European languages. The present, imperfect, and future tenses, with the three corresponding perfect tenses, are all in universal colloquial use in the Portuguese of both continents. Even small children use them easily and well. The future subjunctive is among the first verb forms learned by the Brazilian child, doubtless because it follows "when" and "if" whenever the verb refers to the future. Being learned first and thus more familiar to children, it tends to replace the present subjunctive in any doubtful case.

Portuguese tries to move away from the use of the subjunctive in many constructions, as do other European languages. As in English, the principal instrument to achieve this is the infinitive. For this purpose, Portuguese has an almost unique tool, the personal infinitive, with endings to indicate person and number. Great numbers of studies have been made to determine the origins of this form and to codify its use. Neither purpose has been served with much success. Its origins are still obscure, and its usage is extremely loose. In fact, no rule has ever been drawn up which is not contradicted in passages from the best authors. And there is no idea which cannot be expressed in good Portuguese without the use of this form. It is employed with great frequency by people of all levels of education, however, and it is not difficult to draw up practical instructions for its use. We may classify it as a handy device, rather than as an indispensable tool, in speaking this language. It enables one to use a preposition and the infinitive, whereas another language might require the subjunctive or a whole clause with the indicative. Here are some examples:

Êle pede para fazermos isso.	"He asks us to do that."
Êle diz para tomarem café.	"He tells them to drink coffee."
Deram-nos dinheiro sem termos que pedir.	"They gave us money without our having to ask."

The passive voice, which the other Romance languages use only rarely, occurs very nearly as frequently in spoken Brazilian as in English. This is one of several interesting parallels between the two languages. In both, it is doubtless due to the wish of the speaker to emphasize the object of the action rather than the subject. Even more interesting is the fact (largely ignored by the grammarians), that both languages have two forms of the passive.

Compare English, "He was hurt," "He got hurt," with Portuguese *Êle foi ferido, êle ficou ferido*. As in the case of the progressive form of the verb, the correspondence of usage is not exact, but it is remarkably similar.

The use of the imperative of the verb in the spoken language differs notably from the literary language and from European Portuguese. Although very few persons use the subject pronoun *tu* or the second person of the verb, the imperative, which is historically a second person form, is in general use in the singular. It is heard, not only in the affirmative form, but also in the negative, where it is unacceptable in the literary language even with the subject *tu*. Certain parts of Northern Brazil do use the subjunctive in both cases, but most of the Brazilians consider it a harsh form which should be avoided.

There is still a certain feeling among the people that the imperative is too direct in certain circumstances, for example, when speaking to a much older person or to one who holds an important position. In such cases, they resort to various circumlocutions —the indicative with a subject, the subjunctive with an expressed subject, or a request.

In the plural, the imperative is totally lost on all levels of speech; but the subjunctive is no more popular than in the singular. The speaker usually finds some circumlocution, unless he is able to avoid the plural altogether—an exercise in which he is extremely adept.

For the most part, the actual verb forms used in Brazil are the same as those current in Portugal; that is, they use the same endings. There are some differences, however. A number of verb forms may be used with or without a final *e*. The longer forms are current in Portugal, the shorter ones in Brazil: Portuguese *dize, quere;* Brazilian *diz, quer*. In the preterit tense, the third person plural is written according to the standard language with the ending-*am* but is spoken in the historically correct form -*om*. And in the gerund, the *n* is generally sounded as a consonant, and in extensive areas of the country the *d* is dropped: *falano* for *falando*.

The traditional morphology of the noun and adjective persists largely unchanged, but there is some weakening in the system of distinction of genders and in the formation of the plural.

The Brazilians use a great many more words ending in *a*, which are of the masculine gender or of either gender according to the sex of the person concerned, than do the other Romance languages. Some are of Tupi origin, as *sapurana, jacucanga*. Some are masculine because they resemble masculine words of Greek origin, as *o alabama,* the American state, also used to mean "boll weevil." Some are of African origin, as *o cacula,* "youngest child." Some are feminine nouns which become masculine when they refer to men: *o corneta, o guarda, o cabeleira.* Some are shortened forms of Portuguese words, or slangy inventions: *O carpina, o portuga,* for *carpinteiro* and *português,* respectively.

The effect of these words is increased by the very considerable number which end in stressed *a,* nearly all of which are masculine. Many are of Tupi origin: *xará, jupará, jabá, jabutá, uapucá, ucá, gujará, guará,* etc. Others are African: *aluá, ganzá, gongá, munguzá, vatapá,* etc.

The real distinction of gender is, of course, expressed by the article or other determinative. In many areas of the country, it is common practice to express number solely by this means. Only those words which precede the noun take a plural form; the noun itself and adjectives which follow remain singular, as *moça bonita, êstes homen, três coracão, bons rapaz.* While this phenomenon is limited to a rather low cultural level, all Brazilians avoid the plural to an extent rarely found in other languages. This is done by numerous devices too complex to enumerate, but a few examples will show what is meant. An expression consisting of an indefinite adjective of quantity and a noun is nearly always in the singular: *tanta coisa, muito homen.* General statements are very frequently put in the singular: *Brasileiro come arroz,* "the Brazilians eat rice." Words and expressions which were once regularly used in the plural are often in the singular: *cabelo,* "hair"; *calça,* "trousers"; *bom dia.*

Of all the parts of the sentence, the article seems most refractory to rules. Some irregularity is doubtless due to the sounds involved. The singular forms of the definite article (masculine *o,* feminine *a*) often disappear in pronunciation, since two like contiguous vowels are pronounced as one. Thus, *a ave,* in normal rapid speech, sounds exactly like *ave* alone. In *todo o mundo, toda a casa,* the article is often omitted in writing, since it cannot be heard. The same explanation may apply to *Eu falei com Dr. Peres,* and hence has caused people to say, by analogy, *Eu vi Dr. Peres.* The definite article is especially likely to be omitted in general expressions: *Pássaro voa,* "birds fly," *Eu gosto de cachorro,* "I like dogs."

The indefinite article also consists of a single vowel (*um,* pronounced *u*) in the masculine. The feminine *uma* has a consonant which is frequently omitted. In contemporary newspapers, the usual custom is to write *u'a* before a word beginning with *m* to avoid confusion, for example, *uma mão* and *um mamão,* which would sound alike. In speech there is no such regularity. One may hear *uma* or *ua* before any noun, although some people avoid the full form before certain words which would coincide with an improper expression.

The use of the personal pronoun in spoken Brazilian is one of its outstanding peculiarities.

The subject pronoun is used much more than in Portugal, although still less universally than in English or French. Probably the most important reason for its frequency is the number of verb endings which are either alike or very similar. With the disuse of the second person form, some tenses are reduced to two forms in the singular (*eu falo, você fala, êle fala*), some of them to only one (*eu, você, êle falava*). In the plural, not only is one form used for second and third persons, but it is acoustically not very distinct from the singular. Besides, in many parts of the interior, the nasalization of the final vowel is lost, erasing the small difference entirely. The subject *nós,* "we," is used least, since it has a very easily distinguished verb ending.

A second reason is the conflict between the natural spoken language and the traditional form taught in schools, in the matter of placing the pronoun object in the sentence. The Brazilian says naturally, *Me dá isso.* Traditional rules forbid one to begin the clause with a pronoun object. In order to be both natural and "correct," the speaker resorts to, *você me dá isso.*

The personal pronoun objects corresponding to "him," "her,"

"them," have for all practical purposes disappeared from the language. Except in certain traditional phrases, uneducated persons and children do not use them at all. Even among those who attempt a more literary speech, their use is quite rare. When these words are unstressed they are not needed, and their omission does not in the least impair clarity. The few exceptional cases are expressed by a different construction of the sentence. Even if they were used it would often be impossible to hear them; *eu (o) vi, ela (a) viu,* sound the same whether one uses the object pronoun or not. Sometimes, of course, the object is the important word in the sentence and must be stressed. In such cases, the Brazilian uses the subject form as object. To say, "I saw *him*," he says, *Eu vi êle.* Although this construction is found in Portuguese from the Middle Ages on, it is not acceptable to grammarians. They oppose it with such arguments as the fact that if we say, *Eu vi ela,* the last two words form the word *viela,* "alley."

The indirect objects of the third person are *lhe, lhes.* These spellings, however, represent what the Portuguese use. The Brazilian says *li, lis,* forms current in Portuguese dialects, and etymologically correct.

In the second person, such forms as *você, o senhor,* etc., are used as objects, as well as subjects. This construction is general and accepted. In placing these in sentence order, one treats them as nouns rather than pronouns. In very intimate speech, one hears the old second person pronoun objects along with the third person of the subject and verb: *Que é que você fazia quando te vi?*

In the first person, the object pronoun is always unstressed—a curious contrast to the situation in the third person. In order to call attention to the person who is the object of action, it is necessary to reconstruct the sentence. "He saw me" is *Êle me viu;* "He saw me" might be *Quem êle viu fui eu.* An emphatic form with a preposition, *a mim, a nós,* is sometimes found in literature, but the spoken language ignores it.

The Brazilian speaker never uses both a direct and an indirect object pronoun with the same verb. Such constructions as *êle mo disse, eu lho dei, dá-se-lhe* are rarely written nowadays and never spoken. In the few cases not already resolved by the omission of a third person direct object, the indirect object is expressed with a preposition. In fact, the preposition may be used in all cases. Both *a* and *para* (pronounced *pra*) are used, the latter more frequently. One may say either *Eu lhe disse* or *Eu disse para êle*. But one does not use both in the same phrase, in the Spanish manner.

Apart from the omission of the objects of the third person noted above, spoken Brazilian is very sparing with the use of the others. It has greatly reduced the number of reflexive verbs. Only those which have a somewhat different meaning in the reflexive form are regularly reflexive. One says, usually, *êle casou, êle deitou, êle levantou,* but *êle se chama João, êle se divertiu.* A curious case is the expression *ir-se embora.* One says *eu vou-me embora, êle vai-se embora, êles vão-se embora,* with or without the reflexive pronouns (which, if used, always follow the verb), but only *vamos embora,* without the reflexive object. Like the American, the Brazilian sees no need to distinguish between transitive and intransitive verbs.

One of the most discussed problems of the language is that of placing the object pronouns in relation to the verb. Grammars are filled with rules based on classical literary usage, which is usually also spoken usage in Portugal. But the entire rhythm of the sentence is different in Brazil, and these rules no longer serve. After a few years of school, the Brazilian is torn between his natural speech and that which he is taught. The result is considerable confusion, including constructions not natural in either country. The rules of the natural speech are rather simple and may be summarized as follows, omitting some special cases:

1. The personal pronoun object must precede a negative verb, a verb in a subordinate clause, or a verb preceded by an interrogative word. *Não me viu, o homem que me viu, quando me viu?*

Elsewhere:

2. It precedes a one-word verb, even at the beginning of a sentence. *Me da isso.*
3. It either precedes or follows an infinitive, with some preference to the former. *Pronto para me ajudar,* or *para ajudar-me.*
4. It follows the gerund used alone. *Jogando-se no rio.*
5. It follows the first word of a verb phrase. *Estão se ajudando.*

The possessive adjective in spoken Brazilian has two developments which contradict literary usage. The first is the use of *seu,* which originally belonged to the third person but is now reserved exclusively for the new subjects of the second person. In spite of the fact that all literature, including plays, popular songs, and even public speeches, use the word to mean "his," "her," and "their," as well as "your," in the spoken language it means only "your." Any attempt to use it otherwise results in misunderstanding. To express the other meanings, when it is necessary to do so, one adds *dêle* or *dela* after the noun.

The second development is the extension of the use of the article to replace the possessive adjective to a much wider range than in the other Romance languages. Whenever the reference is to the subject of the verb, it is not necessary to use the possessive. This applies to all three persons but is more used in the third, where the clarifying word *dêle,* etc., is used only when necessary.

Like the pronoun, the preposition has developed new constructions in Brazil. Choice of prepositions varies greatly. Duplicate usages are common, and prepositions are often used where they were not formerly employed. The preposition *a* has had its uses greatly reduced, mostly to the benefit of *em* and *para.* One reason is probably the great number of occurrences of the letter *a,* which is still the most frequent letter in the language. Another is that it consists of a single vowel, which may easily be lost in speech. *Para* has two consonants, and *em,* when combined with an article, begins with a consonant (*no, na,* etc.) . The Brazilian says *chegar em,* rather than *chegar a; está na igreja,* "he is at church," *eu vou em casa,* "I'm going home (for a moment) ." He reserves *a* for expressions of time and a few others in which *em* gives a different meaning, for example, *à mesa,* "at the table," *na mesa,* "on the table."

Para has largely replaced *a* to express the indirect object. After verbs of motion, *a* gives the idea of "go for a while," *para,* "go to stay." But there is some encroachment of the latter on the former.

The use of *a* before direct objects, nouns, or personal pronoun was probably introduced from Spanish in the classical period of Portuguese. If it ever was current in speech, it is not so now in Brazil. There are a few set phrases in which it is heard, such as, *Louvar a Deus*. Only one is used with any frequency: *um ao outro*, "each other."

Many verbs which in theory do not require a preposition are used with one colloquially: *esperei por êle, êle bateu em mim, olha para isso, beija nela.*

Prepositional phrases are often heard in variant forms. In the following examples, the form which occurs most often is placed first. All are taken from books, magazines, or newspapers, but may also be heard in speech.

De automóvel, em automóvel	By car.
No meio de, em meio a	In the midst of.
Em frente de, na frente de, defronte de, à frente de	In front of.
Devagar, com vagar	Slowly.
Mais devagar, com mais vagar	More slowly.
Ao redor de, em redor de	Around.

Expressions of time are especially likely to vary:

Nas quintas, as quintas	On Thursdays.
Aos domingos, nos domingos	On Sundays.
Ontem de manhã, ontem pela manhã, ontem à manhã, na manhã de ontem, pela manhã de ontem	Yesterday morning.
No dia cinco de maio, em cinco de maio, a cinco de maio	On the fifth of May.

Like many other languages, spoken Brazilian has many contractions which are used regularly in speech but are not recognized in writing. At other times, the contraction used in writing is not general in speech.

The standard ones formed with the preposition *em*, although optional, are nearly always used. *Num, no, nêste*, are almost universal. All those written formed with *a* are universal. In addition, any two contiguous *a*'s are automatically contracted, unless both are stressed. In *a avó, dá a êle, na água*, etc., only one *a* is heard. If both are stressed, the increased length reveals the two vowels. With *de*, contractions formed with the definite article and the demonstratives are obligatory. The standard contractions *dum, duma* are optional and rarely heard. Instead, in most of Brazil, the vowel of the preposition becomes a semivowel and coalesces with the consonant to produce a consonant equivalent to English *j*. Before *água, aqui, ali,* and *aí,* the preposition contracts to *d*. *Dali* and *dai* are often so written, but the other two are nowadays usually written in full.

The preposition *para* is always pronounced *pra* in Brazil, except in expressions of the type *para o ano,* "next year." It contracts still more in combination with the articles, forming (in pronunciation only) *pru, pra, prum, pruma*. Before a feminine noun beginning with *a*, there can be further contraction; *para a avenida* becomes *pravenida*.

The adverb in Portuguese includes the usual complement of simple adverbs such as *aqui* and *la,* and those formed from adjectives by the addition of *-mente*. But in the formation of adverbial phrases the Brazilian displays an amazing variety drawn from his linguistic imagination, especially in the combinations formed with *lá, cá, por, para,* and other prepositions and adverbs of place. *Vem cá para fora; leva isto lá para dentro; como vai aquilo lá por baixo; espera pra lá; êle passava por perto de mim; caiu lá de cima; caiu de lá de cima.* A great many distinctions can be made in this way, which other languages frequently do not feel the need of making: *Está em baixo da mesa,* but *passou por baixo da mesa.*

The adverbs *cá* and *lá* are used in ways very difficult for the foreigner to learn or even to translate when he understands the meaning. The following are some examples:

Que é lá isso?	What (in the world) is that?
Eu entendo cá disso?	Do (you imagine that) I understand that?
Conte lá isso como é.	(Come on and) tell us how it is.
Sou lá capaz disso.	I am not capable of that.
Eu sei lá.	I don't know.

THE WORD-STOCK OF BRAZILIAN PORTUGUESE

The vocabulary of the Brazilian language is rich and varied. Not only are there many words in the dictionary, but the vocabulary of individual speakers tends to be quite extensive. The Brazilian loves words, learns new ones easily, uses synonyms in great numbers, and forms new derivatives with astonishing facility. It is considered bad form, both in writing and in speaking, to repeat a word once used in a discourse if there is another one available. One author, in a treatise on grammar, discussed the use of the hyphen for the space of about one page. He found four ways of saying "hyphen," so that he was able to avoid the repetition of any one term. The tenth edition of the *Pequeno dicionário brasileiro da lingua portuguesa* lists ninety-three words for the general meaning of "prostitute." Of course, many vary in connotation, but ample room is left for anyone's synonyms. For the meaning of "uncultured man from the country," it lists sixty-one. Some of these are specialized, referring to persons from a certain section of the country, to those who inhabit the woods, the desert, the seashore, or even an island. For *cachaça,* the strong drink made from sugar cane, the dictionary lists 129 synonyms. Many of these are slang or pure figures of speech, but many are words in common use, with this specific meaning.[2]

The Brazilian forms new derivatives with great facility, using suffixes very freely with old or new words. Diminutives, found with about twenty different suffixes, are limitless. The most easily mastered is *-inho,* with its variant *-zinho,* which may be applied to almost anything—nouns, adjectives, adverbs, even verbs. The nuances of meaning are subtle and vary considerably. Thus, *bonzinho* may at times be slightly pejorative, but *boazinha* is not. *Cedinho* is earlier than *cedo, agorinha* more immediate than *agora,* but *loguinho* may be earlier or later than *logo. Bonito,* a diminutive of *bom,* has nothing to do with the meaning "good," but means "pretty." It has, in turn, a diminutive *bonitinho,* which means "cute." Past participles when used as adjectives usually take a diminutive in *-inho,* but the feminine form, when used as a noun, forms it in *-ela: Elas deram umas chegadelas e agora estão chegadinhas.* The endings are colloquially applied, sometimes to verb forms: *Éle aprendeuzinho da Silva,* "He sure 'nuf learned."

Certain suffixes are used with complete freedom and often have various completely different meanings. Thus, *-eiro* may indicate one who makes the article indicated by the root *(sapateiro)* , one

2. *Pequeno dicionário brasileiro da língua portuguêsa* (10th ed.; Rio de Janeiro: Editora Civilizacão Brazileira, 1961) .

who sells it (*leiteiro*), or one who exercises a profession (*banqueiro, petroleiro*). The same suffix denotes the holder of an article (*acucareiro, saleiro, toalheiro*), or the tree that produces the fruit indicated by the root (*pessegueiro, bananeira*). It has been applied to numerous fruit trees discovered in the New World or imported from elsewhere in the tropics (*assaìzeiro, jabuticabeira, cajuzeiro, juàzeiro*).

The suffix -*ada* is almost as varied. As the feminine form of the past participle of verbs of the first conjugation, it forms nouns denoting the action of the verb (*chegada, chupada*). Sometimes the verb does not exist, but the derivative indicates an action involving this noun (*umbigada*, "a blow with the navel"). It is applied to nouns of many kinds, sometimes with the meaning "action proper to this noun": *macacada*, "monkeyshine"; *molecada*, "child's prank." It may denote a group of the individuals named by the noun: *molecada*, "group of mischievous children"; *cachorrada*, "a gang of dogs." With the name of a fruit, it denotes a cheese-like preparation of that fruit: *bananada, pessegada, marmelada*, made from bananas, peaches, and quinces, respectively.

There are certain suffixes which have a pejorative connotation, but with a denotation also expressed by another suffix. Adjectives which end in -*dor* have a feminine form in -*dora*, but some have forms in -*deira* which are unflattering; *falador*, feminine *faladora* and *faladeira*; *namorador*, feminine *namoradeira*. The very common -*oso* is replaced by -*ento* when the quality is disagreeable: *nojento*, "nauseating"; *lamacento*, "muddy"; *sarnento*, "mangy."

The freedom of composition and the variety of forms can be illustrated with a few examples: From the word *asno*, "ass," we get *asnada*, "a group of asses." It can also mean "a stupid act," and in this sense there are several synonyms: *asneira, asnice, asnidade, asnaria*. An especially aggravated example of ass is an *asneirão*, who commits greater stupidities, known as *asneiradas*. A person of this type is described as *asinino, asnil, asneiro, asneirento, asinal, asinário, asnal, asnático*. The verb, "to commit or say stupid things," is *asneirar*. If one's expression descends to the obscene, it is an *asneirola*. There are, of course, other complete sets of such words derived from *burro*, its feminine form *besta*, and from numerous words having the general meaning of "fool."

The following words are taken from recent publications but do not appear in the most recent edition of the standard Brazilian dictionary: *dodecafonismo,* "system of twelve musical notes"; *roxura,* "purple-ness"; *fantasiacão,* "act of putting on a costume"; *cravável,* "nailable"; *jaguncagem,* "group of, or act of bandits"; *sonhejando,* "dreaming very lightly"; *raivável,* "possible for one to be angry at"; *genista,* "ill-tempered person"; *desmexer-se,* "to get out from among" (although more than 2,200 words formed with this prefix *do* appear); *companheiragem,* "togetherness"; *galhinolagem,* "quality of being like a guinea hen."

The basic word-stock of Portuguese comes directly from the Latin once spoken in Portugal. To these have been added great numbers of new words throughout the history of the language. A perennial source for borrowing from the time that Portuguese became a written language has been literary Latin. Formerly this borrowing was very great, but in modern times it is not much greater than in English, and in general the same words are taken into both modern languages.

Germanic words from the occupation of the country by the Suevi and the Goths are comparatively few and are usually common to all the western Romance languages: *ganar, guardar, guerra, guadanha.*

The Arabic conquest introduced a considerable number of Arabic words, but a great part of them are now obsolete or archaic. We still use *alfaiate,* "tailor," *laranja,* "orange," *alfândega,* "customs house," and a few hundred more.

Portuguese has always borrowed from other European languages, sometimes taking the same word from different sources, with the resulting forms and meaning different from each other. Thus the Latin word *planus* gave two forms in Portuguese (in two dialects, probably): *chão,* meaning "the ground," or as an adjective, "flat"; and *porão,* which means "cellar," or "hold of a ship." From literary Latin it took *plano,* "level," from Spanish *lhano,* "frank," and from Italian *piano,* "piano."

The greatest addition to the vocabulary of the language after its establishment in Brazil came from the Tupi Indian language, or its closely related dialect, Guarani. The words of American origin listed in the *Pequeno Dicionário* number more than twenty thousand. A great number of them are used only locally, since the things they name are not universal. Frequently also the same plant or animal has several different names in various sections of the country. A great many are in general use, however.

Most Tupi words are naturally nouns. They include the names of animals, birds, insects, etc., unknown in Europe: *tapir, manati, colibri, capibara, pium* (a mosquito); plants such as *aipim*, "manioc," and *jerimum*, "pumpkin," *buriti* (a palm), *grumixama* (a fruit); geographical features, such as *pororoca*, "the bore of a river," *piririca*, "a rapid," *igarapé*, "channel between islands"; instruments used by or acquired from the Indians, such as *tacape*, "war club," *igarité* (a kind of boat).

A number of adjectives are in common use. They include: *assu*, "large," *mirim*, "small," *carijó*, "speckled." Also, quite a few verbs are formed by applying Portuguese endings to a Tupi noun: *pererecar*, "to hop like a treefrog (*pererecá*)," *piriricar*, "to ruffle the water," *pipocar*, "to pop like popcorn (*pipoca*)," *entijucar*, "to put into the mud (*tijuca*)," *capinar*, "to pull out the grass (*capim*)," *catingar*, "to have a disagreeable scent (*catinga*)."

All Tupi words are likely to be much altered in passing over to Portuguese. Nasal sounds abound in Tupi but often do not correspond to those used in the same words in Portuguese. One vowel was often described as a "grunt" by the early explorers. It is an unrounded mid-back vowel, very different from anything they were accustomed to. They wrote it in various ways, the favorite ones being *ig* and *y*. Since it was the entire word "water," it entered into innumerable compounds and place-names. It is said that a man who is suddenly struck in the stomach will automatically say "water" in Tupi.

The Africans who arrived in Brazil from the earliest times to the early part of the nineteenth century brought with them numerous African languages. Although these were rapidly replaced by Portuguese, they added to it a considerable number of words. Some of the main categories and examples of each are given below: (translations are often impossible).

Foods: *quiabo, acarajé, vatapá, angu, giló, fubá.*
Religion: *xangô, candomblé, macumba, ogum.*

Music: *carimbó, agê, alufá, lundu, batuque, ganzá, samba.*

Folklore: *quimbundo, banzo, zumbi, pondê.*

Adjectives describing persons: *fulo, capenga, bamba, banguela, dunga, cacula.*

It is very difficult to say whether a group such as the Indians or the Negroes had any general effect on the way a language is spoken. One possible influence of the latter is the widespread loss of final r. Some facts which point this way are the following: this loss occurs elsewhere than in Brazil, wherever there were many Negroes, for example, on the Caribbean islands and coasts; in works of Gil Vicente in the sixteenth century, the dialect of Negroes living in Lisbon is represented without the final *r;* this sound remains most firmly in the South, where there were relatively few Negroes until recently. Of course, it has also been lost in several Romance languages, and in a great part of England.

Portuguese has been borrowing from French since a French family established the monarchy in Portugal. Brazil continues to borrow French words but is less influenced by syntax than is Portugal. Some words have been adapted to Portuguese orthography, but most of them retain French spelling. A few of the main categories, with examples, follow:

Cosmetics and beauty treatments: *baton, maquillage, rouge, massagem, manicure.*

Clothes: *peignoir, soutien, maiô, lingerie, tailleur, decote, echarpe, galocha, paletó, costume, toilete, cachenê, tricô, boné.*

Food: *petit-pois, soufflé, filet-mignon, maionese.*

Automobiles: *camionete, carroceria, chassis, chofer, cupé, garagem, pane.*

More recently, English has become a source of many new words. Perhaps the greatest number has come into popular speech in the field of sports. These include the word *esporte* itself. Some effort has been made to invent new terms in Portuguese or to translate the English term into its Portuguese equivalent. One reads these terms in the sport sections of the newspapers but almost never hears them used in speech. The fans (*fas*) generally prefer the English term, which forms a special technical language. Here follow some examples of parallel terms:

centro-médio	center half
bola ao cesto	basquete
equipe	time (sic).
avante	forward
desporto	esporte
zagueiro	beque (sic)
binômio	doubles
luta livre	catch-as-catch-can
campeão	líder
peleja	match
torcedor	fã
balípodo	futebol (sic)

Many of these words, and others, have come into common use, frequently outside the field of sports:

o scratch	o nocaute	o pôquer
o craque (a "crack" player)	o esparring (-partner)	a sinuca (snooker)
o récorde	o sóccer	o goal
o tênis	o hóquei	o coach
o turfe	o player	o foul
o betting	o half	o jóquei
o referee	o water-polo	chutar (to kick)
o golfe	off-side	o pênalti
o box	o handicap	

Numerous derivatives are made from these words by adding a Portuguese suffix:

driblar	golear	recordista
boxear	esportista	liderar
boxista	futebolista	liderança

After sports, science and technology have probably introduced the greatest number of English words. But the cinema and the press are constantly offering new words to the public. Many of these are not taken into general use, but the number of them known to everybody is quite large. They hold beauty contests to choose a "miss," one who has "glamour," (sic) "sex-appeal," or "it" (pronounced "eachie"). One knows what "shows" are being given by reading the articles of a "repórter." The children like "filmes" about the "far-west," especially if they are really *faruésticos*. They listened, not many years ago, to "bugui-wugui," more recently to "rock and roll" (pronounced "hock and hole"), then danced the "twist." Many people go to a "bar" for a "drinque," or eat "sanduíches" at a "piquenique." Some like "waffles com maple," others prefer *o cachorro quente* (hot dog). The girls wear "suéters" made of "nylon" (pronounced as in English), "jérseis," "shorts," while a man goes more formally wearing his "smoking." There he enjoys a "flerte," if he can find a girl willing to "flertar." If his name is the same as his father's, he may add "júnior" to it. If he frequents "high-life," he meets people who live like "lordes" or "leides." If he discusses the "ianques," he speaks of "Tio Sam," the "gangsters," or the problem of the "coloreds." In politics he hopes to be a "líder," and his chances are improved if he is a "self-made man." In law, he addresses the "júri." He may live in a "dúplex," or in a hotel with a "hall" (lobby). He probably wears a moustache, called *bigode,* a word which goes back to the Peninsular War, when English soldiers twirled their moustaches as they exclaimed, "By God!"

One of the outstanding characteristics of Brazilian speech is its inexhaustible stock of slang. The *carioca* is rarely able to speak at all without using it. It pervades all layers of society, creeps into writing, and reaches its best in informal conversation. The slangiest of American movies, the most colloquial of comic strips (practically all of which appear in newspapers in Brazil) appear with every expression rendered by an equally slangy one in Portuguese. The translators' ability to find an equivalent for a pun, a regionalism, or the group slang of criminals or students, is amazing.

NAMES OF PERSONS

Personal names in Brazil leave the foreigner—and often the native—in confusion. There is really no system, except that everyone has at least one given name and one surname. Beyond that the number is unlimited. If one can distinguish where the first end and the second begin, which is often difficult, there is no way of knowing which is the principal surname. Alphabetization is a nightmare. One system widely used in the schools is to begin the alphabetization with the first given name. Some years ago, the libraries adopted the system of placing all references under the last surname, even if the person rarely used it. Not many years ago, a very well-known American library listed the works of Afonso Arinos (de Melo Franco Filho), some under Arinos, some under Melo, some under Franco, and some even under Filho.

If a man has the same name as his relative, he adds to his name his relationship to the older man. Thus, if he has his father's names, he adds *Filho*, or *Júnior*, if his grandfather's, *Neto*, if an older cousin's, *Primo*. Henrique Coelho Neto became very well known for his books, and the family decided to keep the qualifying word as part of the name. Thus we have the guitar-playing singer, Olga Coelho Neto, who is no one's grandson. A man whom we will call João Silva Sobrinho was named for his uncle. When he was planning a trip to the United States, he had calling cards prepared with his name expressed as follows: João Silva, SOB.

Confusion of names is heightened by the common custom of using only the given names of prominent persons. The unwary reader may find it difficult to look up Afonso Arinos (de Melo Franco Filho), Benjamim Constant (Botelho de Magalhães), João Alberto (Lins e Barros).

In given names, Brazilians often pay no attention to the Catholic custom of naming children for saints. Foreigners are often surprised by the profusion of Greek names, which include those of practically all Greeks known to history or mythology: Aristóteles, Sócrates, Hermógenes, Thales, Cleômenes, Agamenon, Leda, Nicandro, Icaro, even Sátiro. Roman names include Júlio César, Cícero, Marcial, Pompília, Tácito. From the old Germanic peoples they have taken Hildebrando, Ermínio, Clóvis, Leodegário, Segismundo, Xilderico. Hebrew names, biblical or not, are fairly rare, but include Abraão, Isaac, Ismael, Abigail, Abgar, Chaim. Several Slavic names are common: Ivan, Casimiro, Venceslau, Vladimir, Jaroslav. English names, both given names and surnames of famous people, become given names frequently in Brazil: Oscar (and Oscar), Newton, Jéfferson, Wilson, Jackson, Franklin, Gladstone, Edgar (and Edigar), Rônald, James, Alfred. Famous names from any age or country are common: Hamílcar, Haníbal, Mozart, Rubens, Pizarro, Dante, Erasmo, Átila. Even ancient gods are not spared: Hermes, Minerva, Horus. Some seem to be combinations of Portuguese words: Valdivino, Valdemar, Felisbelo. Some would require study to determine the origin: Onestaldo, Walmir, Néri, Adalgisa, Orris, Sinó, Djalma, Djacir, Geir. One fertile source is the Tupi language, either actual names of Indians or Tupi words: Iracema, Ubirajara, Peri, Jaci, Joraci, Jacira. Some families have even "Brazilianized" their surnames by replacing their Portuguese ones with Tupi words, especially the names of trees: Oiticica, Mangabeira, Cambará.

The most common given name for men is José. João is not nearly so frequent, Carlos rather rare, and Jesus almost unknown. The combination José Maria is much used. Girls are named Maria José. Maria is by far the most used name, either alone, in combination with another name, or with a qualifying phrase—Maria das Dores, da Penha, de Lourdes.

The full name of a Brazilian may be quite long. The following examples are real names: Ana Amélia de Queirós Carneiro de Mendonca, and Maria da Soledade Pinto da Fonseca Velinho Rodrigues de Moreira.

REGIONAL SPEECH

Something should be said about the regional variations of Portuguese in Brazil. They are easily noted by anyone who travels in Brazil, but they have not been very thoroughly studied, nor have their boundaries been well defined. Most influential is the speech of Rio de Janeiro, which is carried far and wide by radio, television, and travelers. In its main features, it extends over most of the states of Rio, Minas Gerais, and Espirito Santo.

The south, especially Rio Grande do Sul, constitutes a speech region. It uses clear final vowels, strongly trilled double *r*'s, and numerous regional words and expressions. A large part of São Paulo State once spoke the *caipira* dialect,[3] which is now declining. It was characterized by the change of the *l* at the end of a syllable to *r*, both this and the etymological *r* being pronounced somewhat like that of Chicago English, by the loss of the final *s* in verb

3. Amadeu Amaral, *O dialeto caipira* (São Paulo: Casa Editôra "O Livro," 1920).

forms, in nouns and in adjectives which followed the noun. The Northeast [4] tends to open unstressed vowels more than the rest of the country. It, like nearly every area, has great numbers of regional terms and expressions.

Of all Brazilians, the *carioca* (native of Rio) speaks most rapidly and has departed farthest from the traditional sounds. It should be emphasized that all Brazilian speech is very similar. There are no real dialects within the country which cause difficulty for mutual understanding. On the other hand, Brazilians who have not had much contact with the Portuguese generally have considerable difficulty in understanding them.

CONCLUSIONS

Certain general trends are discernible in the development of the Portuguese language brought to the New World by the colonists from the Iberian Peninsula. The first of these is the tendency to simplify the inflexions of the verb, noun, and adjective, replacing them with separate words when there is a need to express real distinctions. The same means is used to express certain distinctions which did not exist before but which seem to fulfill a requirement of modern communication. This tendency is rather general among the European languages but has often proceeded more rapidly in Brazil.

A second trend might be called the democratization of the language. This is evidenced by such things as the leveling of the formerly complex modes of address, by the breakdown of the traditional rules of grammar both in speech and in writing, and by the acceptance of a large body of slang into the language of educated people. The individual feels free to mold the language to his own needs, rather than attempting to modify his own speech to fit an accepted pattern.

A third trend is the development of an extensive new terminology to deal with modern science and technology. This need has arisen in Portuguese somewhat more slowly than in some other European languages but has not caused any great difficulty. Thirty

4. Mário Marroquim, A língua do Nordeste (São Paulo: Companhia Editôra Nacional, 1934).

years ago there were numerous discussions concerning the form certain new words should take. Today one gets his technical vocabulary from the same source as his science and establishes its usage without reference to the grammarians. Like English, the Portuguese of Brazil has an enormous ability to absorb vocabulary from almost any source and fit it into the framework of the language without doing violence to either.

WHITHER BRAZIL? A POSTSCRIPT
BY ERIC N. BAKLANOFF

WHAT of the future of Brazil? I believe it will rest mainly in the hands of the constructive nationalists—political leaders, the managers of private and public enterprises, military officials and intellectuals—who will shape their country's development in the foreseeable future. Their capacities for effective leadership will be repeatedly challenged by the tensions arising out of the conflict between the values and behavior patterns of Brazilian traditional society and the requirements imposed by modernization. Certainly no challenge is more pressing than that which Baer calls the distributive dilemma, "i.e., the need for both high rates of economic growth and greater equity in the distribution of income." Many advanced industrial societies, including the United States, succeeded in ameliorating the distributive dilemma in the course of their economic "takeoffs" by attracting foreign capital to supplement their domestic savings.

Brazil's economic infrastructure—the railroads, the communications network, electric power, ports, and urban transportation facilities—has been financed largely by foreign private investment and official loans from abroad. The future role of foreign capital in Brazilian development will be conditioned by the policies followed by the nationalist leaders with respect to financial stability and other dimensions of the climate for investment. On the basis of recent trends, we should expect Western European firms (whose stake in Brazil is about equal to that of United States companies) to increase not only their business investments in Brazil but their share of the total as well. Japan, too, may be expected to become a significant source of equity capital and know-how for Brazil. New business investments from abroad will increasingly take the

298

form of joint ventures in which the Brazilian partners will hold the majority of shares.

The World Bank's decision in early 1965 to resume lending operations in Brazil after nearly six years may well be a turning point in that country's capacity to attract official international credits on a massive scale. In addition to the World Bank, the Inter-American Development Bank and the United States Government through the Alliance for Progress will provide Brazil with substantial funds and expertise for key social and economic projects. Increasingly, this public assistance will be channeled in conformance with carefully designed plans and programs at regional, local, and national levels.

While industrialization will continue to be the heart of Brazil's economic expansion, several heretofore neglected sectors will be given much greater attention. Low-cost housing, health and sanitation, basic education and training and other areas falling within the "social" sector will attract a growing share of public resources. Exports will receive priority so that Brazil can pay for the expanding demand for capital goods, fuels, and raw materials associated with investment and current output. And a margin of the rising export proceeds will have to be allocated to the service of Brazil's external debts. As Chardon pointed out, the country's virgin lands of high natural fertility are now sharply limited. He writes that the "key to Brazil's future success will be her ability to develop a new, more intensive and more productive system of agriculture, utilizing the best soils available to her farmers." I expect obsolete land-tenure systems to yield gradually to high-efficiency commercial agriculture with the rising national demand for food and fiber. Political pressures for land-tenure reform, where this is necessary, will grow as industrialists and urban and rural workers find their interests converging on this question.

Brazil's population movements from the rural northeast to urban areas and into pioneer zones will continue in response to a multiplicity of factors. The location of Brasília on the vast expanse of nearly level Pratinha surface will alter future regional oc-cupance patterns of Brazil. According to Ludwig, "developments on the Pratinha will increasingly reflect the sophisticated urban-technical characteristics associated with Brasília and less of the *sertão* in which they occur." Brazilians themselves will have to weigh the benefits flowing from the creation of a new Federal District in the interior against the costs of alternatives foregone.

Concomitantly with continued urbanization and economic modernization, we should expect to see the emergence of true political parties in Brazil. These parties will allow for wider participation in political processes and serve to reconcile conflicting interest groups. The Brazilian's capacity for compromise, his sense of humor, and his low propensity for violent solutions to major national crises, documented in Dulles's essay, will support the adaptation of the political system to the exigencies of modernization. As Santos observed, "the Brazilians may have to deal with their problems and stresses more actively than they have in the past." Their values as well as behavior will undergo reshaping—in family life, in business and professional relations, and in politics. Achievement in a predominantly industrial society will gradually come to outweigh ascription as the main criterion of the individual's position along the social scale.

If our brief prognosis is roughly accurate, we should expect Brazil over the long run to grow away from its dependence on foreign assistance through development and diversification of its economy and the cumulative capabilities of its citizens. A broad, flexible economic base; a unique but modified "Luso-tropical" heritage; and creative leadership should thrust Brazil into the world stage as a leading nation in the ever-shifting balance of international power and prestige.

BIOGRAPHICAL NOTES

WERNER BAER is assistant professor of economics at Yale University. Baer's writings include two monographs, *Industralization and Economic Development in Brazil* (1965), and *The Puerto Rican Economy and United States Economic Fluctuations* (1962), and an extensive list of articles on economic development which have appeared in United States and Latin American journals. These include the *Business History Review, Economic Development and Cultural Change, Trimestre Economico, Quarterly Journal of Economics Economica, American Economic Review,* and *Revista Brasileira de Economia.* He is co-editor (with I. Kerstenetzky) of *Inflation and Growth in Latin America.* Baer spent fifteen months in Brazil in 1962 and 1963 with the assistance of a research grant from the Economic Growth Center of Yale. He returned to Latin America in the summer of 1964 with the support of a Stimson grant.

ERIC N. BAKLANOFF is director of the Latin American Studies Institute and associate professor of economics at Louisiana State University. From 1950 to 1954 he was associated with the International Division of Chase-Manhattan Bank, including three years with its Puerto Rican branches. Before rejoining the Louisiana State University Faculty in September 1965 he was director of Vanderbilt's Graduate Center for Latin American Studies and also taught at the Ohio State University. Baklanoff has published several articles in scholarly and professional journals and is a contributing author of *Foreign Trade and Human Capital* (1962) and *Money and Banking Casebook* (1966) and *Latin America: New Perspectives* (1966). He is a member of the Regional Committee on Critical Languages and World Area Studies, S.R.E.B., and a consultant to the U.S. Armed Forces Institute. In 1964 and 1965 he was a fellow at the Center for Advanced Study in the Behavioral Sciences and was the recipient of a Fulbright grant to Chile in 1957, a Ford Foundation grant through the Harvard Graduate School of Business (summer, 1959), an NDEA postdoctoral fellowship (summer, 1962), a travel-research grant from Vanderbilt University (summer, 1963), and a University of Wisconsin Foundation fellowship to participate in the Political Economy Seminar (June 10–20, 1963).

ROLAND E. CHARDON is assistant professor of geography at Vanderbilt University. Chardon has also taught at the State University of Iowa, the Ohio State

301

University and, during the summer of 1961, at the University of Minnesota. His publications include a monograph, *Geographic Aspects of Plantation Agriculture in Yucatan* (1961), and articles in the *Journal of Geography, Annals of the Association of American Geographers,* and *Focus.* He is coauthor (with Fred A. Carlson) of a forthcoming textbook, *The Geography of Latin America.* Chardon conducted field research in Yucatan with the support of a grant from the National Academy of Sciences–National Research Council (1959) and received a travel-research grant for work in Brazil (summer, 1963) from the Graduate Center for Latin American Studies, Vanderbilt University.

JOHN W. F. DULLES is professor of Latin American studies and Brown-Lupton Lecturer at the University of Texas. He has been associated with United States mining and smelting interests in northern Mexico since 1943 and rose to positions of increasing responsibility with Cia. Minera de Peñoles and Cia. Metalurgica Peñoles as manager of the ore department (1949–1952); manager of the commercial division (1952–1954); assistant general manager (1954–1959); and was promoted to executive vice-president in 1959. Between 1959 and 1962 he served as vice-president of Cia. de Mineracão Novalimense, Belo Horizonte and Rio de Janeiro, Brazil. During the summer of 1965 he was director of the Brazil Peace Corps Training Program at the University of Texas. Dulles published *Yesterday in Mexico: A Chronicle of the Revolution, 1919-1936* (1961) and has contributed to scholarly journals, including *The Hispanic-American Historical Review, The Southwestern Social Science Journal,* and *Stanford Law Review.* Dulles also serves as System Adviser on International Programs, University of Texas.

JUAREZ R. B. LOPES is Professor Catedrático in the Faculty of Architecture and Urbanization of the University of São Paulo, Brazil. Lopes, an eminent Brazilian sociologist, is author of *Sociedade Industrial no Brasil* (Industrial Society in Brazil, 1964) and several monographs dealing with the sociology of industrial relations. He is also a contributing author of *Urbanization in Latin America* (1961) and *Mobilidade e Trabalho* (Mobility and Work, 1960), and has published articles in professional journals including *Sociologie du Travail, Educacão e Ciências Sociais, Revista Brasileira de Estudos Políticos* and *Boletim do Centro Latino Americano de Pesquisas Sociais.* In the fall of 1964, Lopes was visiting professor of sociology at Washington University (St. Louis).

ARMIN K. LUDWIG is assistant professor of geography at Colgate University. Ludwig is a contributing author of two monographs, *Roads and the Advance of Settlement on the Goiás Frontier, the Region of Brazil's New Capital* (1956) and *The Transportation Structure of the Lower Wabash Valley* (1963). In the summer of 1962 he received an NDEA postdoctoral fellowship to participate in an accelerated program in Brazilian-Portuguese at the University of Texas. A grant from the Social Science Research Council enabled Ludwig to pursue field research in Brazil from September 1963 to September 1964. His contribution to this volume draws heavily on that field experience.

VLADIMIR REISKY DE DUBNIC, associate professor of government and foreign affairs at the Woodrow Wilson Department of Government and Foreign Affairs, University of Virginia, was director of the Centro de Estudos Sociais and visiting professor of political science at the Catholic University of Rio de Janeiro. He was also political editor of the *Sintese Politica, Economica, Social,* a quarterly of the University. He published a book, *Communist Propaganda Methods: A Case Study on Czechoslovakia* (Frederic Praeger, New York, 1960) and numerous articles in Brazilian, U.S., and German periodicals. His forthcoming book is *Brazil at the Crossroads: Government, Parties and Politics.*

JOHN F. SANTOS is associate professor of psychology at the University of Notre Dame. Between 1957 and 1965 he was associated with the Research Department of the Menninger Foundation as co-director both of the Perceptual Learning Project and the Program in Reality Testing. He has taught at Tulane University, Texas A. and I. College and was visiting professor of experimental psychology in the Institute of Experimental Pyschology at the Catholic University of São Paulo, Brazil. Since 1962 Santos has also served a social science research associate, the University of Texas, and as co-investigator, for the Brazil II Research Program, Peace Corps San Francisco Valley Project. In 1962–1963, while on leave from the Menninger Foundation, he was responsible for the psychological aspects of the Brazil II Research Program in Brazil. He has published extensively in professional journals including the *British Journal of Psychology,* the *Bulletin of the Menninger Clinic, American Journal of Psychology, Journal of Comparative and Physiological Psychology, Revista de Psicologia Normal e Patológica,* and *Perceptual Motor Skills.*

EARL WESLEY THOMAS is professor of Portuguese at Vanderbilt University. Before joining the Vanderbilt Faculty in 1947, he taught at the University of Michigan and, in 1942 and 1943, was associated with the Instituto Brazil–Estados Unidos in Rio de Janeiro. Thomas contributed to *Brazil: Portrait of Half a Continent* (1949) , *Three Papers: Brazil* (1950) and is author of a forthcoming book, *Brazilian Literature as Seen by American Critics.* Thomas has written for several professional language journals. He plans to continue his research on the syntax of spoken Portuguese in Brazil during 1965–1966 with the support of grants from the Social Science Research Council and the Graduate Center for Latin American Studies of Vanderbilt University.

EMILIO WILLEMS is professor of anthropology at Vanderbilt University. Among his many published works on Brazil are *A acalturacão dos alemães no Brasil* (1946), *Cunha: Tradicão e transicão em uma cultura rural do Brasil* (1948), *Buzios Island: A Caicara Community in Southern Brazil* (1952), and *Uma vila brasileira* (1962). Willems has also provided a Brazilian dimension in his contributions to *The Positive Contributions by Immigrants* (edited by Oscar Handlin, 1955), *The Institutions of Advanced Societies* (edited by Arnold Rose, 1958), and *Religion, Revolution and Reform: New Forces for Change in Latin America* (edited by Frederick Pike, 1964). Willems's articles have appeared in the leading anthropological and sociological journals of the United States, Continental Europe, and Latin America. He has been the recipient of numerous fellowship awards in support of his field research activities, as follows: Guggenheim (1950), UNESCO (1951 and 1952), S.S.R.C. (1951), Rockefeller (1959–1960), Fulbright (1959 and 1960), Ford (1962–1963).

INDEX